KU-044-317

Study Guide for Psychology

Study Guide for
Carlson

Psychology

The Science of Behavior

SECOND EDITION

Prepared by
Madeleine Leveille
GREATER NEW HAVEN STATE TECHNICAL COLLEGE

Eric Carlson
MOUNT HOLYOKE COLLEGE

Mary Carlson

Allyn and Bacon, Inc.

BOSTON LONDON SYDNEY TORONTO

ISBN 0-205-10275-1

Printed in the United States of America

10 9 8 7 6 5 4 3 2 91 90 89 88 87

Contents

CHAPTER 1
The Nature of Psychology

INTRODUCTION

This chapter examines the history of ideas and development of scientific research methods leading to the establishment of psychology as a field of knowledge and investigation. This chapter contains only one lesson, which covers objectives 1-11.

CONCEPT CARDS AND EXERCISES

After you have surveyed and read the text, assemble the concept cards located at the end of this chapter. Use them to learn the important terms, then begin reading the text again, one learning objective at a time, and work through the exercises for the lesson.

SELF TESTS

The lesson is followed by a multiple-choice self test. After you are proficient with the lesson's concept cards and exercises, take the self test to see whether you have mastered the material. Review those objectives for questions you answered incorrectly.

INTEGRATING QUESTIONS

To challenge yourself further, answer the integrating questions at the end of the chapter. These questions ask you to apply the information you have learned to consider larger theoretical or real-life issues.

LESSON I: THE NATURE OF PSYCHOLOGY

1. Describe the history of philosophical systems used to explain behavior, from animism to materialism. (pp. 6-10)

* 1.1 People of early, prescientific cultures adopted _______________ philosophies of nature, which explained natural events by appeal to numerous spirits.

* 1.2 The philosophy of _______________ separates the world into matter (the physical world) and mind or soul (the nonphysical world).

* 1.3 What is the name of the special type of dualism proposed by Descartes?

* 1.4 Identify those features of human behavior that Descartes regarded as a) physical and mechanical in nature and b) nonphysical and nonmechanical in nature.

* 1.5 A ______________ is a simple working system based on known principles employed in an attempt to explain a complex natural phenomenon.

* 1.6 The belief that both personal and scientific knowledge may be derived through direct observation and experience is called ______________, and was advocated by the English philosopher ______________.

1.7 Compare Descartes's rational model of human behavior with Locke's empirical models.

1.8 Briefly describe how Mill's philosophy of materialism contributed to the development of psychology.

2. Describe the biological roots of psychology in the research of French and German physiologists and biologists of the late 19th century. (pp. 10-14)

* 2.1 a) The experimental physiologist Johannes Müller developed the doctrine of

______________ ______________ ______________.

b) Describe this doctrine.

2.2 What are the implications of Müller's doctrine for

a) the general principle of how the brain functions to permit distinctions between various types of stimulation and

b) the empirical investigation of the nervous system?

2.3 How was Müller's doctrine supported by the work of Flourens?

2.4 How did Broca extend the work of Flourens?

2.5 a) What additional method for the analysis of specific brain functions was developed by Fritsch and Hitzig?

b) What did their method indicate about relations between the cerebral cortex and body movements?

2.6 a) Describe Helmholtz's discovery regarding the speed of nerve impulses and

b) explain what his discovery suggested about the potential for measuring or investigating neural events.

3. Describe the methods used by Weber and Fechner to measure human perception. (pp. 14-16)

* 3.1 Psychophysics is an area of psychology developed by Weber and Fechner that measures the relations between changes of stimulus ______________ (a measure of physical properties) and corresponding changes in the reports by subjects of their ______________ (a measure of behavioral properties).

* 3.2 The orderly relations that Weber discovered in the way people discriminate among differences in stimulus magnitude for each type of stimulus modality are presented as ratios called ______________ ______________. These are instances of a more general principle of discrimination referring to the minimum amount of change needed in a stimulus to be detected or ______________ ______________ ______________.

3.3 Describe the method that might be used to obtain the data presented in Figure 1.15 in the text.

4. Describe Wundt's major contributions to psychology and distinguish between those that have lasted and those that have not. (pp. 16-17)

4.1 Wundt adopted the philosophy of structuralism to study the so-called structures or components of the mind. Explain what these structures were supposed to be.

4.2 How were these structures studied? Specify

a) who did the observations (i.e., who served as the subject?).

b) what was being observed.

c) what data were being collected.

4.3 Distinguish Wundt's philosophy of structuralism from his procedure of introspection.

4.4 What was the fate of structuralism and introspection?

5. Describe Ebbinghaus's major contributions to psychology. (pp. 17-18)

5.1 Describe the following features of Ebbinghaus's approach to the study of memory:

a) the subject used for his research,

b) the types of stimuli he used,

c) his method for presenting stimuli,

d) the data he recorded.

5.2 What was his contribution to a) the treatment of variable errors and b) the quantification and graphing of data?

* 5.3 What was his philosophical approach to the study of memory?

6. Describe the development of functionalism. (pp. 18-20)

6.1 Why did the functionalists reject structuralism?

6.2 How was Darwin's concept of natural selection important to the philosophy of functionalism?

6.3 How were the concepts of natural selection and functionalism important to psychologists?

6.4 What were the three features of functionalism identified by Angell?

7. Briefly describe Freud's theory and explain how it integrated structuralism and functionalism. (pp. 20-21)

7.1 In what way did Freud's theory incorporate elements of structuralism?

7.2 In what way did Freud's theory incorporate elements of functionalism?

7.3 How were these two views integrated in Freud's theory?

8. Briefly summarize the work of Thorndike and Pavlov, and explain how their work led to Watson's behaviorism. (pp. 21-23)

8.1 In what ways did behaviorism refine and extend the principles of functionalism?

8.2 How did Thorndike study escape behavior of cats and how did this research lead to his formulation of "the law of effect"?

8.3 How is the law of effect similar to the functionalist account of natural selection?

8.4 What was the significance of Pavlov's research for the field of psychology?

8.5 a) What was the view of psychology espoused by J.B. Watson and b) how was it derived from the research of Thorndike and Pavlov?

9. Describe modern cognitive psychology and and compare it to structuralism. (pp 23-24)

* 9.1 Cognitive psychologists often use the computer as a metaphor for the brain. This analogy suggests that sensory input is received, coded or analyzed and then stored as memory

until it is needed and retrieved and the entire process is referred to as ______________

________________.

9.2 How is the research of modern cognitive psychologists similar to that of structuralists in regard to subject matter?

9.3 How do cognitive psychology and structuralism differ regarding methodology used to study private events?

9.4 Summarize the similarities in subject matter and approach to investigation between cognitive psychology and structuralism.

10. Describe what it means to explain or understand behavior. (p. 25)

* 10.1 Describe the general goal of psychology.

10.2 What elements must an explanation of behavior contain?

11. List and briefly describe the professional activities of modern psychologists. (pp. 25-27)

11.1 Learn the terms and definitions listed on the concept cards for this objective.

LESSON I SELF TEST

1. Descartes departed from earlier thinkers by proposing that

   a. the mind was not subject to the laws of the universe.
   b. truths discovered by human reason and observation could be reconciled with the truth of God's revelation.
   c. free will is an animistic concept.
   d. the body and mind, although separate, were interacting.

2. In contrast to Descartes, Locke believed that knowledge could be obtained through

   a. materialism.
   b. introspection.
   c. observation and experience.
   d. reasoning and discovery of innate ideas.

3. Johannes Müller proposed the doctrine of specific nerve energies to account for the brain's ability to distinguish different kinds of sensory information. This doctrine asserts that

   a. signals from different sense organs send different and unique types of messages to the brain.
   b. signals to different nerve input channels and areas of the brain permit detection of stimulus differences.
   c. the ability to distinguish information from the different sense organs is learned by specific experiences in childhood.

d. the distinguishing ability is produced by stimulation of the nerves and ablation of the brain.

4. Applying the logic behind ablation, Paul Broca

a. claimed an association between a damaged part of the brain and disrupted speech.
b. demonstrated that reflexes did not require participation of the mind.
c. found that the functions of the brain can be mapped by use of electrical stimulation.
d. pioneered functionalism and the science of psychology.

5. Helmholtz is important to psychology because he

a. proposed and tested the doctrine of specific nerve energies.
b. demonstrated that the transmission of impulses through nerves was as fast as the speed of electricity in wires.
c. accurately measured the speed of neural signal transmission.
d. found that the speed of a person's reaction to a stimulus is a function of age and sex.

6. The major problem encountered by structuralism as proposed by Wundt was

a. its reliance on functional explanations for observed behavior.
b. its rigid emphasis on the experimental approach
c. the difficulty of separating basic sensation from complex perception.
d. the difficulty of obtaining students to pursue careers in the new field of psychology.

7. Darwin's work is most closely associated with

a. cognitive psychology.
b. structuralism.
c. functionalism.
d. behaviorism.

8. Functionalists differed from structuralists in their emphasis on

a. the importance of observation and experimentation.
b. ideas and sensations.
c. the relative importance of introspection and animism.
d. the biological significance of natural processes.

9. Thorndike's law of effect proposes that

a. behavior having adaptive results for an organism will be maintained.
b. the mind as well as the body is passive and subject to the effects of the environment.
c. organisms naturally understand the concepts of cause and effect.
d. there is a single, observable cause for each effect.

10. According to Watson, which of the following is the proper study of psychology?

a. feeling of sadness
b. any observable actions
c. the raw data of sensations
d. imagery

11. Contemporary cognitive psychologists follow the principles of methodological behaviorism in that they

a. devalue all forms of self-report.
b. reject the study of the unconscious.
c. abandon humanism for the study of humans as merely another kind of animal.
d. study covert behavioral processes using objective, scientific methods.

12. In contrast to early structuralists, modern cognitive psychologists are concerned with

    a. how simple sensations combine to produce complex perceptions.
    b. using objective research methods to measure aspects of private events.
    c. introspection and the structure of mental operations.
    d. dreams, imagery, and the elements of consciousness.

13. Which of the following is a psychological explanation?

    a. When Elmo gets drunk, he gets mean.
    b. Sam's stomach produced excess acid and Sam developed ulcers.
    c. People who live in large cities are less friendly than people who live in small towns.
    d. Riding in crowded subway cars elevates people's irritability.

14. Which psychologists are most interested in studying species-typical behaviors?

    a. comparative psychologists
    b. experimental neuropsychologists
    c. psychometricians
    d. cognitive psychologists

15. Which of the following type of psychologist is most likely to be employed by colleges and universities?

    a. engineering psychologist
    b. social psychologist
    c. clinical psychologist
    d. school psychologist

INTEGRATING QUESTIONS

1. Match the following researchers or philosophers with their associated methods, findings or philosophies:

_____Broca	a. classical conditioning of salivation by dogs
_____Darwin	b. view that overt action is the proper domain of psychology
_____Descartes	c. interactionism
_____Fechner & Weber	d. measured speed of nerve impulses
_____Flourens	e. materialism
_____Freud	f. law of effect
_____Fritz & Hitzig	g. study of human brain damage
_____Helmholtz	h. functionalist theory
_____Locke	i. doctrine of specific nerve energies
_____Mill	j. experimental ablation
_____Müller	k. psychodynamic theory

Continued on next page

Chapter 1

_____Pavlov	l. empiricism
_____Thorndike	m. electrical brain stimulation
_____Watson	n. just noticeable difference

ANSWERS

1.1 animistic
1.2 dualism
1.3 interactionism
1.4 a) reflexes, observable behavior; b) mind, spirit, thought
1.5 model
1.6 empiricism, Locke
2.1 a) specific nerve energies
3.1 intensity (or magnitude), perceptions (or impressions, estimates, etc.)
3.2 Webber fractions, just noticeable difference
5.3 empiricism
9.1 information processing
10.1 to explain human behavior

Self Test: Lesson I

1. d Obj 1-1
2. c Obj 1-1
3. b Obj 1-2
4. a Obj 1-2
5. c Obj 1-2
6. c Obj 1-4
7. c Obj 1-6
8. d Obj 1-4, 1-5, 1-6, 1-9
9. a Obj 1-8
10. b Obj 1-8
11. d Obj 1-8, 1-9
12. c Obj 1-9
13. d Obj 1-10
14. a Obj 1-11
15. b Obj 1-11

Integrating Question

g-Broca, h-Darwin, c-Descartes, n-Fechner & Weber, j-Flourens, k-Freud, m-Fritz & Hitzig, d-Helmholtz, l-Locke, e-Mill, i-Müller, a-Pavlov, f-Thorndike, b-Watson

1.1 OBJ 1-1

ANIMISM

1.2 OBJ 1-1

DUALISM

1.3 OBJ 1-1

INTERACTIONISM

1.4 OBJ 1-1

EMPIRICISM

1.5 OBJ 1-1

MATERIALISM

1.6 OBJ 1-2

DOCTRINE OF SPECIFIC NERVE ENERGIES

1.7 OBJ 1-2

ABLATION

1.8 OBJ 1-3

JUST-NOTICEABLE DIFFERENCE (JND)

1.9 OBJ 1-4

STRUCTURALISM

1.10 OBJ 1-4

INTROSPECTION

1.11 OBJ 1-6

FUNCTIONALISM

1.12 OBJ 1-6

NATURAL SELECTION

1.13 OBJ 1-8

BEHAVIORISM

1.14 OBJ 1-8

LAW OF EFFECT

1.15 OBJ 1-8

METHODOLOGICAL BEHAVIORISM

1.16 OBJ 1-9

INFORMATION PROCESSING

1.9 Obj 1-4

Wundt's experimental method focusing on the structures of the mind built by consciousness (e.g., ideas, feelings, experiences)

1.10 Obj 1-4

system for discovering elements of consciousness, with trained assistants describing basic stimulus sensations

1.11 Obj 1-6

philosophy that an organism's interactions with the environment result in its adaptation to the environment

1.12 Obj 1-6

tenet of evolutionary theory: individual genetic differences confer reproductive advantages that are passed to succeeding generations

1.13 Obj 1-8

Watson's belief that psychology should study only observable events—the behavior of organisms

1.14 Obj 1-8

Thorndike's view that consequences of behavior strengthen or weaken the probability of similar behavior in similar circumstances

1.15 Obj 1-8

positivistic behaviorism stressing that only observable behavior can be studied because private events cannot be measured or observed objectively

1.16 Obj 1-9

computer-analogue approach to modeling behavior and human cognitive activity

1.1 Obj 1-1

primitive belief that natural phenomena (tides, wind, etc.) are inhabited by individual gods or spirits who control their occurrence

1.2 Obj 1-1

philosophy that divides the world into two separate units: soul, mind, or spirit; and physical or material substances

1.3 Obj 1-1

a form of dualistic philosophy espoused by Descartes that mind and matter can influence one another

1.4 Obj 1-1

philosophy of science; knowledge is fundamentally derived from direct observations, experiments, and experiences

1.5 Obj 1-1

philosophy that the universe and everything in it is composed of the same physical matter and obeying common laws of nature

1.6 Obj 1-2

Müller's hypothesis that particular sets of nerves each had specialized functions and were routed to specific parts of the brain

1.7 Obj 1-2

experimental procedure for removing brain tissue

1.8 Obj 1-3

a minimal physical difference needed between two stimuli to be detected as different by an organism

1.17 OBJ 1-10

CAUSAL EVENTS

1.18 OBJ 1-11

PHYSIOLOGICAL PSYCHOLOGY

1.19 OBJ 1-11

PSYCHOPHYSIOLOGY

1.20 OBJ 1-11

COMPARATIVE PSYCHOLOGY

1.21 OBJ 1-11

EXPERIMENTAL PSYCHOLOGY

1.22 OBJ 1-11

COGNITIVE PSYCHOLOGY

1.23 OBJ 1-11

EXPERIMENTAL NEUROPSYCHOLOGY

1.24 OBJ 1-11

DEVELOPMENTAL PSYCHOLOGY

1.25 OBJ 1-11

SOCIAL PSYCHOLOGY

1.26 OBJ 1-11

PERSONALITY PSYCHOLOGY

1.27 OBJ 1-11

PSYCHOMETRICS

1.28 OBJ 1-11

CLINICAL PSYCHOLOGY

1.29 OBJ 1-11

APPLIED PSYCHOLOGY

1.25 Obj 1-11

study of the effects of individuals on the behavior of other individuals

1.26 Obj 1-11

study of individual differences in disposition and behavior

1.27 Obj 1-11

development and use of psychological tests for measuring personality traits or abilities

1.28 Obj 1-11

area of applied psychology primarily for helping people solve their personal, social, emotional and other behavior problems

1.29 Obj 1-11

non-academic areas of applied psychology for problem-solving in industrial, business, organizational and counseling settings

1.17 Obj 1-10

variables that control or produce subsequent events, results or effects

1.18 Obj 1-11

experimental study of the behavior of nonhuman subjects with emphasis on the physiological correlates of behavior

1.19 Obj 1-11

measurement of the physiological response patterns of human subjects

1.20 Obj 1-11

study of behavior patterns of animals in the laboratory and in natural or field settings; often analyze species-typical behaviors

1.21 Obj 1-11

study of the environmental effects on learning, perception, memory, and motivation in human and nonhuman subjects

1.22 Obj 1-11

study of perception, memory, verbal performance and attention, in terms of structures of the mind, such as imagery and language mechanisms

1.23 Obj 1-11

combines cognitive and physiological study of human subjects with brain damage to discover brain structures needed for cognitive processes

1.24 Obj 1-11

study of psychological change throughout life with special emphasis on childhood

CHAPTER 2
The Ways and Means of Psychology

INTRODUCTION

This chapter examines some of the strategies and tactics used by researchers to answer questions about the behavior of organisms. It is divided into two lessons: Lesson I covers Objectives 1-8 and Lesson II covers Objectives 9-16.

CONCEPT CARDS AND EXERCISES

After you have surveyed and read the text, assemble the concept cards located at the end of this chapter. Use them to learn the important terms, then begin reading the text again, one learning objective at a time, and work through the exercises for each lesson. Answers for questions marked with an asterisk are found at the end of the chapter.

SELF TESTS

Each lesson is followed by a multiple-choice self test. After you are proficient with a lesson's concept cards and exercises, take the self test to see whether you have mastered the material. Review those objectives for questions you answered incorrectly.

INTEGRATING QUESTIONS

To challenge yourself further, answer the integrating questions at the end of the chapter. These questions ask you to apply the information you have learned to consider larger theoretical or real-life issues.

LESSON I

1. Briefly describe the four major steps of the scientific method. (pp. 31-32)

* 1.1 Number the following major steps of the scientific method in the order in which they are performed (1=first, 4=last).

_____ a) identification of the problem and formulation of a hypothesis

_____ b) communication of the findings of the study

_____ c) evaluation of the hypothesis in terms of the results

_____ d) design and implementation of the experiment

* 1.2 Match each of the following with one of the four steps of the scientific method.

_____ a) determining whether observed effects are statistically significant

_____ b) submitting an article describing the study for publication in a specialized scientific journal

_____ c) writing operational definitions of variables

_____ d) manipulating the independent variable(s)

_____ e) comparing the expected results with the actual observed results

_____ f) classifying and operationally defining the variables

_____ g) stating the expected relation between the variables of interest

2. Explain the differences between theories and hypotheses. (pp. 32-33)

* 2.1 A tentative statement about how two or more events are related to one another is called a _______________.

* 2.2 Which of the following statements are hypotheses?

a) The more a person smokes, the more likely it becomes for him or her to develop lung cancer.

b) The world is round.

c) Most people are very aggressive.

d) Aggressive social behavior is related to the number of hours a person must work each day.

e) The less sleep a person gets, the more hallucinations he or she is likely to have when awake.

2.3 Define a scientific theory and compare it to a hypothesis.

3. Describe how psychologists manipulate the environment to study the causes of behavior. (pp. 33-33)

* 3.1 Hypotheses suggest a relationship between _______________.

* 3.2 a) The two variables involved in a hypothesized relationship are the _______________ variable and the _______________ variable.

b) Which of these variables is manipulated by the researcher?

c) Which of these variables is usually measured by the researcher?

* 3.3 Identify the independent and dependent variables in each of the following hypotheses.

a) The more a person smokes, the more likely it becomes for him or her to develop lung cancer.

b) A researcher wishes to study the effects of a particular drug on a person's ability to put together a puzzle. She tests the subject before the drug is taken, fifteen minutes after the drug is taken, and two hours later.

c) The more parental attention a child receives, the more self-confident the child will be.

d) A researcher gives one group of rats a diet sweetened with saccharin and another group a diet sweetened with sugar. He later measures the amount of wheel running displayed by rats in each group.

* 3.4 When we believe that by classifying a phenomenon we have explained it, we are committing the error of ______________ ______________.

* 3.5 Which of these illustrations is an example of the error referred to in 3.4?

a) Sarah came to see me because she wanted to.

b) Sarah came to see me because the clock chimed and reminded her she had been invited to our house in half an hour.

4. Explain what operational definitions are. (pp. 35)

* 4.1 ______________ ______________ consist of descriptions of independent and dependent variables in specific, unambiguous terms.

4.2 How is this description of variables different from that provided in a hypothesis?

5. Describe how to increase the reliability and validity of operational definitions. (pp. 35-37)

* 5.1 The accuracy with which an operational definition represents the actual variable of interest in a study is referred to as its ______________.

* 5.2 a) Two types of validity of operational definitions are ______________ validity and ______________ validity.

b) Contrast these two kinds of validity.

* 5.3 Identify the kind of validity illustrated by the following situations.

a) An investigator defines creativity as the number of different clothes combinations a person wears in a week.

b) A physiological psychologist defines hunger by the concentration of a newly-discovered hormone in the blood. When the level is high, animals eat if offered food; when an animal eats, the level of this hormone decreases; and when an animal is deprived of food, the level of this hormone increases.

* 5.4 The consistency of a measure over repeated times under consistent conditions is referred to as the _______________ of an operational definition.

* 5.5 A reliable measure is necessarily a valid measure. True _____ False _____ Explain your answer.

* 5.6 Evaluate the reliability of the operational definitions involved in each of the following situations. In each case, state what changes should be made to improve the reliability of the measure.

a) In one experiment, creativity was defined as the degree of originality displayed in drawings children made in twenty minutes. Groups of children were given paper and colored pencils and observed in the same room at the same time. Two observers independently rated the children's creativity.

b) In a study similar to a), creativity was defined as the number of original forms drawn by a child in twenty minutes, "original" being defined as a novel form that had not been drawn before in the same session by the same child or other children. Groups of children were given paper and colored pencils and observed in the same room at the same time. One observer rated the children's creativity.

c) In a study on the effects of caffeine consumption on sleep, sleep was defined as a particular brain wave pattern measured by EEGs. Some subjects were observed in the morning, others at night, and others after work.

* 5.7 a) In which of the situations in 5.6 would it be possible to assess interrater reliability?

b) What should a researcher do if observers display low interrater reliability?

6. Describe the problems researchers encounter when they attempt to control independent variables and how they solve these problems. (pp. 37-41)

* 6.1 a) If variables other than the independent variable are changed and these other variables are thought to have affected the dependent variable, these other variables are said to be _______________.

b) Why is it important to make sure that <u>only</u> the independent variable is manipulated in an experiment?

* 6.2 Reread the study by a zoologist that is described in the text. In this experiment order of presentation was confounded with the similarity of the stimulus to a predator. Whenever subjects are exposed to more than one condition as in this study, the

experimenter should use a procedure called ______________.

* 6.3 Read the following example carefully.

An investigator is interested in the effects of a new stimulant drug that increases a person's stamina. He gives the subjects 2 mg. of the drug at the first session, 10 mg. at the second session, and 20 mg. at the third. All three sessions are held on the same day at two hour intervals. Each time, the subjects run on a treadmill until they can no longer keep up a 10-mile per hour pace. The investigator observes that subjects' stamina is less each time. He concludes that contrary to expectations, the drug <u>reduces</u> stamina and that the more drug the subjects consume the less stamina they have.

a) What variables are confounded?

b) What should the investigator do to eliminate the confounded variable?

* 6.4 One way of reducing the possibility that confounding variables will influence the results of a study is to use a "no treatment" group that is exposed to identical procedures as the experimental group but the independent variable is not manipulated. Another name for such a group is the ______________ ______________.

* 6.5 Assume that you are interested in studying the effects of a hormone called vasopressin on memory. You inject all of your rats with vasopressin and then teach them to run a maze. You put the rats back in their home cage for twenty-four hours and then put each of them in the maze to test its memory of the maze. You measure memory by counting the number of errors each rat makes before running through the maze without making an incorrect turn. You find that they do well, making few errors.

a) This experiment lacks a ______________ ______________.

b) Suppose that you compare the performance of the rats that receive the injection of vasopressin with a group of rats that do not. If the injected rats perform better does this mean that vasopressin facilitates learning? Explain.

c) Explain how you would do the experiment correctly.

7. Describe the problems researchers encounter when they attempt to control subject variables and how they solve these problems. (pp. 41-43)

* 7.1 Consider the following experiment.

A researcher wants to evaluate the relation between type of practice ("massed" versus "distributed") on performance of a motor task. Three groups of school children are tested on their skill at writing the alphabet upside down following different amounts of practice. Group M consists of fourth graders who are allowed to practice writing the alphabet upside down for five minutes. Group D consists of fifth graders who practice the same task for one minute periods separated by one minute rest intervals for a total of five minutes of practice. Group O consists of third graders who do not practice the task. After the practice sessions, all three groups are asked to write as many inverted letters as they can in one minute. Group D does the best, writing the most number of correctly inverted letters. Group M does not do as well as Group D, while Group O is the poorest at the task. The researcher concludes that distributed practice improves performance more than massed practice, and that <u>some</u> practice is better than no practice.

a) What is wrong with the researcher's conclusion? Refer to variables that are confounded in your answer.

b) How should the experiment have been conducted in order for the conclusions to be valid?

* 7.2 a) To reduce the likelihood that subject variables will confound the effects of the independent variable, an experimenter may use one of two procedures: ______________ ______________ and ______________.

b) Describe each of these procedures.

* 7.3 Which of the following situations is an example of random assignment and which is an example of matching?

_____ a) Subjects are assigned to experimental groups by having them draw slips of paper marked "A" or "B" from a box.

_____ b) A researcher assesses the personality of subjects who will participate in her experiment by giving them a personality test. Using the test results, she assigns an equal number of subjects scoring high on the extraversion scale to each group and an equal number of subjects scoring low on the extraversion scale to each group.

7.4 What happens to an experiment when some of the subjects in a group drop out? Assume that subjects were randomly assigned to groups.

8. Describe single- and double-blind experiments. (pp. 43-45)

8.1 a) Explain what "subject expectancies" are.

b) In what ways can subject expectancies affect the results of a study?

* 8.2 One way to minimize the effect of subject expectancies is to use a ______________-______________ procedure where subjects are unaware of the exact conditions they are exposed to.

8.3 An experimenter wants to evaluate the hypothesis that teacher's attention increases the hyperactive behavior of hyperactive children. The classroom teacher, who is unaware of the purpose of the study, is asked to pay attention to the subjects (hyperactive children) only when a green light in the corner of the room is on. The experimenter observes the subjects through a one-way mirror and counts the number of times each child leaves his or her seat when the green light is on and when it is off.

a) Explain how experimenter expectancies may influence the results of this study.

* b) This problem could be minimized by using a ______________-______________ procedure. How could you correct this study?

LESSON I SELF TEST

1. As part of the scientific method, once psychologists have identified a problem, they first

   a. need to formulate hypothetical cause-and-effect relations among variables.
   b. share their ideas with other psychologists.
   c. manipulate a potential independent variable.
   d. measure the dependent variable.

2. The statement "Experts are more influential in persuading people than are nonexperts" is an example of a(n)

   a. theory.
   b. hypothesis.
   c. independent variable.
   d. construct.

3. The psychologist frustrated different groups of subjects in different ways, then measured the level of shocks the subjects administered to another person. The dependent variable in this study is the

   a. level of shocks administered by the subjects.
   b. frustration the subjects experienced.
   c. frustration-aggression hypothesis.
   d. different subjects used in this experiment.

4. Which of the following is an example of the nominal fallacy?

   a. Jen hit Sandy because she was frustrated. Sandy had the toy that Jen wanted to play with.
   b. Martha did not want George to go to the party without her because she was jealous.
   c. Dorothy is grumpy because her arthritis is bothering her.
   d. Joan studies hard because she wants to become a physician.

5. Which of the following is an acceptable operational definition of frustration for a test of the hypothesis that frustration causes aggression?

   a. the cause of the subjects' anger towards the experimenter
   b. the number of times subjects strike the experimental victim
   c. subject's failure to solve three insoluble puzzles that they had been told were simple
   d. any experimenter-induced interference in the subjects' goal-directed activities

6. An operational definition has construct validity if it

   a. also has face validity.
   b. produces results similar to previous experiments
   c. measures what it is supposed to measure.
   d. can be easily replicated.

7. If a procedure for operationally defining a variable is reliable, it

   a. has face validity.
   b. will produce similar results under differing conditions.
   c. will have construct validity.
   d. will yield similar results over similar conditions.

8. An experiment is confounded if

   a. its operational definitions are reliable but lack face validity.
   b. it attempts to measure two or more dependent variables.
   c. it attempts to measure two or more independent variables.
   d. its results are the product of extraneous, uncontrolled variables.

9. A research design is counterbalanced if subjects are presented the experimental stimuli in

   a. the same order.
   b. random order.
   c. a consistent fashion across experimental controls.
   d. order of intensity.

10. In a test of the frustration-aggression hypothesis, some subjects served as a control group in which they were not frustrated. The use of the control group allows the experimenter to

    a. assign subjects randomly to conditions.
    b. contrast the effects of manipulating the independent variable with no treatment at all.
    c. counterbalance the presentation of the experimental stimuli.
    d. increase the confounding of the experimental variables.

11. What is the purpose of randomly assigning subjects to experimental groups?

    a. to make sure that subjects are matched by age, sex, and socioeconomic status across groups
    b. to avoid the nominal fallacy
    c. to reduce the possibility of confounding subject variables
    d. to produce a counterbalanced design

12. A researcher wants to test the hypothesis that certain vitamins reduce depression. Half the subjects are given these vitamins and half are given a placebo. This design

    a. uses random selection to reduce confounding.
    b. has confounded independent and dependent variables.
    c. is an observational rather than experimental study.
    d. uses a single-blind method.

LESSON II

9. Compare the advantages and disadvantages of experimental and observational studies and describe the conclusions researchers can draw from each. (pp. 45-47)

* 9.1 a) _______________ studies are useful for studying the relation between variables that cannot be experimentally manipulated.

b) List at least three variables that cannot be experimentally manipulated.

9.2 a) Why are conclusions about causal relations necessarily more limited in the type of study referred to in 9.1, as compared with experimental studies?

b) What type of conclusions are allowed by observational studies?

10. Describe the goal of generality in psychological science. (pp. 47-48)

* 10.1 A group of subjects is a subset of a population. This group is referred to as a ________________.

* 10.2 When working on a scientific study with a particular group of subjects, we want to make causal inferences about the larger population, not just the sample itself. The property of results that can be used to accurately predict from a sample to a population is called ________________.

10.3 Under what conditions may we generalize our conclusions from a specific sample to a larger population?

11. Compare the advantages and disadvantages of retrospective studies and case studies. (pp. 48-49)

11.1 In your own words, describe what is meant by a case study.

11.2 a) Under what circumstances would it be appropriate to use a case study to investigate a phenomenon?

b) In what area of psychology are case studies widely used? Why?

* 11.3 Various issues concerning the safety and health of subjects are confronted by behavioral researchers and are referred to as ________________.

11.4 Describe what measures have been take to ensure that humans and other animals are not treated in unethical ways.

12. Describe the calculations and uses of the two most common measures of central tendency. (pp. 50-51)

* 12.1 a) The single numbers or values that are used as measures to represent a particular variable are referred to as ________________ ________________.

b) Describe the two uses of these measures in an investigation.

* 12.2 The mean and the median are two measures of ________________ ________________.

* 12.3 a) The average is another name for the ________________.

b) Describe how this measure is calculated.

* 12.4 a) If we wish to describe a set of data with a measure that represents its central tendency most accurately, we would probably use the _____________.

b) Give two reasons why we use the mean.

13. Describe the calculations and uses of the three most common measures of variability. (pp. 51-52)

13.1 If we know that the means of two groups are the same, does this imply that both groups are necessarily alike in other respects? Explain your answer.

13.2 How do measures of variability improve our knowledge about the characteristics of a particular variable in a group of subjects?

* 13.3 Three measures of variability are the _____________, the _____________, and the _____________ _____________.

* 13.4 The range of the following set of data is _____.

10, 21, 34, 19, 52

* 13.5 a) The average of the squared deviation of each individual score from the group mean is the _____________.

* b) Fill in the missing information in this table and calculate the variance of the group's score.

scores	scores-mean	(scores-mean)^2
1	-1	1
3	1	1
2	0	_____
2	_____	_____
2	_____	_____

Total=10 Total= _____
Mean=2 Variance= _____

* 13.6 a) A common measure that is used to report the variability of scores is the _____________ _____________.

b) How is this measure calculated?

* 13.7 The standard deviation in the table presented in 23.3 is _____.

14. Explain how the strength of relations can be indicated by use of scatterplots or correlation coefficients. (pp. 53-54)

* 14.1 a) A graph that depicts how two variables are related is called a ______________ ______________.

b) A single value that summarizes the relation between two variables is called a ______________ ______________.

* 14.2 Examine the following graphs.

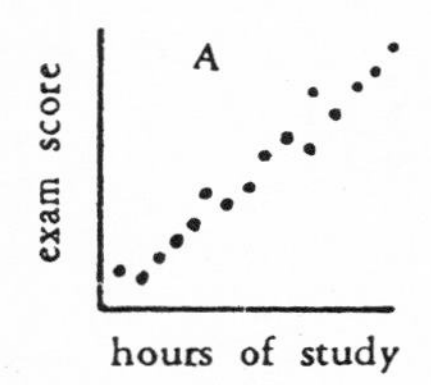

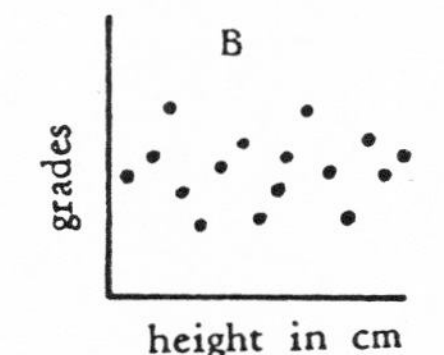

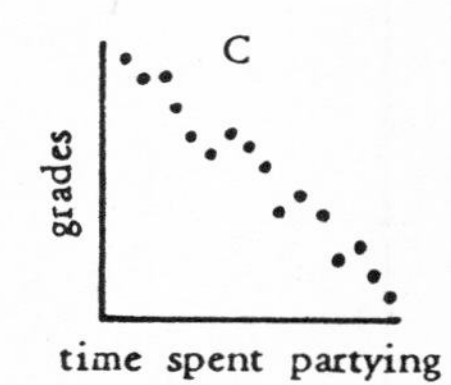

Which of these scatter plots depicts a systematic relation between two variables?

* 14.3 a) The absolute values of a correlation coefficient range from _____ to _____.

b) Arrange the following set of correlation coefficients according to the strength of the relation they indicate, starting with the strongest and progressing to the weakest.

.50, .79, .91, .25

* 14.4 a) When high values on one variable are associated with high values on another variable, we call it a ______________ correlation.

b) When high values on one variable are associated with low values on another variable, we call it a ______________ correlation.

* 14.5 Refer to question 14.2 and answer the following.

a) Which scatter plot depicts a positive correlation?

b) Which scatter plot depicts a negative correlation?

* 14.6 For each of these examples, indicate whether the correlation is likely to be positive or negative.

a) number of cigarettes smoked per day and probability of developing lung cancer

b) standardized test scores and grade point average

c) price of gasoline and rate of gasoline consumption

d) amount of light present and amount of photosynthesis in plants

14.7 Give one example of a positive correlation and one example of a negative correlation.

* 14.8 Consider the following correlation coefficients.

-.89, +.26, -.64, +.52

a) Which of these represent positive correlations?

b) Which of these represent negative correlations?

c) Arrange these correlation coefficients according to the strength of the relation they represent from strongest to weakest.

15. Explain why psychologists assess the statistical significance of their results. (pp. 55-56)

* 15.1 When working on an experiment, the differences we observe between the means of the groups may be due to 1) the manipulation of the independent variable, 2) the influence of confounded variables (which we hope to have minimized), or 3) it may be due to

_________________.

* 15.2 a) Assuming that we have minimized the influence of confounded variables, we must determine whether the difference between the means of the groups in our experiment is "real" (due to the independent variable) or due to chance. This problem refers to the

_________________ _________________ of our results.

b) All other things being equal, the larger the difference observed between the means of different groups, the less likely it is that the difference was due to chance. True _____ False _____

16. Explain in general terms how statistical significance is assessed. (pp. 56-59)

16.1 In evaluating whether the observed difference between the mean scores of two groups was due to chance or to the effect of the independent variable, an investigator consults a table. What does this table tell the investigator?

* 16.2 An investigator conducts a study to evaluate the effects of the drug methylphenidate (commonly called Ritalin) on the behavior of hyperactive children. Seven-year-old children are randomly assigned to one of two groups. Subjects in Group R are given 10 mg/kg of Ritalin for five consecutive days. Subjects in Group P are given a placebo for five consecutive days. The investigator observes the frequency of out-of-seat behavior during a morning class.

Assume these are the results of the experiment.

Frequency of out-of-seat behavior in a 30 minute period

Group R	Group P
16	39
5	22
4	17
10	23
9	38
7	26

a) List three steps the investigator must take in order to assess whether or not the results are statistically significant.

b) If, according to the table, the probability of obtaining the observed difference between the means of Group R and Group P by chance alone is greater than five times in 100 (five percent), what would the investigator conclude?

c) If, according to the table, the probability of obtaining this difference by chance alone is less than one percent, what would the investigator conclude?

LESSON II SELF TEST

1. A researcher is told that he cannot generalize the results of his study of birth order and leadership behavior to other people. This criticism suggests that

   a. the subjects of this study were aware of the researcher's hypothesis.
   b. there were not enough operational definitions of the dependent variables.
   c. the control group in this study was inadequate.
   d. the results of this study do not apply to other groups of subjects.

2. Amelia was the victim of incest. A clinical psychologist might infer that some of Amelia's passivity is due to sexual victimization. This hypothesis is derived from

   a. introspection.
   b. experimental study.
   c. case study.
   d. theory building.

3. The primary purpose of review committees in departments of psychology is to

   a. determine whether a piece of research merits publication.
   b. evaluate the importance of a piece of research.
   c. critique the design of a piece of research.
   d. safeguard the rights and well-being of subjects.

4. Descriptive statistics helps researchers

   a. control extraneous variables found in manipulation of the independent variable.
   b. select subjects.
   c. obtain useful information about properties of a sample.
   d. generalize their results to others.

5. An instructor tells you that the class mean was 61 but the median was 75. You know that

   a. an incorrect measure of central tendency has been used.
   b. some students must have performed very poorly but most performed satisfactorily.

c. the average deviation of the median is greater than the average deviation of the mean.
d. the mean represents the score most students earned.

6. An instructor finds that the difference between the highest and lowest scores on a test with a maximum score of 100 is 80. The instructor has obtained a(n)

a. measure of central tendency.
b. average deviation.
c. standard deviation.
d. range.

7. A measure of variability tells a psychologist how

a. close together the scores in a sample tend to be.
b. good a measure of central tendency the median is.
c. valid scores across the sample are.
d. well subjects performed on a test.

8. A team of psychologists presented their data in the form of a scatterplot. A scatterplot shows

a. how spread out scores are.
b. that scores on one measure are related to another measure.
c. the average person performed on a group of tests.
d. the causal relationship among a set of variables.

9. Which of the following correlations indicates the greatest degree of relationship between two variables?

a. -.89
b. +.20
c. -.13
d. +.61

10. A psychologist concluded that the difference between the drug group and the placebo group was statistically significant. This conclusion means that the

a. research produced important results.
b. difference between the groups is not likely to have occurred by chance.
c. drug is safe to use in most cases.
d. variability in the drug group was greater that the variability in the placebo group.

11. To determine if differences between two groups are statistically significant, researchers

a. must estimate the reliability of the independent variable.
b. compare the measures of central tendency across the different groups.
c. run a computer simulation of their experiment.
d. use a table and formula to determine the probability of obtaining the difference between groups by chance.

INTEGRATING QUESTIONS

1. a) Try to think of an original question about human behavior that might be difficult to answer using experimental methods because of ethical concerns. b) Think about whether you could use a case study approach to answer the question. c) If you did use the case study method, how are the kinds of conclusions that can be drawn limited relative to experimental procedures?

2. a) Now try to simplify the question to ask if you could study the phenomenon of interest with nonhuman subjects. Be aware that ethical issues are also of concern in research with nonhuman animals. b) How does the use of animals and the use of an experimental procedure enable you to make stronger conclusions?

ANSWERS

1.1 a) 1, b) 4, c) 3, d) 2
1.2 Step 1: f, g; Step 2: d; Step 3: a, e; Step 4: b, c
2.1 hypothesis
2.2 Statements a), d), and e) are hypotheses.
3.1 variables
3.2 a) independent, dependent; b) the independent variable; c) the dependent variable
3.3 a) IV: amount of smoking (or, perhaps, the amount of "tar" and nicotine), DV: lung cancer
b) IV: drug, DV: ability to put together a puzzle
c) IV: parental attention, DV: self-confidence of child
d) IV: type of sweetener, DV: activity (wheel running)
3.4 nominal fallacy
3.5 Example A illustrates the nominal fallacy.
4.1 operational definitions
5.1 validity
5.2 a) face, construct
5.3 a) face, b) construct
5.4 reliability
5.5 False. While a valid measure must be reliable, a measure may be reliable without being valid. You should provide an example of the latter.
5.6 a) "Original" is not defined explicitly; therefore, raters must use their own judgment to determine whether the children displayed creativity.
b) Interrater reliability cannot be assessed because only one observer is present. A second rater should be used. Otherwise, the conditions are adequate.
c) The subjects are observed under different conditions; thus, the measure would have poor reliability. All subjects should be observed at the same time of day.
5.7 a) Situation "a"
6.1 a) confounded
6.2 counterbalancing
6.3 a) Drug dose and order of presentation; the subjects may still feel the effects of exercise from the previous session and become more and more fatigued.
b) Counterbalance the order of presentation of the different doses of the drug. One group would receive the order 30, 20, 10; another 20, 10, 30; another 10, 30, 20, etc.
6.4 control group
6.5 a) control group
b) No. The rats may be aroused by receiving an injection (being handled by the experimenter and stuck with a needle), which may simply make them more alert. We cannot conclude that the drug itself had an effect.
c) Use a control group that receives a placebo injection of a salt solution to control for the activating effects of receiving an injection.
7.1 a) The groups consist of children of different ages, so developmental (age-related) differences may account for differences in the groups' performance.
b) All groups should consist of children of the same age.
7.2 a) random assignment, matching
7.3 a) random assignment, b) matching
8.2 single-blind
8.3 b) double-blind, Hire an observer who does not know the purpose of the experiment.
9.1 a) observational, b) Any three of the following: sex, age, socioeconomic status, race, personality
10.1 sample
10.2 generality

Chapter 2

11.3 ethics
12.1 a) descriptive statistics
12.2 central tendency
12.3 a) mean, b) the sum of all scores divided by the number of scores
12.4 a) median
13.3 range, variance, standard deviation
13.4 42
13.5 a) variance
b) scores scores-mean (scores-mean)^2

scores	scores-mean	(scores-mean)^2
1	-1	1
3	1	1
2	0	0
2	0	0
2	0	0
Total=10		Total= 2
Mean=2	Variance= 2/4=0.5	

13.6 a) standard deviation, b) the square root of the variance
13.7 .707, the square root of 0.5
14.1 a) scatter plot, b) correlation coefficient
14.2 Graphs A and C illustrate a systematic relation between two variables.
14.3 a) 0, 1; b) .91, .79, .50, .25
14.4 a) positive, b) negative
14.5 a) graph A, b) graph C
14.6 a) positive correlation, b) negative correlation, c) negative correlation, d) positive correlation
14.8 a) +.26, +.52; b) -.89, -.64; c) -.89, -.64, +.52, +.26
15.1 chance
15.2 a) statistical significance, b) True
16.2 a) 1. Calculate the mean and standard deviation. 2. Consult a table, using a particular formula. 3. Decide whether the observed difference between the means is likely to be due to chance or to the independent variable.
b) The investigator would probably conclude that the observed difference between the means was due to chance.
c) The investigator would probably conclude that a difference this large is not likely to occur by chance, so the difference is probably due to the effect of the independent variable.

Self Test: Lesson I

1. a Obj. 2-1
2. b Obj. 2-2
3. a Obj. 2-3
4. b Obj. 2-3
5. c Obj. 2-4
6. c Obj. 2-5
7. d Obj. 2-5
8. d Obj. 2-6
9. b Obj. 2-6
10. b Obj. 2-6
11. c Obj. 2-7
12. d Obj. 2-8

Self Test: Lesson II

1. d Obj. 2-10
2. c Obj. 2-11
3. d Obj. 2-11
4. c Obj. 2-12
5. b Obj. 2-12
6. d Obj. 2-13
7. a Obj. 2-13
8. b Obj. 2-14
9. a Obj. 2-14
10. b Obj. 2-15
11. d Obj. 2-16

2.1 OBJ 2-1

SCIENTIFIC METHOD

2.9 OBJ 2-5

VALIDITY

2.2 OBJ 2-2

HYPOTHESIS

2.10 OBJ 2-5

FACE VALIDITY

2.3 OBJ 2-2

SCIENTIFIC THEORY

2.11 OBJ 2-5

CONSTRUCT VALIDITY

2.4 OBJ 2-3

VARIABLE

2.12 OBJ 2-5

RELIABILITY

2.5 OBJ 2-3

INDEPENDENT VARIABLE

2.13 OBJ 2-5

INTERRATER RELIABILITY

2.6 OBJ 2-3

DEPENDENT VARIABLE

2.14 OBJ 2-6

CAUSE-AND-EFFECT RELATION

2.7 OBJ 2-3

NOMINAL FALLACY

2.15 OBJ 2-6

CONFOUNDING OF VARIABLES

2.8 OBJ 2-4

OPERATIONAL DEFINITION

2.16 OBJ 2-6

COUNTERBALANCING

2.9 Obj 2-5

extent to which an operational definition or psychological test accurately represents a variable

2.10 Obj 2-5

means of evaluating validity; uses intuitive, common sense criteria

2.11 Obj 2-5

means of evaluating validity; criteria involves how well it integrates a wide range of related effects

2.12 Obj 2-5

extent to which a measure is consistent when applied under similar conditions

2.13 Obj 2-5

extent to which there is agreement between observations of a same event by two independent observers

2.14 Obj 2-6

special kind of relation between two variables in which the value or occurrence of one is dependent on (caused by) the other

2.15 Obj 2-6

inadvertent manipulation of variables other than the independent variable, which may influence the dependent variable in an experiment

2.16 Obj 2-6

method for minimizing confounding of variables due to sequential presentation of conditions

2.1 Obj 2-1

system of inquiry for gaining knowledge about the causes of natural phenomena

2.2 Obj 2-2

statement about the possible relation between two or more variables

2.3 Obj 2-2

comprehensive system that organizes several related hypotheses in accounting for some aspect of natural events

2.4 Obj 2-3

events, characteristics or quantities of interest in a scientific experiment; components of hypothesis

2.5 Obj 2-3

variable that is typically manipulated in an experiment

2.6 Obj 2-3

variable that is typically measured in an experiment in order to see how it is affected by the independent variable

2.7 Obj 2-3

belief that by merely naming an event the event has been explained

2.8 Obj 2-4

specific, unambiguous description of the variables involved in an experiment

2.17 OBJ 2-6

CONTROL GROUP

2.25 OBJ 2-9

OBSERVATIONAL STUDY

2.18 OBJ 2-7

SUBJECT VARIABLES

2.26 OBJ 2-9

MATCHING

2.19 OBJ 2-7

RANDOM ASSIGNMENT
(RANDOM SELECTION)

2.27 OBJ 2-10

SAMPLE

2.20 OBJ 2-7

SUBJECT EXPECTANCIES

2.28 OBJ 2-10

GENERALITY

2.21 OBJ 2-8

PLACEBO

2.29 OBJ 2-11

CASE STUDY

2.22 OBJ 2-8

SINGLE-BLIND STUDY

2.30 OBJ 2-11

ETHICS

2.23 OBJ 2-8

EXPERIMENTER EXPECTANCIES

2.31 OBJ 2-12

DESCRIPTIVE STATISTICS

2.24 OBJ 2-8

DOUBLE-BLIND STUDY

2.32 OBJ 2-12

MEASURES OF CENTRAL TENDENCY

2.25 Obj 2-9

type of scientific study; relations between variables are assessed but manipulation of independent variables is not attempted (nonexperimental)

2.26 Obj 2-9

procedure for minimizing the confounding effects of subject variables; equates subjects across groups on relevant characteristics

2.27 Obj 2-10

subset of a population used as subjects in a particular experiment

2.28 Obj 2-10

extent to which the conclusions obtained from a particular sample may be extended (generalized) to the population of interest

2.29 Obj 2-11

study evaluating changes in individual behavior in order to make inferences about its causes

2.30 Obj 2-11

in psychology, cultural criteria for defining appropriate and humane treatment of living experimental subjects

2.31 Obj 2-12

values representing the central tendency or variability of a variable

2.32 Obj 2-12

measures representing the most "typical" values of the dependent variable

2.17 Obj 2-6

method for minimizing confounding of variables using a "no treatment" group

2.18 Obj 2-7

characteristics of subjects that may influence the dependent variable and thus confound the results of an experiment

2.19 Obj 2-7

procedure for assigning subjects to groups by chance; minimizes the confounding effects of subject variables

2.20 Obj 2-7

predisposition of subjects that may alter their behavior in a study and thus confound the results

2.21 Obj 2-8

procedure used to minimize the effects of subject expectancies by making them believe they are being treated when, in fact, they are not

2.22 Obj 2-8

procedure used to minimize the effect of subject expectancies by withholding information about treatment

2.23 Obj 2-8

predisposition of experimenter or observers that may influence the dependent variable; confounds results of an experiment

2.24 Obj 2-8

procedure used to minimize the effects of both experimenter and subject expectancies

2.33 OBJ 2-12

MEAN

2.34 OBJ 2-12

MEDIAN

2.35 OBJ 2-13

MEASURES OF VARIABILITY

2.36 OBJ 2-13

RANGE

2.37 OBJ 2-13

VARIANCE

2.38 OBJ 2-13

STANDARD DEVIATION

2.39 OBJ 2-14

SCATTER PLOT

2.40 OBJ 2-14

CORRELATION COEFFICIENT

2.41 OBJ 2-14

POSITIVE CORRELATION

2.42 OBJ 2-14

NEGATIVE CORRELATION

2.43 OBJ 2-15

STATISTICAL SIGNIFICANCE

2.44 OBJ 2-16

FREQUENCY DISTRIBUTION

2.33 Obj 2-12

measure of central tendency; sum of scores divided by the number of scores in the sample = mean (average)

2.34 Obj 2-12

measure of central tendency; divides the sample in half (fifty percent of the scores fall above it, fifty percent of the scores fall below it)

2.35 Obj 2-13

measures representing the degree of dispersion of scores in a set of data

2.36 Obj 2-13

measure of variability; highest score minus lowest score

2.37 Obj 2-13

measure of variability; average squared deviation of each score from the group's mean

2.38 Obj 2-13

measure of variability; square root of the variance

2.39 Obj 2-14

graph depicting the relation between two variables

2.40 Obj 2-14

value summarizing the extent to which two variables are related

2.41 Obj 2-14

relation between two variables; high values on one associated with high values on other, low values on one associated with low values on other

2.42 Obj 2-14

relation between two variables; high values on one associated with low values on other, low values on one associated with high values on other

2.43 Obj 2-15

criterion for evaluating whether the observed difference between means of groups are due to chance or to the independent variable

2.44 Obj 2-16

an index of the number of times all particular values in a sample of scores are repeated

CHAPTER 3
Biology of Behavior

INTRODUCTION

Chapter 3 examines the biological contribution of the structure and function of the nervous system to behavior. This chapter is divided into two lessons. Lesson I (Objectives 1-14) is an introduction to the structure and function of the nervous system. Lesson II (Objectives 15-26) covers the mechanisms of neural communication and the mechanisms by which various drugs affect behavior.

CONCEPT CARDS AND EXERCISES

After you have surveyed and read the text, assemble the concept cards located at the end of this chapter. Use them to learn the important terms, then begin reading the text again, one learning objective at a time, and work through the exercises for each lesson. Answers for questions marked with an asterisk are found at the end of the chapter.

SELF TESTS

Each lesson is followed by a multiple-choice self test. After you are proficient with a lesson's concept cards and exercises, take the self test to see whether you have mastered the material. Review those objectives for questions you answered incorrectly.

INTEGRATING QUESTIONS

To challenge yourself further, answer the integrating questions at the end of the chapter. These questions ask you to apply the information you have learned to consider larger theoretical or real-life issues.

LESSON I: STRUCTURE AND FUNCTION OF THE NERVOUS SYSTEM

1. Describe the three basic areas of research in behavioral biology. (pp. 67-68)

1.1 What does a neurologist specialize in?

1.2 What early contribution did neurologists make to physiological psychology?

1.3 What are the scientific objectives of neuropsychologists?

1.4 How are the observational and inferential procedures of neurologists and neuropsychologists similar?

1.5 How do the goals of neuropsychologists and neurologists differ?

1.6 Describe the kinds of experiments that physiological psychologists can perform with animals that neurologists and neuropsychologists cannot perform with humans.

2. Describe the common experimental research methods used in physiological psychology. Explain what psychologists use CAT scans for. (pp. 68-73)

2.1 Describe how lesion production differs from the ablation method used by neurologists and neuropsychologists.

2.2 What is a stereotaxic apparatus used for?

2.3 Describe three different types of physiological procedures that can be accomplished using a stereotaxic apparatus.

2.4 Summarize the most common research procedures used by physiological psychologists.

* 2.5 The acronym CAT stands for ______________ ______________ ______________.

2.6 In general terms, what does a CAT scanner do?

2.7 What does a CAT scanner provide?

2.8 What are the advantages of a CAT scan over older methods of determining the location and severity of lesions?

3. Describe the basic structural features and functions of the central nervous system. (pp. 73-74)

* 3.1 What part of the central nervous system is protected by vertebrae? by the skull?

3.2 Describe the three layers of the meninges.

3.3 What is CSF, what is its function, where is it produced, and where does it go?

3.4 Describe the two basic parts of the central nervous system, the bones that protect them, and the nature and location of the meninges.

4. Describe the basic structural features and functions of the peripheral nervous system. (p. 75)

4.1 What is the function of the peripheral nervous system (PNS)?

4.2 What is the role of the PNS when sense organs detect changes in the environment?

4.3 What is the role of the PNS when the brain sends signals to the muscles and glands?

4.4 Describe the structural connections of the CNS and PNS above and below the neck.

4.5 Describe the functions of the CNS and PNS above and below the neck.

5. Describe the basic features of the sensory systems, including the thalamus and sensory areas of the cerebral cortex. (pp. 76-79)

5.1 What complex human behaviors are mediated primarily by the cerebral cortex?

5.2 Where is the cerebral cortex located? How thick is it?

5.3 What is the position of the cerebral cortex relative to the cerebral hemispheres?

5.4 What are gyri?

* 5.5 The thalamus is located in the _____________ area of the brain.

5.6 What is the shape of the two parts of the thalamus, and where are they located?

* 5.7 What are the five sensory modalities by which we interact with the environment?

5.8 Explain what a primary sensory area is. From what brain structure does it receive its information?

5.9 State the name, location, and function of the primary sensory cortex area associated with sight.

5.10 State the name, location, and function of the sensory cortex area associated with hearing.

5.11 State the name, location, and function of the cortex area associated with "body" senses.

5.12 Which sensory modality inputs are relayed to various parts of the brain by the thalamus? Which one is not?

* 5.13 Label the locations of the three primary sensory areas on figure 3.1, below.

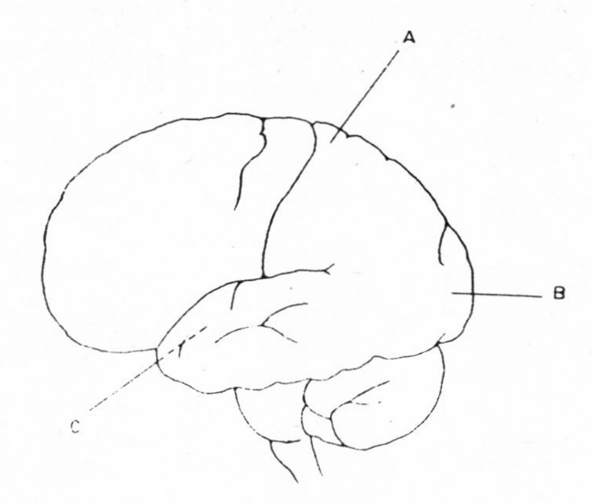

FIGURE 3.1

6. Describe the major neural structures that control motor activity and their primary function. (pp. 79-80)

6.1 What is the principal role of primary motor cortex and where is it located?

6.2 What does the word cerebellum mean and why is it called that?

6.3 What are the functions of the cerebellum and where is it located?

6.4 List the three major portions of the brain associated with motor activity, their approximate location, and the specific motor activity each structure mediates.

7. Describe the locations and functions of the areas of association cortex. (pp. 80-83)

7.1 Where is the frontal lobe located? What fissure is it in front of?

7.2 Where is the temporal lobe located? What fissure is it below?

7.3 Where is the parietal lobe located relative to the central sulcus?

7.4 Where are the parietal and frontal lobes located relative to the temporal lobe?

7.5 Where is the occipital lobe located relative to the other lobes?

* 7.6 Label the central sulcus, lateral fissure, frontal lobe, temporal lobe, occipital lobe, and parietal lobe on figure 3.2 in the study guide.

7.7 Sketch in the location of the various areas of association cortex on figure 3.2, below.

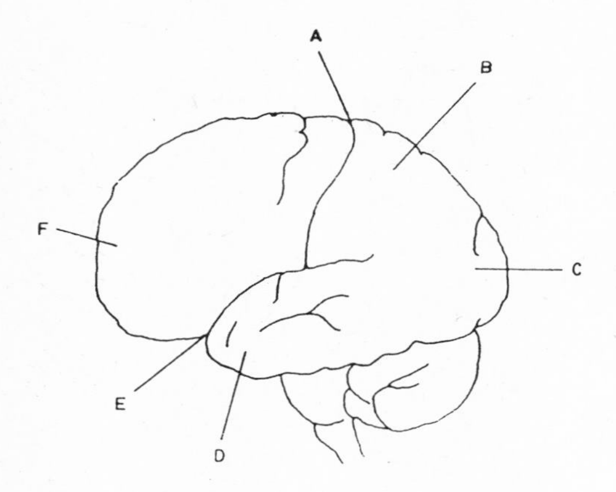

FIGURE 3.2

7.8 Describe the general functions of association cortex.

7.9 Describe the functions of the motor association areas of the cortex.

7.10 Which area of association cortex is involved in the planning and execution of movements?

8. Describe the location, size, and functions of the hypothalamus. (pp. 83-86)

8.1 Describe the location and two major functions of the hypothalamus.

8.2 What are the functions of the endocrine glands? Why is the pituitary gland such an important endocrine gland?

8.3 Where is the pituitary gland located?

* 8.4 Because the ______________ controls the pituitary gland and the pituitary gland controls the ______________ system, it follows that the ______________ indirectly controls the endocrine system.

9. Describe the basic structure and functions of each of the following brainstem regions: midbrain, pons, medulla and reticular formation. (pp. 86-87)

9.1 Where is the midbrain located and what are its primary functions?

9.2 a) What does the pons look like?

b) How was its name derived?

c) What general functions are performed by the pons?

9.3 Where is the medulla located and what are the "vital functions" controlled by the medulla?

9.4 List several other physiological functions that are mediated by the medulla.

9.5 Describe the structural features and functions performed by the reticular formation.

10. Describe the lateralization of brain functions involved in behavior. (pp. 87-88)

10.1 Which general area of the brain is concerned with motor activity and which area mediates sensory activity?

10.2 Describe lateralization of function.

10.3 Describe the general lateralized functions of the left hemisphere.

10.4 Describe the general lateralized functions of the right hemisphere.

10.5 Are there any exceptions to your answer to question 10.4? If so, what are they?

11. Describe the visual functions of the occipital lobe. Differentiate between the visual functions of the left and right hemispheres. (pp. 88-89)

11.1 Distinguish between the effects of damage to primary visual cortex and damage to visual association cortex.

11.2 Which hemisphere's visual association cortex is specialized for recognition of familiar objects? What is the other hemisphere's visual association cortex specialized for?

12. Describe the principal functions of the temporal lobes and relate them to lateralization of function. (pp. 89)

12.1 In what parts of the temporal lobe are the primary auditory cortex and the auditory association cortex found?

12.2 Describe the effects of damage to left auditory association cortex.

12.3 Describe the effects of damage to right auditory association cortex.

12.4 Describe the effects on memory resulting from bilateral damage to the temporal lobes.

12.5 Describe the abnormal social, emotional and sexual activities that appear to be related to temporal lobe damage.

13. Describe the principal functions of the parietal lobe and relate them to lateralization of function. (pp. 89-91)

13.1 What is the principal function of the parietal lobe?

13.2 Describe the functions of the parietal lobe that overlap with those of the occipital lobe and the temporal lobe.

13.3 Describe the contribution of the parietal lobe to our perception of spatial relations.

13.4 Suppose someone you know sustained damage to the right parietal lobe, and was later seen wearing a pair of shoes with only the right shoe laced and tied. What common symptom would this exemplify?

13.5 Describe how mathematical ability is impaired by parietal lobe damage and offer a reasonable explanation in terms of basic functions of the parietal lobe.

14. Describe the functions of the frontal lobe by relating damage to this area to corresponding behavior changes. (pp. 91-93)

14.1 a) Briefly describe the four types of symptoms associated with damage to the forward portions of the frontal lobes.

b) Explain how they differ from a simple decline in intellectual ability.

14.2 Provide an original example of perseveration.

14.3 Describe the kinds of personality changes seen in those with frontal lobe damage.

14.4 Describe the effects frontal lobe damage has on planning and anticipation.

LESSON I SELF TEST

1. The neural basis of behavior is most likely to be investigated by

   a. neurologists, neuropsychologists, and physiological psychologists.
   b. behaviorists, cognitivists, and physiologists.
   c. behaviorists, cognitivists, and developmentalists.
   d. physiologists, neuroanatomists, and ethologists.

2. Physiological psychologists use a stereotaxic apparatus to

   a. electrically stimulate part of an animal's brain.
   b. electrically create a lesion in part of an animal's brain.
   c. insert a wire into a specific area of an animal's brain.
   d. record the brain waves of a subject.

3. The CNS is composed of the _________ and _________.

   a. ventricles; meninges
   b. brain; spinal cord
   c. PNS; meninges
   d. skull; vertebrae

4. Auditory and visual information is sent to the _________ before it reaches the cerebral cortex.

   a. frontal lobe
   b. thalamus
   c. cerebellum
   d. basal ganglia

5. Damage to the frontal lobe is most likely to disrupt functioning of the _________ cortex.

   a. visual
   b. somatosensory
   c. auditory
   d. motor

6. Which of the following regions of the brain contain association cortex?

   a. temporal fissure, thalamus, hypothalamus, basal ganglia
   b. basal ganglia, frontal lobes, temporal lobes
   c. thalamus, basal ganglia, cerebellum
   d. frontal, parietal, temporal, occipital lobes

7. The pituitary gland has been called the "master gland" because it controls

   a. the flow of information to and from the brain.
   b. the rest of the endocrine system.
   c. heart rate, blood pressure, and respiration.
   d. self-awareness and higher cognitive functions.

8. The critical or "vital functions" are mediated by

   a. midbrain.
   b. pons.
   c. medulla.
   d. reticular formation.

9. Gabe, who knows basic neurology, says he is a left-brained person. He really means that he is

   a. more of an athlete than a scholar.
   b. able to analyze information well.
   c. a very visual person.
   d. a very sensual person.

10. As a result of the accident, George suffered brain damage. He has difficulty recognizing familiar objects by sight. George probably suffers from __________ caused by damage to the __________.

   a. dyslexia; occipital lobe
   b. sensory neglect; reticular formation
   c. visual agnosia; occipital lobe
   d. dyslexia; reticular formation

11. Individuals with bilateral temporal lobe damage suffer from

   a. severe loss of recall for new events.
   b. an inability to recognize speech sounds.
   c. an inability to recognize non-speech sounds.
   d. an inability to utter meaningful word combinations.

12. Linda has exhibited a continuous behavior pattern of sensory neglect since her car accident. She probably sustained damage to her

   a. left parietal lobe.
   b. right parietal lobe.
   c. left frontal lobe.
   d. right occipital lobe.

13. One of the usual behavioral changes resulting from frontal lobe damage is a deficit in

   a. memory.
   b. motor coordination.
   c. perception of speech sounds.
   d. planning.

LESSON II: NEURAL COMMUNICATION AND BEHAVIORAL EFFECT OF DRUGS

15. Identify and describe the functions of the basic parts of a neuron. (pp. 93-94)

* 15.1 The cell body of the neuron is called the _______________. What is its size relative to other parts of the neuron? Describe its functions.

15.2 What do dendrites resemble? How are they connected to the rest of the neuron? What are their functions?

15.3 What is the principal function of an axon?

15.4 Distinguish between the signals carried by an axon and those transmitted through an electrical wire.

* 15.5 Signals traveling along an excited axon are called _______________ _______________.

* 15.6 The swellings at the end of the axon are called _______________ _______________.

15.7 Describe the structure of an axon and the terminal buttons found at its end.

15.8 Explain the functions of terminal buttons. Be sure to describe the signal that a terminal button sends and how it differs from the action potential of the axon.

15.9 Describe the structure and function of the myelin sheath.

16. Describe how neurons communicate by means of synapses. (pp. 94-95)

16.1 What is a synapse?

16.2 What is a motor neuron?

16.3 Explain how muscles are activated. How does the number of activated neurons affect the magnitude of the muscular response?

17. Describe two basic effects that synapses have on postsynaptic neurons and relate them to starting and stopping motor responses. (pp. 95-96)

17.1 What happens when an action potential activates an excitatory neuron?

* 17.2 Imagine two neurons labelled A and B. If neuron A sends a signal to neuron B, which is the postsynaptic neuron? the presynaptic neuron?

* 17.3 If neurons A and B are connected by an inhibitory synapse and neuron A is fired, what will be the effect on neuron B?

* 17.4 If a neuron simultaneously receives input from many of its inhibitory synapses but from

only a few of its excitatory ones, what its rate of firing be?

18. Explain the process of synaptic transmission. (pp. 96-97)

* 18.1 In terminal buttons, transmitter substance is stored in _______________ _______________.

18.2 Describe how the synaptic vesicles release transmitter substance from the terminal buttons.

18.3 Describe the interaction between molecules of transmitter substance and postsynaptic receptors.

* 18.4 Name the two processes that terminate the effects of the transmitter substance on the postsynaptic neuron.

19. Describe the basic circuit involved in a withdrawal reflex. (pp 98-101)

19.1 Describe the three types of neurons involved in a withdrawal reflex and then explain their functions.

19.2 Draw a schematic diagram of a simple withdrawal reflex circuit.

19.3 Indicate on your diagram where in this circuit an inhibitory effect from the brain may be introduced.

20. Summarize the four basic mechanisms by which drugs may alter normal synaptic activity: production of transmitter substances, release of transmitter substances, activation of postsynaptic receptors, and re-uptake of transmitter substances. (pp. 101-103)

20.1 Explain why the symptoms of Parkinson's disease are alleviated following administration of L-DOPA.

* 20.2 a) Drugs can alter the release of transmitter substance by _______________ and _______________.

b) For each of the effects you named in question 20.2, supply an example and name the affected transmitter substance.

* 20.3 a) Drugs can either inhibit or stimulate the activity of postsynaptic _______________.

b) Provide an example of a drug that stimulates receptors and a drug that blocks them.

20.4 a) What usually happens to the transmitter substance shortly after it is released into the synaptic cleft?

b) What is the effect of this process on the duration of the activity of the post-synaptic neuron?

21. Describe the effects of alcohol, alcohol withdrawal, and chronic alcohol use. (pp. 104)

21.1 Describe the effects of alcohol withdrawal after prolonged heavy consumption.

21.2 Alcohol is properly classed as a depressant. Explain why small or moderate doses of alcohol are usually considered to have stimulating effects?

21.3 Name and describe the effects of the syndrome that can be caused by chronic alcohol abuse.

22. Compare the effects of tranquilizers, barbiturates and aromatic solvents to those of alcohol. (p. 104)

* 22.1 The effects of barbiturates, tranquilizers, and aromatic solvents are (similar to/different from) those of alcohol.

22.2 If nonlethal doses of two or more depressant drugs are taken together, what is the effect?

22.3 Compare the potential for damage of chronic barbiturate use and chronic alcohol use. Explain your answer.

23. Describe the physiological processes and behavioral effects of chronic use of opiates. (pp. 105-106)

23.1 Name and briefly describe three well-known types of opiates.

23.2 Explain how opiates produce their effects by referring to the role of endorphins and opiate receptors.

23.3 What are the effects of opiate receptor stimulation?

* 23.4 The class of chemicals that block opiate receptor sites is ______________

______________.

23.5 Why are these drugs of little use in controlling opiate addiction?

24. Compare the primary pharmacological and behavioral effects of LSD and related compounds with the behavioral effects of marijuana. (pp. 106-107)

24.1 a) What is the apparent effect of hallucinogenic drugs on serotonin secreting neurons?

b) What is the suggested role of serotonin secreting neurons in dreaming?

c) Explain an LSD "trip" by referring to the interaction between the drug, these neurons, and dreaming.

24.2 Briefly summarize what we know about the effects of tetrahydrocannabinol—the active ingredient in marijuana—on neuron activity.

24.3 What are the effects of LSD and marijuana on the reproductive process?

25. Describe the physiological and behavioral effects of the two major stimulant drugs, amphetamine and cocaine. (pp. 107-108)

* 25.1 _______________ and _______________ are two commonly used drugs that are central nervous system stimulants.

25.2 Describe the initial effects of amphetamine use and compare then with the initial effects of cocaine use.

25.3 Describe some of the serious consequences of chronic heavy use of amphetamine and cocaine.

LESSON II SELF TEST

1. The action potential is

a. a chemical message carried by the dendrites.
b. a mechanism in the soma that controls the metabolism and maintenance of a cell.
c. another name for transmitter substance secreted by the terminal buttons.
d. an electrical message sent by and along the axon of a cell.

2. If an inhibitory synapse increases firing, it will cause

a. the postsynaptic neuron to increase firing.
b. the postsynaptic neuron to decrease firing.
c. an excitatory synapse to decrease firing.
d. a slowing down of the presynaptic neuron.

3. When a transmitter substance is released from the synaptic vesicles it goes

a. into the synaptic cleft to the postsynaptic receptors.
b. into the synaptic cleft to the presynaptic membrane.
c. from the dendrites to the terminal buttons.
d. from the terminal buttons to the presynaptic membrane.

4. A sensory neuron, an interneuron, and a motor neuron form the components of a simple

a. nerve cell.
b. neural integration.
c. withdrawal reflex.
d. inhibitory synapse.

5. Which of the following is <u>not</u> a way that drugs can affect the nervous system?

   a. directly affect the electrical transmission of messages among neurons
   b. mimic the effects of neurotransmitter substances
   c. interfere with mechanisms that deactivate neurotransmitters
   d. increase the production of neurotransmitter substances

6. Sudden withdrawal from prolonged acute alcohol dependence results in

   a. no withdrawal symptoms.
   b. mild withdrawal symptoms.
   c. moderate withdrawal symptoms.
   d. severe withdrawal symptoms.

7. Compared to the chronic use of alcohol, the chronic use of barbiturates is

   a. less likely to lead to addiction and withdrawal symptoms.
   b. more likely to lead to a drug-induced psychosis.
   c. less likely to produce long-term damage.
   d. less likely to lead to increased tolerance of the drug.

8. Analgesia may be induced by

   a. tranquilizers.
   b. opiates.
   c. cocaine.
   d. barbiturates.

9. Research on the pharmacological effects of marijuana suggests that

   a. the causes of its effects are still unknown.
   b. it inhibits the secretion of the neurotransmitter substance, serotonin.
   c. it mimics the effects of the body's own analgesics.
   d. it facilitates the release of the neurotransmitter substance, norepinephrine.

10. Which drug are most likely to produce psychotic reactions in chronic and heavy users?

   a. tranquilizers
   b. barbiturates
   c. heroin
   d. amphetamines

INTEGRATING QUESTIONS

1. Now that you know more about the brain, turn back to Chapter 1 and think about Descartes's model of the brain's control of behavior. How would you, with your modern knowlegde of brain functioning, go about solving the mind-body problem? Does the word "mind" have a different meaning for you after having studied this chapter? If so, how? Will the research of neuroscientists in this century and the next fundamentally alter the way we think about ourselves?

2. If brain transplants were possible (they are not, and what we know about the nervous system suggests that they never will be), what would the identity of the "person" be, the original owner of the brain or the original owner of the body? What if <u>parts</u> of the brain of a recently-dead person could be implanted into the brain of a living person to repair parts that had been damaged?

Chapter 3

ANSWERS

2.5 Computerized Axial Tomography
3.1 spinal cord, brain
5.5 subcortical
5.7 audition (sound), olfaction (smell), somatosensory ("body"—touch, heat pressure, etc.), taste, and vision
5.13 a) primary somatosensory cortex, b) primary visual cortex, c) primary auditory cortex
7.6 A. central sulcus, B. parietal lobe, C. occipital lobe, D. temporal lobe, E. lateral fissure, F. frontal lobe
8.4 hypothalamus, endocrine, hypothalamus
15.1 soma
15.5 action potentials
15.6 terminal buttons
17.2 neuron A is presynaptic, neuron B is postsynaptic
17.3 decreases rate of firing
17.4 a low rate of firing
18.1 synaptic vesicles
18.4 rapid chemical destruction or deactivation of the transmitter substance and/or re-uptake of the transmitter substance by the terminal button
20.2 a) stimulation, inhibition, b) black widow spider venom, butolinum toxin
20.3 a) receptors, b) nicotine, curare or chlorpromazine
23.4 opiate antagonists
25.1 cocaine, amphetamines

Self Test: Lesson I

1. c Obj. 3-1
2. c Obj. 3-2
3. b Obj. 3-3
4. b Obj. 3-5
5. d Obj. 3-6
6. d Obj. 3-7
7. b Obj. 3-8
8. c Obj. 3-9
9. b Obj. 3-10
10. c Obj. 3-11
11. a Obj. 3-12
12. b Obj. 3-13
13. d Obj. 3-14

Self Test: Lesson II

1. d Obj. 3-15
2. b Obj. 3-17
3. a Obj. 3-18
4. c Obj. 3-19
5. a Obj. 3-20
6. d Obj. 3-21
7. c Obj. 3-22
8. b Obj. 3-23
9. a Obj. 3-24
10. d Obj. 3-25

3.1 OBJ 3-1

NEUROLOGIST

3.2 OBJ 3-1

NEUROPSYCHOLOGIST

3.3 OBJ 3-1

PHYSIOLOGICAL PSYCHOLOGIST

3.4 OBJ 3-2

LESION PRODUCTION

3.5 OBJ 3-2

STEREOTAXIC APPARATUS

3.6 OBJ 3-2

CAT SCANNER

3.7 OBJ 3-3

CENTRAL NERVOUS SYSTEM (CNS)

3.8 OBJ 3-3

MENINGES

3.9 OBJ 3-3

CEREBROSPINAL FLUID (CSF)

3.10 OBJ 3-3

VENTRICLES

3.11 OBJ 3-4

PERIPHERAL NERVOUS SYSTEM (PNS)

3.12 OBJ 3-4

SPINAL NERVES

3.13 OBJ 3-4

CRANIAL NERVES

3.14 OBJ 3-5

CEREBRAL CORTEX

3.15 OBJ 3-5

CEREBRAL HEMISPHERES

3.16 OBJ 3-5

GYRI

3.9 Obj 3-3

liquid bathing and cushioning brain; inside meninges

3.10 Obj 3-3

hollow chambers in the brain full of CSF

3.11 Obj 3-4

nerves that connect CNS to sense organs, muscles, and glands

3.12 Obj 3-4

nerves attached to the spinal cord

3.13 Obj 3-4

nerves attached directly to the brain

3.14 Obj 3-5

"gray matter"; thin layer of nerve cell tissue covering the cerebral hemispheres

3.15 Obj 3-5

two large masses of brain tissue; one on the left and one on the right

3.16 Obj 3-5

bulges on the outer surface of the brain (cerebral cortex)

3.1 Obj 3-1

a physician specializing in diseases of the nervous system

3.2 Obj 3-1

scientist studying the organization of the nervous system and its contribution to human behavior

3.3 Obj 3-1

a scientist who experimentally investigates nervous system structure and function with non-human subjects

3.4 Obj 3-2

a technique for producing specific, localized damage to brain tissue for physiological research

3.5 Obj 3-2

a device for precisely locating a particular location in the brain using a three-dimensional coordinate system

3.6 Obj 3-2

Computerized Axial Tomography—a diagnostic medical tool; takes x-rays of cross sections of the body

3.7 Obj 3-3

brain and spinal cord

3.8 Obj 3-3

set of three layers inside the skull and vertebrae protecting the CNS

3.17 OBJ 3-5

FISSURES

3.18 OBJ 3-5

THALAMUS

3.19 OBJ 3-5

WHITE MATTER

3.20 OBJ 3-5

PRIMARY VISUAL CORTEX

3.21 OBJ 3-5

PRIMARY AUDITORY CORTEX

3.22 OBJ 3-5

PRIMARY SOMATOSENSORY CORTEX

3.23 OBJ 3-6

PRIMARY MOTOR CORTEX

3.24 OBJ 3-6

CEREBELLUM

3.25 OBJ 3-7

CENTRAL FISSURE

3.26 OBJ 3-7

FRONTAL LOBE

3.27 OBJ 3-7

PARIETAL LOBE

3.28 OBJ 3-7

TEMPORAL LOBE

3.29 OBJ 3-7

OCCIPITAL LOBE

3.30 OBJ 3-7

SENSORY ASSOCIATION CORTEX

3.31 OBJ 3-7

MOTOR ASSOCIATION CORTEX

3.32 OBJ 3-8

HYPOTHALAMUS

3.25 Obj 3-7

division of anterior and posterior regions of cerebral cortex: motor cortex in front, sensory cortex behind

3.26 Obj 3-7

brain mass above the lateral fissure and forward of the central sulcus; contains motor cortex

3.27 Obj 3-7

brain mass behind the central sulcus and above the lateral fissure; contains somatosensory cortex

3.28 Obj 3-7

brain mass below the lateral fissure; contains auditory cortex

3.29 Obj 3-7

brain mass behind the parietal and temporal lobes; contains visual cortex

3.30 Obj 3-7

areas adjacent to primary sensory cortex regions; receives signals from primary cortex

3.31 Obj 3-7

area involved in coordination of muscular activity

3.32 Obj 3-8

small region below the thalamus: regulates homeostasis and species-typical behavior

3.17 Obj 3-5

large grooves in the outer surface of the brain (cerebral cortex)

3.18 Obj 3-5

part of the subcortical area of the cerebral hemispheres

3.19 Obj 3-5

shiny white coated fiber bundles connecting the cortex and other areas of the brain

3.20 Obj 3-5

area at the back of the brain receiving visual signals

3.21 Obj 3-5

area on the surface of the lateral fissures receiving auditory signals

3.22 Obj 3-5

area behind the central fissure receiving body senses

3.23 Obj 3-6

area just in front of the central sulcus controlling hand and finger movement

3.24 Obj 3-6

"little brain"; beneath rear halves of the cerebral hemispheres; coordinates rapid motor activity

3.33 OBJ 3-8

HOMEOSTASIS

3.34 OBJ 3-8

PITUITARY GLAND

3.35 OBJ 3-8

ENDOCRINE GLANDS

3.36 OBJ 3-8

AUTONOMIC NERVOUS SYSTEM

3.37 OBJ 3-9

PONS

3.38 OBJ 3-9

MEDULLA

3.39 OBJ 3-9

RETICULAR FORMATION

3.40 OBJ 3-13

SENSORY NEGLECT

3.41 OBJ 3-15

NEURONS

3.42 OBJ 3-15

SOMA

3.43 OBJ 3-15

DENDRITES

3.44 OBJ 3-15

AXON

3.45 OBJ 3-15

ACTION POTENTIAL

3.46 OBJ 3-15

TERMINAL BUTTONS

3.47 OBJ 3-15

TRANSMITTER SUBSTANCE

3.48 OBJ 3-15

MYELIN SHEATHS

3.41 Obj 3-15

nerve cells; convey signals from sensory cells to the brain and from the brain to muscle cells and glands

3.42 Obj 3-15

cell body; largest part of the neuron; controls metabolism of the cell

3.43 Obj 3-15

tree-like branches receiving signals from other cells and bringing the signals toward soma or axon

3.44 Obj 3-15

part of the neuron that carries signals from soma toward other cells

3.45 Obj 3-15

electrical pulse or signal transmitted along the axon

3.46 Obj 3-15

nodes at the end of the axon; release chemical signals to other cells

3.47 Obj 3-15

chemical signal released by terminal buttons to other cells

3.48 Obj 3-15

special "flat" cells that wrap around sections of the axon to "insulate" action potentials of adjacent axons from "short-circuiting" each other

3.33 Obj 3-8

an organism's self-regulation of physiological variables, such as temperature, water, sleep, etc.

3.34 Obj 3-8

"master endocrine gland"; controlled by hypothalamus; controls endocrine system

3.35 Obj 3-8

hormone secreting system of glands in the body

3.36 Obj 3-8

controls "automatic" response systems—sweating, emotions, salivation, digestion, etc.

3.37 Obj 3-9

large bulge in the brainstem; regulates arousal and sleep states

3.38 Obj 3-9

lowest brain part; controls "vital functions"—heart, blood pressure, respiration

3.39 Obj 3-9

structure in the pons; controls waking and alert states

3.40 Obj 3-13

inability to attend to objects in the left field of vision; produced by right parietal lobe damage

3.49 OBJ 3-16

SYNAPSES

3.50 OBJ 3-16

MOTOR NEURON

3.51 OBJ 3-17

INHIBITORY AND EXCITATORY SYNAPSES

3.52 OBJ 3-17

PRE- AND POSTSYNAPTIC NEURONS

3.53 OBJ 3-18

SYNAPTIC VESICLES

3.54 OBJ 3-18

SYNAPTIC CLEFT

3.55 OBJ 3-18

RE-UPTAKE

3.56 OBJ 3-19

SENSORY NEURONS

3.57 OBJ 3-19

INTERNEURONS

3.58 OBJ 3-19

WITHDRAWAL REFLEX

3.59 OBJ 3-20

DOPAMINE

3.60 OBJ 3-20

ACETYLCHOLINE

3.61 OBJ 3-23

OPIATE RECEPTORS

3.62 OBJ 3-23

ENDORPHINS

3.63 OBJ 3-24

SEROTONIN

3.64 OBJ 3-26

NOREPINEPHRINE

3.57 Obj 3-19

convey signals from sensory neurons to motor neurons

3.58 Obj 3-19

a simple motor response removing sensory contact with aversive stimuli

3.59 Obj 3-20

a transmitter substance synthesized from precursor enzyme L-DOPA; dopamine neuron deficiency produces Parkinson's disease

3.60 Obj 3-20

a transmitter substance necessary for remembering

3.61 Obj 3-23

postsynaptic receptor sites on neurons that are activated by opiate-like chemicals

3.62 Obj 3-23

naturally produced chemical in the brain; similar to opiates in chemical structure and in affects on opiate receptors

3.63 Obj 3-24

a transmitter substance whose releasing neurons are inhibited by hallucinogens

3.64 Obj 3-26

a transmitter substance similar to dopamine; re-uptake is retarded and release facilitated by amphetamines and cocaine

3.49 Obj 3-16

junctures between terminal buttons of one neuron and dendrites of another neuron

3.50 Obj 3-16

a neuron that synapses on a muscle fiber; signals from the terminal buttons of the motor neuron produce muscle contractions

3.51 Obj 3-17

synapses whose signals increase or decrease the probability of firing by the neuron receiving the signal, respectively

3.52 Obj 3-17

neuron sending a signal over a synapse to a postsynaptic neuron or receiving a signal from a presynaptic neuron, respectively

3.53 Obj 3-18

small sacs containing transmitter substance; located in terminal buttons; release transmitter substance into synaptic cleft

3.54 Obj 3-18

space between the terminal button's presynaptic membrane and the membrane of the postsynaptic neuron

3.55 Obj 3-18

"recycling" of previously released transmitter substance by "repackaging" it in new presynaptic vesicles within the terminal button

3.56 Obj 3-19

convey signals from environmental stimuli to interneurons

CHAPTER 4
Sensation and Perception

INTRODUCTION

This chapter examines the mechanics of stimulus detection by the nervous system and how these signals are interpreted and integrated. It is divided into two lessons: Lesson I (Objectives 1-19) covers vision and Lesson II (Objectives 20-30) covers the other sense modalities—hearing, taste, smell, and the body senses.

CONCEPT CARDS AND EXERCISES

After you have surveyed and read the text, assemble the concept cards located at the end of this chapter. Use them to learn the important terms, then begin reading the text again, one learning objective at a time, and work through the exercises for each lesson. Answers for questions marked with an asterisk are found at the end of the chapter.

SELF TESTS

Each lesson is followed by a multiple-choice self test. After you are proficient with a lesson's concept cards and exercises, take the self test to see whether you have mastered the material. Review those objectives for questions you answered incorrectly.

INTEGRATING QUESTIONS

To challenge yourself further, answer the integrating questions at the end of the chapter. These questions ask you to apply the information you have learned to consider larger theoretical or real-life issues.

LESSON I: VISION

1. Describe transduction and sensory coding. (pp. 113-115)

* 1.1 The process by which stimuli are transformed from environmental energy into

_______________ _______________ is referred to as transduction.

* 1.2 Specialized _______________ _______________ are sensitive to specific kinds of stimuli and are responsible for the process of transduction.

1.3 List at least three parts of your body where you would expect to find receptor cells.

1.4 In general terms, explain what a code is.

* 1.5 The system by which sensory information is conveyed by the nerves that connect sense organs with the brain is referred to as _______________ _______________.

1.6 Explain why different stimuli must be encoded by means <u>other</u> than differences in size or duration of action potentials.

* 1.7 The two forms of sensory coding that have been identified are _______________ coding and _______________ coding.

* 1.8 Identify the type of sensory coding used in each of the following examples.

_____ a) activity of nerve fibers originating in the eye versus activity of nerve fibers originating in the tongue

_____ b) activity of nerve fibers originating in the skin of the right cheek versus activity of nerve fibers originating in the left cheek

_____ c) a high rate of firing of nerve fibers originating from the ear versus a lower rate of firing of the same nerve fibers

1.9 Summarize the nature of temporal and anatomical coding.

2. Identify the parts of the eye and describe their function. (pp. 115-117)

2.1 Use the following set of terms, label the drawing of the eye in figure 4.1, below: pupil, iris, cornea, posterior chamber, lens, sclera, retina, optic disk

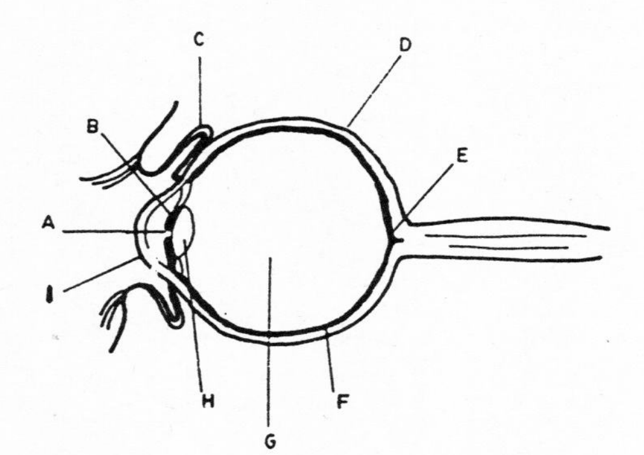

FIGURE 4.1

2.2 Describe the functions of the iris, aqueous humor, lens, and retina.

2.3 Describe the path taken by light as it enters the eye.

3. Describe how photoreceptors transduce light into neural activity. (pp. 117-119)

* 3.1 The specialized cells that are sensitive to light and transduce it into neural activity are called _______________, and they are located in the _______________.

* 3.2 The three layers of cells that make up the retina are the _______________ layer, the _______________ _______________ layer, and the _______________ _______________ layer.

3.3 a) Draw a schematic diagram illustrating the position of each of the cell layers of the retina.

b) Which of these layers responds directly to light?

c) Describe the function of each of the cell layers.

* 3.4 Fill in the missing information indicating the path of visual information.

_______________ → bipolar cell → _______________ cell → brain

* 3.5 The two types of photoreceptors found in the retina are _______________ and _______________.

3.6 Distinguish between the kinds of visual stimulation that each of the two types of photoreceptors respond.

3.7 Describe the relative concentration of rods and cones in different areas of the retina. Use the term fovea in your answer.

* 3.8 a) A chemical compound whose structure is modified when a photon (particle of light) impinges upon it is called a _______________.

b) What happens when a particle of light strikes the molecules that form a photopigment?

* 3.9 The human eye has _______________ kinds of photopigments. The photopigment of rods is called _______________.

3.10 Boll discovered the phenomenon of bleaching when he exposed the eye of a dead animal to a bright scene and then examined it under dim light.

a) Describe bleaching.

b) State the importance of Boll's discovery for our understanding of the transduction of light.

4. Describe the process of light and dark adaptation. (pp. 119-120)

Chapter 4

4.1 a) Explain why we are not able to see very well when going from the sunny outdoors into a house with all the curtains closed.

* b) After being in the dark for several minutes, the rods become replenished with unbleached rhodopsin, and we are able to see again. At this point, we say that the eye

has undergone ______________ ______________.

4.2 a) Describe how Hecht and Schlaer (1938) investigated the process of dark adaptation.

b) Describe the resulting dark-adaptation curve obtained by these investigators.

* 4.3 The abrupt change in the threshold of detection occurring during the dark-adaptation process after about seven minutes of being in the dark corresponds to the

______________ - ______________ break.

4.4 What would the dark-adaptation curve look like in each of the following situations.

a) The fovea alone is stimulated by light.

b) The entire retina is stimulated by light.

c) The entire retina of a person who lacks cones is stimulated by light.

5. Describe the categories of involuntary and voluntary eye movements and explain their functions. (pp. 120-121)

5.1 Even when our eyes are resting, they are not completely passive, but rather they move in systematic involuntary patterns. Describe each of these patterns.

* 5.2 Three types of "active" eye movements are ______________, ______________, and

______________ movements.

5.3 a) Describe a stabilized image and explain what happens when one is projected onto the retina.

b) Explain what this observation tells us about the role and importance of involuntary eye movements.

* 5.4 Which of these eye movements is illustrated by each of the following situations?

_____ a) abrupt shifts in gaze from one point to another

_____ b) following the movement of a tennis ball across the field

_____ c) coordinating the gaze of both eyes on a single same object that moves toward or away from you

6. Describe the electromagnetic spectrum and its relation to color vision. (pp. 121-122)

* 6.1 The frequency of vibration of light energy determines its ______________, which is measured in ______________.

* 6.2 Check which of the following fall within the visible range of light.

_____ a) 460 nm _____ b) ultraviolet light

_____ c) x-rays _____ d) 300 nm

* 6.3 Three physical dimensions of light that are relevant to the perception of color are ______________, ______________, and ______________.

6.4 Give two reasons why it is not appropriate to say that "a wavelength of 650 nm is red."

7. Describe the three physical dimensions of color and their corresponding perceptual dimensions. (pp. 122)

* 7.1 Supply the psychological perceptual counterparts to each of the following dimensions of light.

a) wavelength ______________

b) intensity ______________

c) purity ______________

7.2 Compare the level of saturation of the following:

a) violet light

b) yellow light mixed with white light

7.3 All other factors being equal, compare how we would perceive each of the following in terms of the three dimensions of color.

a) pure 540 nm, low intensity

b) 650 nm plus white light, high intensity

c) pure 650 nm, high intensity

8. Compare synthetic and analytic sensory systems. (pp. 122-123)

* 8.1 A sense modality that integrates different sensory inputs and perceives them as a whole is referred to as a(n) ______________ sensory modality, while one that takes apart incoming sensory inputs breaking them up into their components is called a(n) ______________ sensory modality.

8.2 To which of these categories do vision and audition belong?

8.3 Explain the phenomenon of color mixing in terms of synthetic versus analytic sensory modalities.

9. Describe two kinds of color coding that occur in the cones and ganglion cells of the body. (pp. 123-124)

* 9.1 The three types of photoreceptors hypothesized by Young were assumed to be sensitive to

_______________, _______________, and _______________ light.

9.2 a) List the three types of photopigments that have been discovered in cones of the human eye.

b) What are the common names of the photoreceptors that contain each of these pigments?

9.3 Explain how Young's color synthesis hypothesis accounts for our ability to perceive a wide variety of colors on a color television screen.

* 9.4 According to Hering, the reason we cannot imagine a yellowish blue or a reddish green is

that color is encoded by two types of photoreceptors in an _______________

_______________.

9.5 How was Hering's theory correct? How was it incorrect?

* 9.6 Describe how the normal (steady) firing rate of a ganglion cell is affected when the retina is struck by the following hues of light.

_____ a) a red/green ganglion cell, red light

_____ b) a yellow/blue ganglion cell, blue light

_____ c) a red/green ganglion cell, green light

_____ d) a yellow/blue ganglion cell, yellow light

_____ e) a black/white ganglion cell, red light

_____ f) a black/white ganglion cell, yellow light

10. Explain how negative afterimages occur. (pp. 124-125)

* 10.1 After staring for a while at a particular spot of red light and then shifting immediately to a gray spot, we will probably "see" the complementary color of red, which is green.

This effect is referred to as a _______________ _______________.

10.2 What are complementary colors?

* 10.3 a) Two processes of our visual system seem to be responsible for negative afterimages:

_______________ _______________, and _______________ _______________

_______________.

b) Explain how each of these processes contributes to the phenomenon of negative afterimages.

11. Describe three types of defective color vision. (p. 125)

11.1 Why are males more frequently affected by color vision defects than females?

* 11.2 a) Two color vision deficiencies involving the red/green system are _______________ and

_______________.

b) Describe the characteristic of cone pigmentation associated with each of the color defects you named in question 11.2.

* 11.3 a) _______________ is the extremely rare color defect involving the yellow/blue system. Describe how a person with this defect sees the world.

b) What seems to be the pattern of cone pigmentation of people with this defect?

c) Explain what causes this pattern.

12. Describe the research of Hubel and Wiesel on hierarchical coding of visual information on the brain. (pp. 125-129)

* 12.1 Hubel and Wiesel (1977, 1979) recorded the activity of individual neurons in the visual

system of monkeys and cats by inserting _______________ in different areas of the visual cortex.

12.2 What is a receptive field?

12.3 Describe the kinds of stimuli to which the following type of cells in visual cortex respond best.

a) simple cells

b) complex cells

* 12.4 According to Hubel and Wiesel, the analysis of shape and form is integrated at the level

of the _______________ _______________ cortex.

12.5 Describe the kinds of stimuli to which cells in the visual association cortex respond best.

13. Describe the phenomenon of brightness constancy. (pp 129-130)

13.1 Explain what is meant by brightness constancy.

13.2 Describe Katz's experiment. In particular, note

a) the kinds of stimuli presented to the subjects.

b) the subjects' task.

c) the findings of this study.

d) the implications of this study for our perception of brightness.

13.3 Explain what the results of Katz's study suggest regarding our perception of brightness.

14. Explain how the features that distinguish figure and ground contribute to the perception of form. (pp. 130-132)

* 14.1 In perceiving the world around us visually, we tend to organize it in terms of object and background, or _______________ and _______________, respectively.

14.2 Explain how familiarity with an object and the existence of boundaries contribute to the figure/ground distinction.

14.3 State the main proposition made by Gestalt psychologists about the way in which we perceive stimuli.

14.4 Explain how the main Gestalt thesis applies to the following example.

15. Describe the five organizational laws of gestalt psychology. (pp. 132-134)

* 15.1 List the five principles of Gestalt psychology.

15.2 In your own words, define each of the five Gestalt principles.

15.3 What principle of Gestalt psychology is best illustrated by our perception of ripples or waves in water?

15.4 Give an example that illustrates the closure principle.

16. Describe how the role of experience with objects affects perception of size and shape. (pp. 134-135)

16.1 a) How did Hirsch and Spinelli (1971) control the type of visual stimulation received by kittens?

b) What did these investigators observe after several weeks during which the kittens had been exposed to specific kinds of visual stimulation?

16.2 Explain what Hirsch and Spinelli's findings tell us about the role of experience in the perception of visual elements.

16.3 Briefly describe a study with humans that suggests that even the adult visual system can be changed by experience.

17. Describe how experience with objects affects perception of size and shape. (pp. 135-136)

* 17.1 a) When we see an elephant on a distant field, the image it casts on our retina is very small compared to the image of the same elephant when it is right in front of us. Nevertheless, we perceive the elephant as being the same size in both cases. This example illustrates _______________ _______________.

b) Define this phenomenon in its general sense.

17.2 How did von Helmholtz account for form constancy?

* 17.3 Two types of form constancy are _______________ constancy and _______________ constancy.

17.4 Give an original example to illustrate shape constancy.

18. Describe two types of binocular cues and three types of monocular cues for perception of distance. (pp. 136-141)

18.1 What are binocular cues?

* 18.2 Two types of binocular cues that are used in perceiving distance or depth are _______________ and _______________ _______________.

18.3 Explain how each type of binocular cue works.

18.4 Describe three types of monocular cues used in our perception of depth or distance.

19. Describe the factors that contribute to visual perception of movement. (pp. 141-143)

19.1 Try the "experiment" described in your text that asks you to passively move your eye. Describe what you see, and explain why this perception occurs.

19.2 If you stand next to a large building and look up at the clouds moving past it overhead, it looks like the building is falling in the opposite direction. Explain this illusion, using the phenomenon shown in Figure 4.35 in your text.

19.3 Describe the phi phenomenon. Give two examples of this phenomenon from daily life.

LESSON I SELF TEST

1. Information that has been transduced has been

   a. transformed so that the sensory organs can respond to it.
   b. bypassed in favor of information that is more psychologically compelling.
   c. has been incorrectly interpreted by the brain.
   d. translated into a message that can be interpreted by the brain.

2. To relay information to the brain that a stimulus is very strong, the neurons of the sense organs

   a. increase the action potentials of their axons.
   b. increase their rate of firing.
   c. transduce chemically rather than electrically.
   d. send messages to additional areas of the brain.

3. Visual information passes through a three-cell chain to the brain in the following order:

   a. retina, cornea, optic nerve, brain.
   b. aqueous humor, vitreous humor, lens, brain.
   c. photoreceptor, bipolar cell, ganglion cell, brain.
   d. optic disk, basal cells, photoreceptors, brain.

4. Driving on a dark road, Randy found himself momentarily blinded by the high beams of an oncoming car. The bright light of the oncoming car caused

   a. the photopigments in his eye to be bleached.
   b. his brain to override signals from his cones.
   c. the precipitous joining of vitamin A and proteins in his ganglion cells.
   d. the bipolar cells to misfire and release rhodopsin.

5. The rod-cone break explains why

   a. it hurts to move too quickly from a darkened room to bright sunlight.
   b. there is discontinuity in the dark-adaptation curve.
   c. color vision is best if light is focussed on the rods.
   d. directing light at the fovea produces less detailed vision.

6. Hue is to wavelength as

   a. intensity is to amplitude.

b. physical dimension is to psychological dimension.
c. wavelength is to color.
d. saturation is to purity.

7. To explain why the human eye can see all the colors that it does, Thomas Young proposed that the eye contains __________ types of color receptors that are sensitive to the psychologically "pure" colors of __________.

   a. ten; the spectrum
   b. three; red, blue, green
   c. four; red, blue, green, yellow
   d. six; red, green, blue, yellow, orange, purple

8. Your eyes jump from point to point as you scan a scene. This movement is a __________ movement.

   a. pursuit
   b. conjugate
   c. saccadic
   d. resting

9. What would happen if an image of an object was fixated on one part of the retina?

   a. Over time the object would be seen more clearly.
   b. The colors of the object would be perceived as painfully bright.
   c. No change in visual acuity would occur.
   d. The object would disappear.

10. Individuals who experience negative afterimages

   a. have protanopia, a disorder in which red cones are filled with green photopigment.
   b. see a complementary color after having turned their gazes away from the stimulus object.
   c. see colors darker or lighter than they actually are.
   d. have cones that work in opposition to each other rather than in synchrony.

11. The investigations of Hubel and Wiesel suggest that

   a. neurons in the visual cortex respond best to gradual changes in brightness.
   b. there is a point-to-point relation between the real world and the surface of the primary visual cortex.
   c. complex cells in the primary visual cortex use messages from the retina to analyze the shape and form of environmental stimuli.
   d. simple cells in the thalamus analyze information in gross detail from a wide receptive field.

12. A study by Hirsch and Spinelli (1971) suggests that some neurons in the visual cortex

   a. can develop to respond to particular stimuli.
   b. can only respond to vertical stimulus arrays.
   c. are able to respond to any kind of input.
   d. cannot respond at all to vertical stimulus arrays

13. When a person walks away from you, the image of this person grows smaller on your retina, yet you do not perceive this person as shrinking. This phenomenon is known as

   a. object permanence.
   b. size constancy.
   c. the Gestalt.
   d. pursuit movement.

14. Each eye sees slightly different images. This phenomenon is called

a. retinal disparity; it makes it difficult to maintain form constancy.
b. retinal disparity; it contributes to our perception of depth.
c. stereopsis; it forces us to fuse separate moving images into continuous moving images.
d. stereopsis; it is responsible for the resting and purposive movements that aid vision.

15. The light on a theater marquee flicks on and off such that the light appears to move around the marquee. This is as example of

a. sine-wave grating.
b. the phi phenomenon.
c. the autokinetic effect.
d. ballistic movement.

LESSON II: AUDITION, GUSTATION, OLFACTION, AND THE SOMATOSENSES

20. Describe the physical properties of sound and their corresponding perceptual dimensions. (p. 144)

20.1 What does sound consist of?

* 20.2 The measure of sound waves is frequency units of cycles per seconds or ______________.

* 20.3 Pair the following perceptions of sound with the corresponding physical characteristics of sound waves.

loudness and ______________

pitch and ______________

timbre and ______________

21. Describe the structure and functions of the auditory system. (pp. 144-147)

* 21.1 Label the parts of the ear in Figure 4.2, below.

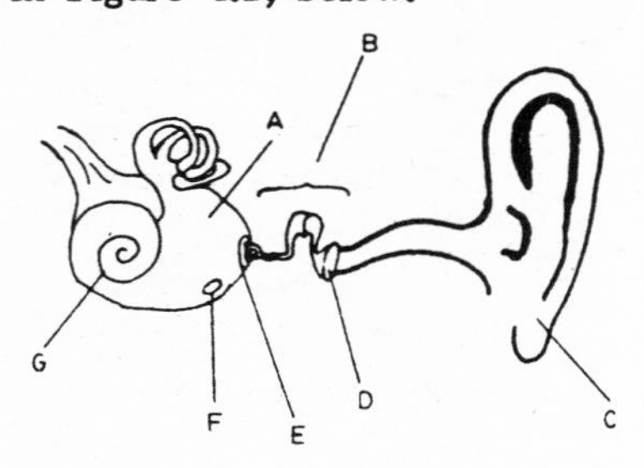

FIGURE 4.2

* 21.2 List the structures of the ear that are found in each of the following areas.

a) middle ear

b) inner ear

21.3 What structure of the ear is the first to respond to sound waves?

* 21.4 The ossicles are located in the middle ear and consist of the _____________, the _____________, and the _____________.

21.5 Where is the receptive organ of audition located?

* 21.6 The _____________ _____________ divides the cochlea into two parts.

22. Describe how low and high frequency sounds are detected. (pp. 147-148)

22.1 Explain why it is unlikely that pitch is encoded by the rate of axonal firing.

* 22.2 Sound frequency is encoded by different parts of the _____________ _____________.

22.3 Describe the effects of some antibiotics on the basilar membrane.

22.4 Describe the procedure used by Stebbins et al. (1969) for studying the relation between damage to the basilar membrane and pitch perception.

* 22.5 a) Kiang (1965) observed that when a tone lower than _____________ Hz stimulates the basilar membrane, anatomical coding of pitch does not appear to take place.

b) In what part of the basilar membrane are the neurons that are stimulated by low frequencies located?

22.6 Explain how temporal coding of low frequency tones occurs.

* 22.7 a) A mixture of all perceptible sound frequencies is referred to as _____________ _____________.

b) What regions of the basilar membrane are stimulated by this type of sound?

22.8 a) Describe the stimuli that Miller and Taylor (1948) presented to their subjects.

b) What results were obtained in this study?

c) Summarize the ways in which different sound frequencies are encoded.

23. Explain two ways that we perceive the directions of sounds. (pp. 148-150)

* 23.1 In locating the source of a particular sound, we make use of two processes:

______________ ______________ and ______________ ______________.

* 23.2 The following examples illustrate which of the two processes that aid us in locating sound sources?

__________ a) the differences in the intensity of sound reaching the right and left ear.

__________ b) the difference in arrival time of sound pressure waves at each tympanic membrane.

24. Explain the perception of timbre. (p. 150)

* 24.1 The difference we perceive between the sound of a trumpet and the sound of a human voice that are of equal pitch and loudness is referred to as ______________.

24.2 What is a complex tone?

* 24.3 a) The timbre of a sound is composed of a fundamental tone and a number of ______________.

b) Briefly explain how a complex tone with a particular timbre is perceived.

25. Describe the transduction of gustatory stimuli. (p. 152)

25.1 How does flavor differ from taste?

* 25.2 The taste receptor cells are contained in the ______________ ______________, which in turn are contained in the ______________ of our tongue.

25.3 Summarize the way that we believe taste receptors transduce chemical stimulation into neural activity.

26. Describe the four categories of taste and the regions of the tongue that detect each of them. (pp. 152-154)

* 26.1 The four basic qualities of taste are ______________, ______________, ______________, and ______________.

* 26.2 List the types of substances that most typically correspond to the following qualities of taste.

a) saltiness

b) bitterness and sweetness

c) sourness

26.3 Describe the locations on the tongue that detect each of the four basic qualities of taste.

27. Describe the anatomy of the olfactory system and explain the problems in understanding the physiological basis of odor detection. (pp. 154-156)

* 27.1 The olfactory receptor cells are located in the ______________ ______________, under the nasal sinuses.

* 27.2 a) The axons of the olfactory receptor cells synapse with neurons located in the

______________ ______________.

b) Describe the structure referred to in question 27.2.

27.3 How does the transduction of olfactory stimuli into neural activity appear to take place?

27.4 Explain why it is unlikely that we have specific receptors for each odor that we perceive.

* 27.5 a) According to Amoore (1970), there are ______________ primary odors.

b) Describe Amoore's theory regarding the way in which primary odors interact with olfactory receptor cells.

27.6 Describe evidence that supports Amoore's theory and evidence that challenges it.

28. Describe the somatosensory system, including the specialized systems for detecting temperature, pressure and pain. (pp. 158-162)

* 28.1 The most common type of nerve ending in the skin is the ______________.

* 28.2 Describe the function of Pacinian corpuscles.

* 28.3 Describe the relative location of warmth detectors and coolness detectors.

* 28.4 The cessation of neural impulses from the sensory receptors in the skin, once the movement of an object sinking into the skin stops, is called ______________

______________.

* 28.5 a) A common measure of the sensitivity of a region of the skin is known as the

______________-______________ ______________ ______________.

b) Describe how the above measure is taken and what it means.

28.6
* Two kinds of pain seem to be elicited by noxious stimuli: _________ pain and _________ pain.

28.7
How do we assume pain detectors are stimulated? Cite some evidence that tentatively supports this hypothesis.

29. Describe the information detected by our internal senses. (p. 162)

29.1 Describe the type of internal stimulation that results in pain for each of the following structures.

a) the walls of the internal organs such as the intestine and bladder

b) the innervated membrane that covers the bones

c) the membranes in joints between bones

d) the muscles

* 29.2 Some internal receptors located at the junction of muscle and tendon, responds to _______________.

* 29.3 a) _______________ _______________ are another type of stretch detectors.

b) Where are these stretch detectors located?

c) Describe the type of information conveyed by these detectors to the brain.

30. Describe the structure and functions of the vestibular system. (pp. 162-163)

* 30.1 In order for a tight-rope walker to maintain her balance walking from one end of the rope to the other, she must make use of sensory information from her _______________, _______________ and _______________, _______________ _______________.

* 30.2
The vestibular apparatus consists of the _______________ _______________ and the _______________. Describe each of these structures.

30.3 How do the semicircular canals respond to head rotation?

30.4 a) How do the vestibular sacs respond to head tilt?

b) Describe two functions of the vestibular sacs.

LESSON II SELF TEST

1. The pitch of a sound is determined primarily by the _________ of the sound waves.

   a. timbre
   b. frequency
   c. intensity
   d. amplitude

2. The receptive organ for sound is the _________, which is in the _________.

   a. tectorial membrane; cilia
   b. tympanic membrane; inner ear
   c. organ of Corti; cochlea
   d. basilar membrane; round window

3. The pitch of most frequencies of sound are encoded

   a. anatomically.
   b. temporally.
   c. chemically.
   d. thermally.

4. Tom cannot hear high frequency sounds. This hearing loss may be due to

   a. damaged cilia on the basilar membrane farthest away from the oval window.
   b. damage to the basilar membrane closest to the oval membrane.
   c. middle ear disease that causes bone to grow over the round window.
   d. reduced action potentials of the auditory hair cells.

5. High frequency auditory stimuli are coded _________ and low frequency auditory stimuli are coded _________.

   a. as white noise; as sound
   b. anatomically; temporally
   c. by the movement of the basilar membrane farthest from the oval window; by movement closest to the oval window
   d. simple cells; complex cells

6. We determine the locations of the sources of sounds by

   a. phase differences and relative loudness
   b. echo location and sound shadows
   c. frequency of the sound relative to the position of the head
   d. the pitch and amplitude of the sound

7. Which of the following sounds is more difficult to localize?

   a. the slow, steady hum of a refrigerator
   b. the shill sound of a firetruck
   c. the blare of the noon whistle
   d. the territorial song of a male bird

8. Timbre is

   a. the synthesis of two or more complex tones having multiple frequencies.
   b. the relative phasing of frequencies by temporal coding.
   c. the distinctive combination of overtones with the fundamental tone.

d. the analysis of the ratio of periodicity and frequency of sound.

9. Unlike taste, flavor depends on

a. gustation.
b. the vestibular sense.
c. internal senses.
d. olfaction.

10. The hairlike projections on the tongue that contain the receptors for taste are

a. papillae.
b. microvilli.
c. cilia.
d. ossicles.

11. According to Amoore's hypothesis concerning odor transduction, how does a person detect if dinner is burning?

a. The burnt smell, one of the seven odor primaries, stimulates the odor receptors.
b. The nose has separate receptors for each kind of odor so the nose analyzes the smells from the different foods that are burning.
c. The burning foods cause the olfactory receptors to vibrate at certain frequencies.
d. The odor molecules of the burning foods wholly or partially fit into the olfactory receptors.

12. The skin senses

a. have no separate receptor cells.
b. transport information from the face to the brain by way of the spinal nerves.
c. have specific sensory endings for specific classes of stimuli.
d. have Pacinian corpuscles that are very sensitive to pain.

13. The sensation of pressure

a. occurs even the skin is touched lightly by an object.
b. is most pronounced when elbows and knees come into forceful contact with an object.
c. occurs only when the skin is actually moving.
d. is measured by a three pronged discrimination threshold.

14. Which of the following treatments might be offered to individuals who experience chronic pain that cannot be alleviated by other means?

a. surgery similar to but less drastic than prefrontal lobotomy
b. removal of the part of the thalamus that controls sharp pain
c. prescription for the drug, cantharides
d. removal of the free nerve endings in the area of chronic pain

15. Debra has an ear infection that has affected her ability to hear and to

a. detect temperature changes.
b. see colors.
c. feel pain.
d. maintain her balance.

INTEGRATING QUESTIONS

1. Of the five senses, the loss of our ability to see or hear would be the most difficult to

adjust to. What kind of changes would you have to make in your life if you were to loose your sight? How would blindness affect your career goals? Now consider what your life would be like if you could see, but not hear. How would you communicate with your friends? Which sensory loss do you think it would be the most difficult to adjust to?

2. Make a list of the characteristics of things that you can detect with your somatosenses (for example, stickiness, slipperiness, oilyness, softness, etc.). What do you think are the biological advantages of your ability to detect these sensations? What is tickle? Do you have any idea why we often laugh when we are tickled? What if you lost somatosensation rather than vision or audition? What effect would such a loss have on your life?

ANSWERS

1.1 neural activity
1.2 receptor cells
1.5 sensory coding
1.7 anatomical, temporal
1.8 a) anatomical b) anatomical c) temporal
3.1 photoreceptors, retina
3.2 photoreceptor, bipolar cell, ganglion cell
3.4 photoreceptor, ganglion cell
3.5 rods, cones
3.8 a) photopigment
3.9 three, rhodopsin
4.1 b) dark adaptation
4.3 rod-cone
5.2 conjugate, saccadic, pursuit
5.4 a) saccadic b) pursuit c) conjugate
6.1 wavelength, nanometers
6.2 only a) is visible
6.3 wavelength, intensity, purity
7.1 a) hue b) brightness c) saturation
8.1 synthetic, analytic
9.1 blue, green, red
9.4 opponent process
9.6 a) increases b) decreases c) decreases d) increases e) increases f) increases
10.1 negative afterimage
10.3 a) photopigment bleaching, ganglion cell adaptation
11.2 a) protanopia, deuteranopia
11.3 a) tritanopia, in greens and reds
12.1 microelectrodes
12.4 visual association
14.1 figure, ground
15.1 proximity, similarity, good continuation, closure, common fate
17.1 a) form constancy
17.3 shape, size
18.2 convergence, retinal disparity
20.2 Hertz
20.3 loudness—intensity, pitch—frequency, timbre—complexity
21.1 A. vestibule B. ossicles C. pinna D. tympanic membrane E. oval window F. round window G. cochlea
21.2 a) middle ear: tympanic membrane, ossicles b) inner ear: vestibule, oval window, round window, cochlea, basilar membrane, malleus, incus, stapes
21.4 malleus, incus, stapes
21.6 basilar membrane

Chapter 4

22.2 basilar membrane
22.5 a) 200
22.7 a) white noise
23.1 relative loudness, phase difference
23.2 a) relative loudness b) phase difference
24.1 timbre
24.3 a) overtones
25.2 taste buds, papillae
26.1 sourness, sweetness, bitterness, saltiness
26.2 a) NaCl (sodium chloride) b) nonionizing molecules c) H^+ (hydrogen ions) in acid solutions
27.1 olfactory mucosa
27.2 a) olfactory bulbs
27.5 7
28.1 a) free nerve endings
28.2 detection of vibration
28.3 a) deep in the skin b) close to skin surface
28.4 sensory adaptation
28.5 a) two-point discrimination threshold
28.6 bright, dull
29.2 a) stretch
29.3 a) muscle spindles
30.1 eyes, joints and muscles, vestibular apparatus
30.2 semicircular canals, vestibular sacs

Self Test: Lesson I

1. d Obj. 4-1
2. b Obj. 4-1
3. c Obj. 4-3
4. a Obj. 4-4
5. b Obj. 4-4
6. b Obj. 4-6
7. c Obj. 4-8
8. b Obj. 4-9
9. d Obj. 4-9
10. b Obj. 4-10
11. b Obj. 4-12
12. a Obj. 4-16
13. b Obj. 4-17
14. b Obj. 4-18
15. b Obj. 4-19

Self Test: Lesson II

1. b Obj. 4-20
2. c Obj. 4-21
3. a Obj. 4-22
4. b Obj. 4-22
5. b Obj. 4-22
6. d Obj. 4-23
7. a Obj. 4-23
8. a Obj. 4-24
9. c Obj. 4-25
10. d Obj. 4-25
11. b Obj. 4-27
12. d Obj. 4-28
13. a Obj. 4-28
14. c Obj. 4-28
15. a Obj. 4-30

4.1 OBJ 4-1

TRANSDUCTION

4.2 OBJ 4-1

RECEPTOR CELLS

4.3 OBJ 4-1

CODE

4.4 OBJ 4-1

SENSORY CODING

4.5 OBJ 4-1

ANATOMICAL CODING

4.6 OBJ 4-1

TEMPORAL CODING

4.7 OBJ 4-2

SCLERA

4.8 OBJ 4-2

CORNEA

4.9 OBJ 4-2

IRIS

4.10 OBJ 4-2

AQUEOUS HUMOR

4.11 OBJ 4-2

LENS

4.12 OBJ 4-2

RETINA

4.13 OBJ 4-2

OPTIC DISK

4.14 OBJ 4-2

PHOTORECEPTORS

4.15 OBJ 4-2

PHOTORECEPTOR LAYER

4.16 OBJ 4-2

BIPOLAR CELL LAYER

4.9 Obj 4-2

two bands of muscle; dilates or contracts the pupil and thus control amount of light entering the eye

4.10 Obj 4-2

transparent fluid that fills anterior chamber; nourishes front parts of the eye

4.11 Obj 4-2

flexible, clear tissue lying behind the iris; allows for focusing on near or distant objects

4.12 Obj 4-2

innermost membrane of the eye; contains the photoreceptors

4.13 Obj 4-2

point where axons from cells in retina converge and exit to optic nerve; corresponds to the "blind spot"

4.14 Obj 4-2

specialized receptor cells located in the retina; sensitive to light

4.15 Obj 4-2

bottom layer of cells in retina; consists of the receptor cells

4.16 Obj 4-2

cell layer between photoreceptor layer and ganglion cell layer; cells are stimulated chemically by photoreceptors

4.1 Obj 4-1

conversion of a particular form of energy into neural activity; process by which brain and environment interact

4.2 Obj 4-1

specialized nerve cells located in sense organs; respond to specific kinds of stimuli

4.3 Obj 4-1

rules that allow us to translate information from one form to another

4.4 Obj 4-1

rules by which sensory neurons translate environmental stimuli into neural activity

4.5 Obj 4-1

form of sensory coding; uses different nerve fibers as a basis for conveying sensory information

4.6 Obj 4-1

form of sensory coding; rate of neuron firing is the basis for conveying information

4.7 Obj 4-2

outer membrane surrounding and protecting the eye; very tough

4.8 Obj 4-2

transparent membrane in front of anterior chamber of eye; continuation of sclera

4.17 OBJ 4-2

GANGLION CELL LAYER

4.18 OBJ 4-2

RODS

4.19 OBJ 4-2

CONES

4.20 OBJ 4-2

FOVEA

4.21 OBJ 4-3

PHOTOPIGMENT

4.22 OBJ 4-3

RHODOPSIN

4.23 OBJ 4-4

DARK-ADAPTATION CURVE

4.24 OBJ 4-4

ROD-CONE BREAK

4.25 OBJ 4-5

STABILIZED IMAGE

4.26 OBJ 4-5

CONJUGATE EYE MOVEMENTS

4.27 OBJ 4-5

SACCADIC EYE MOVEMENTS

4.28 OBJ 4-5

PURSUIT MOVEMENTS

4.29 OBJ 4-6

WAVELENGTH

4.30 OBJ 4-6

NANOMETER

4.31 OBJ 4-6

SPECTRAL COLORS

4.32 OBJ 4-7

HUE

4.25 Obj 4-5

image projected continuously onto the same spot of the retina by coordinating the image source with eye movements

4.26 Obj 4-5

coordinated movements of both eyes, keeps them fixed on the same target; important in perception of space and distance

4.27 Obj 4-5

jerky eye movements from one point to another when scanning a scene

4.28 Obj 4-5

slow movement of the eyes when following a moving target

4.29 Obj 4-6

frequency of vibration of radiant energy

4.30 Obj 4-6

billionth of a meter; measure of wavelengths

4.31 Obj 4-6

colors we see in a rainbow; span the entire spectrum of visible light (380 nm -760 nm)

4.32 Obj 4-7

sensory dimension of color determined by wavelength

4.17 Obj 4-2

outermost layer of cells in retina that receives information from bipolar cells; axons of cells in this layer travel to optic nerve

4.18 Obj 4-2

type of photoreceptor in human retina; sensitive to very low levels of light; provides little visual acuity

4.19 Obj 4-2

type of photoreceptor in human retina; provides great detail of vision; sensitive to different hues; concentrated in fovea

4.20 Obj 4-2

small region of retina; contains only cones and thus provides greatest visual acuity

4.21 Obj 4-3

substance in photoreceptors formed by two molecules; structure is split apart when struck by a photon

4.22 Obj 4-3

photopigment contained in rods

4.23 Obj 4-4

graph of visual detection threshold as a function of time since entering a dark environment

4.24 Obj 4-4

discontinuity in the dark-adaptation curve after approximately seven minutes of being in the dark

4.33 OBJ 4-7

BRIGHTNESS

4.34 OBJ 4-7

SATURATION

4.35 OBJ 4-8

COLOR MIXING

4.36 OBJ 4-8

SYNTHETIC SENSORY SYSTEM

4.37 OBJ 4-8

ANALYTIC SENSORY SYSTEM

4.38 OBJ 4-10

NEGATIVE AFTERIMAGE

4.39 OBJ 4-10

COMPLEMENTARY COLORS

4.40 OBJ 4-11

PROTANOPIA

4.41 OBJ 4-11

DEUTERANOPIA

4.42 OBJ 4-11

TRITANOPIA

4.43 OBJ 4-12

RECEPTIVE FIELD

4.44 OBJ 4-12

SIMPLE CELLS

4.45 OBJ 4-12

COMPLEX CELLS

4.46 OBJ 4-13

BRIGHTNESS CONSTANCY

4.47 OBJ 4-18

BINOCULAR CUES

4.48 OBJ 4-18

CONVERGENCE

4.41 Obj 4-11

color vision defect resulting from lack of green-sensitive photopigment

4.42 Obj 4-11

extremely rare color vision defect; seems to result from lack of blue-sensitive photopigment or blue photoreceptors

4.43 Obj 4-12

portion of visual field to which particular neurons in visual cortex respond

4.44 Obj 4-12

cells in primary visual cortex; correspond to lines of particular orientation; restricted receptive fields

4.45 Obj 4-12

cells in visual cortex; respond to lines that move at right angles to their angle of orientation

4.46 Obj 4-13

perceiving an object as having the same brightness regardless of the level of illumination

4.47 Obj 4-18

cues obtained from both eyes in perceiving depth or distance

4.48 Obj 4-18

binocular cue; uses the angle of focus between the eyes

4.33 Obj 4-7

sensory dimension of color determined by intensity of light

4.34 Obj 4-7

sensory dimension of color determined by the purity of light

4.35 Obj 4-8

mixing of light beams of different wavelengths; results in a brighter light

4.36 Obj 4-8

sensory system that integrates different sensory inputs

4.37 Obj 4-8

sensory system that breaks apart sensory inputs into its components

4.38 Obj 4-10

perceptual phenomenon; "seeing" complementary colors of those which we had been staring at recently

4.39 Obj 4-10

colors that are perceived as white or gray when their wavelengths are added together

4.40 Obj 4-11

color vision defect resulting from lack of red-sensitive photopigment

4.65 OBJ 4-21

TECTORIAL MEMBRANE

4.66 OBJ 4-24

TIMBRE

4.67 OBJ 4-24

FUNDAMENTAL FREQUENCY

4.68 OBJ 4-25

GUSTATION

4.69 OBJ 4-25

PAPILLAE

4.70 OBJ 4-25

TASTE BUDS

4.71 OBJ 4-25

MICROVILLI

4.72 OBJ 4-27

OLFACTORY MUCOSA

4.73 OBJ 4-27

OLFACTORY BULBS

4.74 OBJ 4-28

SOMATOSENSES

4.75 OBJ 4-28

FREE NERVE ENDINGS

4.76 OBJ 4-28

PACINIAN CORPUSLE

4.77 OBJ 4-28

TWO-POINT DISCRIMINATION THRESHOLD

4.78 OBJ 4-30

VESTIBULAR APPARATUS

4.79 OBJ 4-30

SEMICIRCULAR CANALS

4.80 OBJ 4-30

VESTIBULAR SACS

4.73 Obj 4-27

enlargements at ends of olfactory nerves; receive information from olfactory receptor cells

4.74 Obj 4-28

body senses; includes skin senses, internal senses, and vestibular senses

4.75 Obj 4-28

most common nerve endings in skin; surrounds hair follicles in hairy skin

4.76 Obj 4-28

specialized skin nerve ending; responds to movement

4.77 Obj 4-28

common measure of skin sensitivity to pressure and touch

4.78 Obj 4-30

structure in inner ear; aids in sense of balance

4.79 Obj 4-30

liquid-filled part of vestibular apparatus; responds to head rotation

4.80 Obj 4-30

part of vestibular system: contains calcium carbonate crystals; responds to changes in head tilt

4.65 Obj 4-21

rigid structure hanging over the basilar membrane in which cilia are embedded

4.66 Obj 4-24

perceptual dimension of sound; specific combinations of fundamental tones and overtones

4.67 Obj 4-24

basic pitch of a sound

4.68 Obj 4-25

sensory modality of taste

4.69 Obj 4-25

bumps on surface of tongue; contain the taste buds

4.70 Obj 4-25

structures in the papillae: contain the taste receptor cells

4.71 Obj 4-25

hairlike projections of taste receptors that come into direct contact with saliva

4.72 Obj 4-27

patches of mucous membrane under nasal sinuses; contain the olfactory receptor cells

4.49 OBJ 4-18

RETINAL DISPARITY

4.50 OBJ 4-18

STEREOPSIS

4.51 OBJ 4-18

MONOCULAR CUES

4.52 OBJ 4-19

PHI PHENOMENON

4.53 OBJ 4-20

HERTZ (HZ)

4.54 OBJ 4-20

LOUDNESS

4.55 OBJ 4-20

PITCH

4.56 OBJ 4-21

EARDRUM

4.57 OBJ 4-21

OSSICLES

4.58 OBJ 4-21

OVAL WINDOW

4.59 OBJ 4-21

ROUND WINDOW

4.60 OBJ 4-21

COCHLEA

4.61 OBJ 4-21

BASILAR MEMBRANE

4.62 OBJ 4-21

ORGAN OF CORTI

4.63 OBJ 4-21

AUDITORY HAIR CELLS

4.64 OBJ 4-21

CILIA

4.57 Obj 4-21

a set of three bones in middle ear that transmit vibrations from eardrum to inner ear

4.58 Obj 4-21

vestibule opening to inner ear

4.59 Obj 4-21

opening of vestibule; allows for fluid displacement in inner ear

4.60 Obj 4-21

bony snail-shaped structure; contains auditory receptor organ

4.61 Obj 4-21

flexible membrane; divides the cochlea lengthwise; contains the organ of Corti

4.62 Obj 4-21

receptor organ for sound

4.63 Obj 4-21

auditory receptor cells; contain cilia

4.64 Obj 4-21

hairlike protrusions of auditory hair cells; embedded in the tectorial membrane

4.49 Obj 4-18

binocular cue consisting of different images of a same object falling on each of the eyes

4.50 Obj 4-18

perception of depth due to retinal disparity

4.51 Obj 4-18

cues available from only one eye that allow for perception of depth

4.52 Obj 4-19

perception of alternating lights as a continuous movement, given certain timing limits

4.53 Obj 4-20

frequency units of cycles per second: a measure of sound waves

4.54 Obj 4-20

perceptual dimension of sound, corresponds to intensity of a sound wave

4.55 Obj 4-20

perceptual dimension of sound; corresponds to frequency of a sound wave

4.56 Obj 4-21

a flexible membrane; the first structure in the ear to respond to sound waves

CHAPTER 5
Human Development

INTRODUCTION

This chapter reviews development of the person across the lifespan from conception and birth (Objectives 1-4) through the physical and perceptual development of the infant (Objectives 4-7), cognitive development (Objectives 8-13), social development in infancy (Objectives 14-17), sexual development (Objectives 18-22), and adult development (Objectives 23-25). The chapter is divided into two lessons. Lesson I covers Objectives 1-13 and Lesson II covers Objectives 14-25.

CONCEPT CARDS AND EXERCISES

After you have surveyed and read the text, assemble the concept cards located at the end of this chapter. Use them to learn the important terms, then begin reading the text again, one learning objective at a time, and work through the exercises for each lesson. Answers for questions marked with an asterisk are found at the end of the chapter.

SELF TESTS

Each lesson is followed by a multiple-choice self test. After you are proficient with a lesson's concept cards and exercises, take the self test to see whether you have mastered the material. Review those objectives for questions you answered incorrectly.

INTEGRATING QUESTIONS

To challenge yourself further, answer the integrating questions at the end of the chapter. These questions ask you to apply the information you have learned to consider larger theoretical or real-life issues.

LESSON I: CONCEPTION AND BIRTH and PHYSICAL, PERCEPTUAL, AND COGNITIVE DEVELOPMENT

1. Describe the relations between chromosomes, genes, and proteins (especially enzymes) and the role of each in human development. (pp. 169-170)

* 1.1 The functional units containing the necessary information for the construction of a human being are the ______________, which reside in the ______________.

* 1.2 The production of proteins is controlled by the ______________. The proteins that break

up and create complex molecules from simple ones are ______________. These proteins act as ______________ ______________.

1.3 Summarize, in your own words, the process by which genes contribute to human development. (Relate chromosomes, genes, proteins and enzymes in your answer.)

2. Describe the production of gametes and the process of fertilization and differentiation. (pp. 170-173)

* 2.1 In order for fertilization to occur, it is necessary that a female produce ______________ and a male produce ______________, which together are referred to as ______________.

* 2.2 When a woman's ______________ is ripe, it is released into the ______________ through a process known as ______________.

* 2.3 How many chromosomes do human gametes contain, in contrast to all other cells in our body? Briefly explain how this happens.

* 2.4 When a sperm unites with an ovum travelling through one of the fallopian tubes, this event is called ______________ and it results in a single cell called a(n) ______________.

2.5 In order for a single fertilized egg to develop into a fully formed human being, the egg must undergo a series of self-replicating divisions. If this process continued, however, we would end up being nothing more than a large amorphous mass of identical cells. Explain what <u>other</u> process must occur in order for development to proceed as it does.

2.6 Offer reasons why humans produce so many gametes.

3. Describe development in the uterus and the process of birth. (pp. 174-175)

* 3.1 Fertilization of the ovum occurs in the ______________. The fertilized egg attaches itself to the wall of the ______________. When the cells of the fertilized ovum begin to specialize, it becomes a(n) ______________.

* 3.2 The ______________ encases the embryo and the ______________, which allows ______________ of nourishment from and waste to the mother.

* 3.3 a) A common drug-induced abnormality that can be seen in many offspring of alcoholic women is the ______________ ______________ syndrome.

b) Describe the characteristics of children for whom an excessive amount of alcohol was present in their prenatal environment.

3.4 Describe the birth process.

4. Describe the causes, symptoms, and prognosis of Down's syndrome and phenylketonuria (PKU). (pp. 175-177)

4.1 Describe the characteristics and usual cause of Down's syndrome.

4.2 Explain what is meant by the statement, "Down's syndrome is not inherited, but it is genetic."

* 4.3 a) Phenylketonuria (PKU) is a disease caused by a genetic abnormality in which the enzyme responsible for converting _______________ into _______________ is lacking.

b) Explain what produces the damage to brain cells in children with PKU.

4.4 Compare the life expectancy and treatment possibilities for persons with Down's syndrome and those with PKU.

5. Describe infant motor development and the factors that affect it. (pp. 177-179)

* 5.1 The period of _______________ lasts from birth to _______________ years of age. The word infant means _______________.

* 5.2 Three major reflexes displayed by a newborn baby are _______________, _______________, and _______________. Describe situations that would elicit these reflexes.

5.3 What did Shirley's (1933) study of the development of the ability to walk show?

* 5.4 Two important trends in the development of motor control in infants are _______________ and _______________. Describe these trends.

* 5.5 The two elements that are required for the development of motor skills are _______________ and _______________.

* 5.6 The development of the central nervous system has reached its final stage at birth. True _____ False _____ Explain your answer.

5.7 a) Compare the level of motor skills attained by children who have spent much of their infancy lying in cribs with that of children who had ample opportunity for movement and exploration during this time.

b) How can the effects of early deprivation of the opportunity to practice motor skills be remediated?

6. Describe the methods used to study infants' preferences for visual stimuli, and the results these methods have produced. (p. 179-181)

6.1 What senses appear to be present in a newborn baby?

6.2 Explain the difficulties researchers have had in studying perceptual development of infants.

6.3 Describe two refinements of Stirnimann's technique to study the development of infants' visual perception.

6.4 William James, an early American psychologist, described the world as a "booming, buzzing place of confusion" for the infant. This belief has lead caregivers to greatly simplify infants' environments, to offer them soft, pastel colors and simple shapes. What does current research [for example, studies by Salapatek (1975) and Riesen (1961)] suggest about this approach?

7. Explain what current research suggests about the development of depth perception during infancy. (p. 181-183)

7.1 Describe the "visual cliff" and its uses.

7.2 What happens to the heart rate of young infants who are placed on a visual cliff? What does this suggest about their perception of depth?

7.3 What is stereopsis? How does it develop?

7.4 Describe the findings and implications of the research that earned a Nobel Prize for Hubel and Wiesel (1970).

8. Describe the role of a responsive environment in an infant's cognitive development. (p. 183)

8.1 Define cognition and explain how it develops.

8.2 Consider the following examples. Which of these examples provides conditions that would stimulate an infant's cognitive development? Justify your answer by citing work by Watson and Ramey (1972), Goldfarb (1955), and Lewis and Golddberg (1969). answers.

a) Whenever an infant babbles, one of the caregivers in the day care center comes toward it, smiles, and caresses it playfully.

b) A caregiver decides that infants need "attention" in order to develop normally. She routinely goes by all of the infants in the day care center every hour, smiles at them, and caresses them playfully. She does this regardless of whether an infant is babbling, crying, or lying still.

c) A caregiver never smiles or caresses the infants under her care regardless of what they are doing.

9. Describe what Piaget means by schema, concept, assimilation, and accommodation, and explain their interrelations. (pp. 184-186)

* 9.1 _______________ are rules used for understanding and dealing with the world, for thinking and solving problems, according to Piaget. The two basic types of cognitive structures are _______________ and _______________.

9.2 Identify each of the following examples as illustrating the application of (mainly) a schema or a concept. Note: These cognitive structures are assumed to be "unconscious," in the sense that an infant cannot verbalize them; nevertheless, they can be inferred by an observer, according to Piaget.

* __________ a) When food is in her mouth, she swallows.

* __________ b) The child seems to know that apples, bread, soup, and candy are things to eat.

* __________ c) She has learned that knives, forks, and spoons, cups and plates go on tables.

* __________ d) When his mother speaks, he turns his head in the direction of the sound of her voice.

* 9.3 The process by which concepts become coordinated with schemas as the infant interacts with its environment is referred to by Piaget as the process of _______________, whereas the adjustment or modification of schemas as a result of acquiring new concepts is referred to as _______________.

9.4 Identify the processes of assimilation and accommodation in the following situations.

* a) An adult throws a big ball to a child. The child opens and stretches out his arms and catches the ball. Next the adult throws a small ball to the child. The child again opens and stretches out his arms, but fails to catch it. The adult keeps throwing balls of different sizes to the child, and this sort of interaction is repeated on different days. The child learns that some balls are big and some are small. He also learns that opening and stretching out the arms is useful only for catching big balls, but not small ones.

* b) Eventually, he begins to use his hands to catch and grasp the small balls, keeping the arms flexed. Whenever he wants to catch a big ball, he stretches out his arms. He becomes quite adept at catching balls of all sizes.

10. Name and describe Piaget's six stages of development during the sensorimotor period. (pp. 186-188)

10.1 Identify the stage of sensorimotor development illustrated in each of the following examples.

situation	child reaction
* _____ a) adult partially hides doll under a cloth	child reaches for doll
adult completely hides doll under a cloth	does not reach for doll
* _____ b) adult shows an apple to the child	looks at the apple
screen comes down covering the apple	looks elsewhere
* _____ c) toy train moves along a track	follows train with eyes
train disappears into tunnel	looks toward the place where train disappeared; after a while seems to lose interest
* _____ d) adult hides doll under one cloth, then under a different cloth while the child watches	looks for doll in the first place it was hidden,
* _____ e) adult hides doll in a novel place	actively and systematically searches for the doll until it is found
* _____ f) adult hides doll under three different cloths, leaving it under the last one, while child watches	looks for doll in the last place it was hidden

10.2 According to Piaget, an infant's object concept changes throughout the sensorimotor period.

a) Explain what the terms <u>passive expectation</u> and <u>object permanence</u> mean relative to the development of the object concept.

b) At which stages of sensorimotor development does object permanence appear to be present? At what stage is it assumed to be fully developed?

* 10.3 According to Piaget, the stage of sensorimotor development in which "thinking" begins is

stage _______________.

11. Describe Piaget's preoperational period and the research regarding this period. (pp. 188-190)

* 11.1 A child shapes a piece of modeling clay and refers to it as "mommy." Another child pretends she is a doctor. A third child puts pieces of wood together and calls his construction a "castle."

According to Piaget, these examples illustrate the appearance of the _______________ function, which develops along with language ability during the _______________ period of development.

11.2 Distinguish between a symbol and a sign and give an example of each.

11.3 A child is shown a glass containing several colored marbles. The marbles are then poured from the glass into a tall, narrow container. When the child is asked whether the tall container has more, less, or the same number of marbles than were in the glass, he reports that the tall container has more marbles.

Using this example, explain what Piaget meant by conservation.

11.4 According to Piaget, at what ages do the various aspects of conservation develop?

11.5 Some psychologists believe that children develop the ability to conserve at earlier ages than Piaget hypothesized.

a) Cite research evidence to support this view.

b) Explain what factors may explain the differences observed by Piaget and these other psychologists such as Gelman.

12. Describe the major changes in cognition that occur during the periods of concrete operations and formal operations. (pp. 190-192)

12.1 Consider the following situation.

A child is shown two balls, marked A and B, and is asked which of the two is larger. She answers correctly that ball B is. These balls are then removed from her sight, and she is shown a new ball marked C. The child is then told that ball C is larger than ball B. Finally she is asked to say which ball she thinks is larger, ball A or C.

Identify at what point during the period of concrete operations (generally speaking) each of the following responses would be likely to be observed in a child.

* a) The child unhesitatingly answers that C must be larger than A.

* b) The child says that she does not know, or simply guesses.

12.2 a) According to Piaget, what is responsible for the child's ability to analyze and solve the above problem?

b) Describe an alternative explanation for the child's behavior.

12.3 Define egocentrism from a developmental perspective and give an example of egocentric behavior that you may have observed in children.

12.4 Compare the academic and social behavior of an adolescent who has achieved formal operations and one who has not.

13. Describe Piaget's explanation for progression from one stage of development to the next and discuss the strengths and weaknesses of his theory. (pp. 192-193)

* 13.1 According to Piaget, the process that is responsible for a child passing from one developmental stage to another is _______________ _______________.

13.2 Define cognitive disequilibrium and provide an example.

13.3 State two criticisms of Piaget's work regarding the methods he used.

13.4 Despite the above limitations Piaget's contribution to our understanding of cognitive development is considered by many to be extremely valuable. In your own words, summarize the ways in which Piaget's work has been important.

LESSON I SELF TEST

1. The functional unit of the chromosome is the

   a. gene.
   b. phenotype.
   c. gamete.
   d. enzyme.

2. Each parent contributes twenty-three __________ to their offspring.

   a. chromosomes
   b. genes
   c. gametes
   d. enzymes

3. Which of the following statements is correct?

   a. There are twenty-three single genes in sperms and ova respectively.
   b. Genes produce behavior.
   c. Genes contain recipes.
   d. Genes differentiate as the organism matures.

4. Fetal alcohol syndrome occurs

   a. only in cases when the mother is a chronic alcoholic.
   b. occasionally as a result of a single alcoholic binge during a critical stage of pregnancy.
   c. when alcohol passes through the placenta and causes the fetus to suffer oxygen deprivation.
   d. when alcohol causes a mutation, an extra twenty-first chromosome.

5. Which of the following is an inherited, recessive disorder that is associated with mental retardation?

   a. Down's syndrome
   b. phenylketonuria
   c. fetal alcohol syndrome
   d. polygenic determined phenotype

6. Don wants the baby to turn its face to the left in order to face the camera. If he touches the

   a. left side of the baby's face, it will turn toward the left.

b. baby's face, it will cry and show organized withdrawal movements.
c. baby's stomach, it will face the camera and show the rooting reflex.
d. right side of the baby's face, it will move its head toward the left.

7. Research on infants' vision suggests that

a. there is an innate ability to recognize the human face.
b. soft, pastel colors facilitate the development of visual skills.
c. depth perception does not develop until an infant is able to crawl.
d. an infant's gaze is attracted to contrasts.

8. Research on the development of visual skills suggests that if a child

a. has unrestricted movement, it will be overstimulated and slower to develop.
b. cannot coordinate its eyes, stereoscopic vision will not develop.
c. has a choice of which pictures to look at, it will select the quieter, simpler picture.
d. does not develop depth perception by the age of two months, corrective surgery may be necessary.

9. Rita cares for ten infants and must follow a set routine in order to attend to all of them. It is likely that the infants under her care will

a. not learn anything from this environment.
b. become irritable and demanding.
c. learn that what they do has little effect upon their environment.
d. spontaneously develop motor and visual skills as their nervous systems develop.

10. The baby throws a toy outside the crib. The parent returns the toy to the baby. This sequence of behaviors is repeated many times. The baby will develop a

a. dropping schema.
b. dropping concept.
c. rooting reflex.
d. dropping signifier.

11. According to Piaget, individuals begin to think

a. during the stage of formal operations.
b. during the later part of the sensorimotor stage.
c. at birth.
d. during the preoperational period.

12. Gelman's research on the development of conservation suggests that

a. testing methods affect estimates of children's cognitive abilities.
b. the sequence of cognitive development proposed by Piaget is wrong.
c. children's language ability determines their ability to conserve.
d. the use of signifiers retards language development.

13. According to Piaget's theory of cognitive development, at about what age is a child likely to be ready to learn algebra?

a. age ten
b. age seventeen
c. age thirteen
d. age six

14. In telling a story to any group of people Katie assumes that her listeners know her background and share her perspective. Katie

a. has not yet gotten through the period of concrete operations.
b. shows cognitive disequilibrium.
c. does not distinguish between signs and signifiers.
d. shows a failure of the contingency game.

15. Piaget's theory and work can be criticized because Piaget

a. did not explain how individuals move from one stage to another.
b. used his own children as subjects.
c. did not always define his terms operationally.
d. minimized the role of the environment in cognitive development.

LESSON II: SOCIAL DEVELOPMENT DURING INFANCY, SEXUAL DEVELOPMENT, AND ADULT DEVELOPMENT

14. Define attachment and explain how the behaviors of sucking, cuddling, looking, smiling, and crying shape and maintain attachment between infants and their primary caregivers. (pp. 193-200)

14.1 What is attachment?

* 14.2 a) List the special behaviors exhibited by an infant that appear to be important in establishing care-giving behavior on the part of adults.

b) Describe the main characteristics of each of the above behaviors.

14.3 What do Harlow's studies of infant monkeys and surrogate mothers suggest about the causes of attachment? Make sure you discuss the cupboard theory, conditioned reinforcement, and the importance of close physical contact.

14.4 Describe the behavior of infants and caregivers in visual interaction with one another. What happens when the caregiver fails to respond to the infant's looking behavior?

14.5 Describe the "contingency game" and explain its importance in development.

14.6 A friend is concerned that if he responds to all the cries of his two-month-old baby he will reinforce the child's crying and thus spoil him. What does the research by Bell and Ainsworth (1972) suggest about this situation?

15. Summarize and evaluate research on the possibility that attachment between infants and primary caregivers must occur during a critical period. (pp. 200-201)

15.1 What happens if a newly hatched duckling is isolated during the first two days of its life? Use this example to explain what imprinting and critical periods are.

15.2 Barbara's newborn had to be placed in an incubator. Among Barbara's concern is her fear that the baby will have missed the critical period for bonding to her. Review the research on bonding and develop a response that may ease Barbara's worry.

16. Describe research with humans and monkeys concerning the importance of attachment between infant and caregiver in environmental exploration. (pp. 201-202)

16.1 What is meant by the term secure base, and what role does it play in an infant's exploration of the environment?

16.2 Use the studies by Harlow and his colleagues to suggest a possible explanation of the attachment abused children feel towards their abusive parents.

17. Describe research with humans and monkeys concerning the role of interactions with peers. (pp. 202-205)

17.1 Describe the effects of depriving an infant monkey of social contact with peers on its subsequent sexual, social, and maternal behavior.

17.2 Explain under what conditions the effects of early social deprivation in monkeys can be remediated later in life, as suggested by the research of Harlow and his colleagues. What do these findings suggest about the nature of critical periods for social interaction?

17.3 a) Describe the "juvenile therapist" technique used by Fuhrman et al. (1979) with children and b) the findings, and c) implications of this investigation for making inferences from studies of nonhuman primates to humans.

18. Describe the role of chromosomes in determining people's gender and the prenatal development of the sex organs. (pp. 205-207)

* 18.1 The sex of a person is determined by the _______________ and the two types of sex chromosomes are _______________ chromosomes and _______________ chromosomes.

* 18.2 If the sperm fertilizing an ovum contains an X chromosome, what will the sex of the offspring be?

* 18.3 Up to the fourth week of gestation male and female fetuses have a pair of _______________ gonads.

18.4 a) Describe the development of the internal sex organs of the human males and females and

b) contrast it with the development of the external sex organs.

* 18.5 If _______________ are present, the _______________ gonads become _______________.

The most important androgen is _______________.

18.6 What does the expression, "nature's impulse is to create a female" mean? Offer a) a clinical example and b) a research example to support your answer.

19. Describe the sexual development that occurs during puberty. (pp. 207-212)

* 19.1 The transition from childhood to adulthood begins with the onset of ______________. Briefly characterize this stage.

* 19.2 At puberty the hypothalamus stimulates the ______________ to secrete ______________ hormones.

19.3 How do males and females differ in terms of their

a) primary sex characteristics?

b) secondary sex characteristics?

* 19.4 The testes of pubescent males secrete ______________ and the ovaries of pubescent females secrete ______________, which is the most important ______________ or female ______________ hormone.

19.5 What do you think would happen in the following cases? Offer reasons for your answers.

a) A male takes estrogen pills.

b) An adult female takes testosterone tablets.

c) A grade school girl swallows her grandmother's estrogen tablets.

20. Explain the role of sex hormones in the behavioral masculinization and defeminization of laboratory animals. (pp. 212-213)

20.1 State the main advantage of using mice, rats, and hamsters as subjects for research on the effects of prenatal androgens on sexual behavior.

* 20.2 Unlike ______________, ______________ rats develop sexual behavior through activation of ______________ in the ______________ itself.

20.3 Contrast the adult sexual behavior of male and female rats whose internal sexual organs had been removed shortly after birth.

* 20.4 In ______________ masculinization, ______________ presented during a(n) ______________ ______________ causes rats to develop neurons that activate ______________ sexual behavior. The same hormone also ______________ female behavior, a phenomenon called ______________ ______________.

20.5 If testosterone, the male sex hormone, is needed to masculinize a male rat's brain, is estrogen, the female sex hormone, needed to feminize a female rat's brain? Give reasons for your answer.

21. Describe research on the effects of hormones on human behavior, and the possibility of these effects being reversed by socialization. (pp. 213-216)

21.1 Describe the research by Money and Ehrhardt on androgenized girls in terms of

a. the two experimental groups and the control group.

b. the results.

c. the implications of these results for causes of gender-related behavior.

d. other factors that may have contributed to the behavioral differences among the groups.

21.2 Compare the play and sexual behavior of androgenized female rhesus monkeys to that of normal females in the study by Goy and Goldfoot (1973).

21.3 Why is the interpretation of this study less ambiguous than that of studies of androgenized human females?

21.4 a) Describe the traditional behavior of parents with respect to male and female children in our society.

b) How does this presumably affect gender-related behavior in children?

21.5 a) What did the parents of the boy who accidentally lost his penis as a baby decide to do (Money and Ehrhardt (1972)?

b) On the basis of the reports on the development of this child, what would you advise parents to do if their baby's penis was destroyed? Offer reasons for your answer.

22. Describe the hypotheses and summarize the research on the development of sexual orientation. (pp. 216-219)

22.1 In what aspect does homosexuality in humans differ from that observed in other animals?

22.2 Explain why the observation that homosexuals may have more problems adjusting socially is <u>not</u> evidence for considering homosexuality a "disorder."

22.3 Using the study by Bell et al. as a reference, provide the appropriate information for each of the following:

a) What population was studied?

b) According to this study, at what point in a person's development is sexual preference established?

c) How did most homosexual men and women in this study perceive their early heterosexual experiences?

d) What does the relation between gender-related play behavior and homosexuality appear to be?

e) How does the type of interaction with one's father and mother seem to relate to sexual preference?

22.4 Discuss the implications of the Bell et al. study for the notion that

a) homosexual behavior results from disordered social adjustment.

b) homosexuality is at least partially determined by biological factors.

22.5 Explain what is meant by masculinization and defeminization in humans, and relate these to possible preference for sexual partners.

22.6 What evidence suggests that a tendency for a male to become homosexual may be "inherited"?

22.7 Discuss the evidence for the biological basis of female homosexuality.

23. Describe the nature of adult development, including physical changes that occur then and their psychological consequences. (p. 219)

23.1 Explain why it is more difficult to catalogue adult development than child development.

23.2 Using Erikson's notion of the identity crisis, explain how Erikson views development.

23.3 Using concrete examples, summarize what happens to most of our physical functions during adult life.

23.4 What effect does a changing physical appearance have upon a person's social life during adulthood?

* 23.5 Mental deterioration in the elderly may be caused by many factors; for instance, ______________, a prevalent form of ______________, or ______________. Describe the symptoms of these conditions.

23.6 Describe the relationship between the actual and functional changes in sensory functions that occur with age.

24. Summarize the difficulty with assessing the effects of aging on intellectual abilities. (pp. 219-222)

24.1 Describe cross-sectional studies and contrast them with longitudinal observations.

24.2 State some of the problems in interpreting the results of cross-sectional studies.

24.3 Describe some of the problems inherent in longitudinal studies.

25. Compare the specific intellectual abilities of younger and older adults. (pp. 222-226)

25.1 Distinguish between Cattell's notions of crystallized and fluid intelligence.

25.2 State three possible reasons for the decline of fluid intelligence with age.

25.3 Describe Kogan's (1973) findings regarding the classifying strategies of young and older people. What do these suggest about cognitive development in older people?

25.4 Describe some reasons for the decrease in speed of intellectual performance found in older people.

LESSON II SELF TEST

1. Harlow's studies of monkeys suggests that the reason infants form attachments to their primary caregivers is that

   a. physical contact is innately reinforcing.
   b. primary caregivers provide food, a primary reinforcer.
   c. infants imprint on their mothers while they are in the womb.
   d. they are exposed to the caregivers more than to other people.

2. Modern psychology believes that infants

   a. are programmed to emit behaviors that shape parental concern.
   b. are like blank slates, as John Locke theorized several centuries ago.
   c. have predetermined and inflexible behavior patterns.
   d. are overwhelmed by the stimulation around them.

3. Which of the following bits of advice on child rearing and development has been supported by psychological research?

   a. Newborns' smiles are really grimaces in response to gas pains.
   b. Decorating a baby's room in soft pastels is more conducive for later learning.
   c. If you pick infants up every time they cry, you will spoil them.
   d. Infants love patty-cake and other contingency producing games.

4. Infants' exploratory behaviors are

   a. inhibited by the presence of their parents.
   b. enhanced by the presence of their parents.
   c. are limited if they have not been bonded to their mothers at birth.
   d. depressed by peer contact.

5. Harlow's studies of isolate monkeys have shown that

   a. mating behavior and care of one's young is innate.
   b. if a monkey has not interacted with peers, it will never be able to form peer relationships.
   c. isolated monkeys when first introduced to other monkeys become overly social and aggressive.

d. adaptation to peers by previously isolated monkeys can be successful if the introduction to peers is gradual.

6. If a father contributes an X chromosome to his offspring, this child will be

a. male.
b. female.
c. male if autosomes are present.
d. female if androgens are present.

7. The widening of a female's hip during puberty is an example of
a. a secondary sex characteristic.
b. a primary sex characteristic.
c. behavioral demasculinization.
d. behavioral feminization.

8. The primary sex hormone in males is

a. progesterone.
b. testosterone.
c. estrogen.
d. estradiol.

9. Male rats will not behave as males unless

a. the male sex organs have been fully developed.
b. receptive females are present.
c. they have been both masculinized and defeminized.
d. unless they have had an opportunity to learn male behavior.

10. A chromosomal female who has been prenatally androgenized is likely to

a. become oriented towards the helping professions.
b. have greater verbal skill than female peers.
c. be more responsive to pain and touch.
d. become active and athletic.

11. John Money and other researchers have studied the case of the twin who was raised as a female after his penis had been destroyed. This case demonstrated that

a. the relationship between socialization and prenatal androgenization still remains to be specified.
b. socialization can completely override the effects of a person's prenatal hormone exposure.
c. the effects of prenatal exposure to androgens are irreversible.
d. behavioral masculinization is necessary for behavioral defeminization to occur.

12. One of the implications of the study by Bell, Weinberg, and Hammersmith (1981) is that

a. people are seduced into homosexuality by older persons of the same sex.
b. homosexual behavior is unnatural and peculiar to the human species.
c. homosexuals have poor relationships with their parents.
d. most homosexuals have had heterosexual experience.

13. As adults age, they can reasonably expect that they will

a. become more immune to psychological disorders such as depression.
b. become more like other people of their age group.
c. experience fewer functional changes than sensory changes.
d. suffer extensive loss of the gray matter of the cerebral cortex.

14. Which of the following is a limitation of cross-sectional studies of intelligence and aging?

    a. They cannot control for differences in environments of the people of different ages.
    b. They tend to minimize the drop in intelligence associated with aging.
    c. They frequently exceed the time parameters set by funding agencies.
    d. In order to ensure comparability at each time of measurement, researchers may be forced to use outdated tests of intelligence.

15. Declines in intellectual performance throughout adulthood are

    a. attributable to declines in crystallized intelligence.
    b. associated with the tendency of the elderly to answer test items carelessly.
    c. may be associated, in part, with decline in sensory abilities.
    d. associated with the tendency of the elderly to categorize items by physical characteristics.

INTEGRATING QUESTIONS

1. Your friend wants to raise her child to be intelligent and loving. Offer advice to your friend based on the current psychological research regarding the cognitive and social development.

2. Offer an answer to the philosophical question, "Do we learn to see?" by reviewing the research regarding the development of visual perception.

3. Psychologists have studied laboratory animals in order to understand their development and also to learn through inference something about our own development. Identify the areas in which psychologists have used laboratory animals in these ways. Review representative studies of these areas, and the implications they have for human development.

ANSWERS

1.1 genes, chromosomes
1.2 genes, enzymes, biological catalysts
2.1 ova, sperm, gametes
2.2 ovum, fallopian tube, ovulation
2.3 Human gametes contain twenty-three single chromosomes, half of the chromosomes of other cells in the body. This occurs through the division of cells in the ovaries and testes.
2.4 fertilization, zygote
3.1 fallopian tube, uterus, embryo
3.2 amniotic sac, placenta, transfer
3.3 a) fetal alcohol
4.3 phenylalanine, tyrosine, in that order
5.1 infancy, two, unable to speak
5.2 rooting, sucking, swallowing
5.4 proximodistal, cephalocaudal
5.5 maturation of the nervous system, practice
5.6 False. The nervous system continues to develop during infancy and even into early adulthood.
9.1 cognitive structures, concepts, schemas
9.2 a) schema, b) concept, c) concept, d) schema
9.3 assimilation; accommodation
9.4 a) assimilation, b) accommodation
10.1 a) Stage 3, b) Stage 1, c) Stage 2, d) Stage 4, e) Stage 6 f) Stage 5
10.3 6

Chapter 5

11.1 symbolic; preoperational
12.1 a) late in the preoperational period; b) early in the preoperational period
13.1 cognitive disequilibrium
14.2 a) rooting, sucking, cuddling, looking, smiling, crying
18.1 sex chromosomes; X, Y
18.2 female
18.3 identical primordial or undifferentiated
18.5 androgens, undifferentiated, male, testosterone
19.1 puberty
19.2 anterior pituitary gland, gonadotropic
19.4 testosterone, estradiol, estrogen, sex
20.2 males, female, neurons, hypothalamus
20.4 behavioral, testosterone (or androgen), critical period, male, inhibits, behavioral defeminization
23.5 Alzheimer's disease, dementia, depression

Self Test: Lesson I

1. a Obj. 5-1
2. a Obj. 5-1
3. c Obj. 5-2
4. b Obj. 5-3
5. b Obj. 5-4
6. a Obj. 5-5
7. d Obj. 5-6
8. b Obj. 5-7
9. c Obj. 5-8
10. a Obj. 5-9
11. b Obj. 5-10
12. a Obj. 5-11
13. c Obj. 5-12
14. a Obj. 5-12
15. c Obj. 5-13

Self Test: Lesson II

1. a Obj. 5-14
2. a Obj. 5-14
3. d Obj. 5-15
4. b Obj. 5-16
5. d Obj. 5-17
6. b Obj. 5-18
7. a Obj. 5-19
8. b Obj. 5-19
9. c Obj. 5-20
10. d Obj. 5-21
11. a Obj. 5-21
12. d Obj. 5-22
13. c Obj. 5-23
14. a Obj. 5-24
15. c Obj. 5-25

5.1 OBJ 5-1

GENES

5.2 OBJ 5-2

OVULATION

5.3 OBJ 5-2

GAMETES

5.4 OBJ 5-2

ZYGOTE

5.5 OBJ 5-2

DIFFERENTIATION

5.6 OBJ 5-3

PLACENTA

5.7 OBJ 5-3

FETAL ALCOHOL SYNDROME

5.8 OBJ 5-4

DOWN'S SYNDROME

5.9 OBJ 5-4

PHENYLKETONURIA
(PKU)

5.10 OBJ 5-5

ROOTING

5.11 OBJ 5-5

CEPHALOCAUDAL DEVELOPMENT

5.12 OBJ 5-9

SCHEMA

5.13 OBJ 5-9

CONCEPT

5.14 OBJ 5-9

ASSIMILATION

5.15 OBJ 5-9

ACCOMMODATION

5.16 OBJ 5-10

SENSORIMOTOR PERIOD

5.9 Obj 5-4

genetic recessive disorder; results in accumulation of phenylalanine, which damages brain; can be controlled by diet

5.10 Obj 5-5

infant's reflex; turns head when cheek touched so that object reaches lips

5.11 Obj 5-5

development of motor control over upper parts of body before lower parts

5.12 Obj 5-9

according to Piaget, rules governing a particular behavior or behavioral sequence

5.13 Obj 5-9

according to Piaget, mental structures or rules describing properties of objects and events in the environment

5.14 Obj 5-9

construction of new concepts or modification of old ones as a result of interaction with the environment; leads to accommodation

5.15 Obj 5-9

adjustment of behavioral schemas to concepts as a result of interaction with objects and events in the environment; follows assimilation

5.16 Obj 5-10

Piaget's first period of development; lasts from birth through age two; cognition represented by behavior; closely tied to environmental stimulation

5.1 Obj 5-1

units of information determining characteristics of individual or species; contained in chromosomes; produce proteins

5.2 Obj 5-2

burst of follicle, releasing ovum into abdominal cavity

5.3 Obj 5-2

cells (sperm and ova) produced by sexual organs; contain half the normal number of chromosomes

5.4 Obj 5-2

fertilized egg

5.5 Obj 5-2

process by which cells develop into different, specialized body tissues

5.6 Obj 5-3

tissue developed by the embryo; allows exchange of substances between mother and fetus through the umbilical cord

5.7 Obj 5-3

alcohol-induced developmental abnormality; includes physical and mental defects

5.8 Obj 5-4

mental retardation produced by extra twenty-first chromosome

5.17 OBJ 5-10

PASSIVE EXPECTATION

5.18 OBJ 5-10

PERMANENCE

5.19 OBJ 5-11

PREOPERATIONAL PERIOD

5.20 OBJ 5-11

SYMBOLIC FUNCTION

5.21 OBJ 5-11

SIGNIFIER

5.22 OBJ 5-11

SIGN

5.23 OBJ 5-11

CONSERVATION

5.24 OBJ 5-12

PERIOD OF CONCRETE OPERATIONS

5.25 OBJ 5-12

EGOCENTRISM

5.26 OBJ 5-12

PERIOD OF FORMAL OPERATIONS

5.27 OBJ 5-13

COGNITIVE DISEQUILIBRIUM

5.28 OBJ 5-14

ATTACHMENT

5.29 OBJ 5-18

AUTOSOMES

5.30 OBJ 5-18

X CHROMOSOME

5.31 OBJ 5-18

Y CHROMOSOME

5.32 OBJ 5-18

GONADS

5.25 Obj 5-12

child's belief that others perceive the world exactly the way he or she does

5.26 Obj 5-12

Piaget's final period of cognitive development; begins at 12 years; adult logic and symbolic representation, hypothesis testing

5.27 Obj 5-13

Piaget: motivates changes from one cognitive stage to another; arises from contact with novel stimuli that do not fit existing schemas

5.28 Obj 5-14

close bond between parent or other caregiver and infant; important for social development; result of mutual reinforcement

5.29 Obj 5-18

chromosomes that determine a person's physical development independent of sex

5.30 Obj 5-18

chromosome from mother, which when combined with X chromosome from father, determines that child will be female

5.31 Obj 5-18

chromosome that can only be produced by male; when combined with woman's X chromosome, produces a male

5.32 Obj 5-18

testes or ovaries

5.17 Obj 5-10

infants' actions suggesting they expect object moved out of sight to reappear but they do not actively search for it. characteristic of Stage 2, sensorimotor period

5.18 Obj 5-10

belief that object that is moved out of sight continues to exist; acquired during Piaget's 4th stage of sensorimotor development

5.19 Obj 5-11

Piaget's second period of development (2-7 yr.); symbolic and language ability develop rapidly

5.20 Obj 5-11

ability to represent things through symbols such as words and actions; rapidly develops during Piaget's preoperational period

5.21 Obj 5-11

Piaget: movements that symbolically represent a concept; acquired through interaction with concept

5.22 Obj 5-11

Piaget: abstract symbols such as words, acquired through social convention

5.23 Obj 5-11

ability to recognize and say that an object retains its mass, volume, weight, or number after various transformations

5.24 Obj 5-12

Piaget's third period of development (7-11 yr.); logical analysis, social empathazing, and symbolic thought developed and refined

5.33 OBJ 5-18

ANDROGENS

5.34 OBJ 5-18

TURNER'S SYNDROME

5.35 OBJ 5-19

PUBERTY

5.36 OBJ 5-19

ANTERIOR PITUITARY GLAND

5.37 OBJ 5-19

GONADOTROPIC HORMONES

5.38 OBJ 5-19

PRIMARY SEX CHARACTERISTICS

5.39 OBJ 5-19

SECONDARY SEX CHARACTERISTICS

5.40 OBJ 5-19

ESTROGEN

5.41 OBJ 5-20

BEHAVIORAL MASCULINIZATION

5.42 OBJ 5-20

BEHAVIORAL DEFEMINIZATION

5.43 OBJ 5-21

ADRENOGENITAL SYNDROME

5.44 OBJ 5-24

ALZHEIMER'S DISEASE

5.45 OBJ 5-24

CROSS-SECTIONAL STUDY

5.46 OBJ 5-25

LONGITUDINAL STUDY

5.47 OBJ 5-25

CRYSTALLIZED INTELLIGENCE

5.48 OBJ 5-25

FLUID INTELLIGENCE

5.41 Obj 5-20

behavioral androgenization whereby male sexual behavior is organized

5.42 Obj 5-20

inhibition of tendency to display female sexual behavior induced by androgens

5.43 Obj 5-21

abnormal sexual development induced by high levels of androgens in female fetuses

5.44 Obj 5-24

most prevalent presenile dementia; loss of neurons in cerebral cortex; affects memory, language, and motor ability

5.45 Obj 5-24

observations and measurements that compare different age groups at the same time

5.46 Obj 5-25

observations and measurements that compare individuals at different times in their lives

5.47 Obj 5-25

according to Cattell, intellectual abilities that depend on knowledge and experience

5.48 Obj 5-25

according to Cattell, abstract reasoning; speed-related; flexibility; strategy; necessary for development of crystallized intelligence

5.33 Obj 5-18

class of hormones, secreted by males' testes

5.34 Obj 5-18

disorder produced by lack of one sex chromosome, known as XO condition; primordial gonads fail to develop

5.35 Obj 5-19

final stage of child development; physical and social changes mark transition from childhood to adulthood

5.36 Obj 5-19

organ that secretes gonadotropic hormones

5.37 Obj 5-19

hormones that induce the ovaries or testes to secrete sex hormones

5.38 Obj 5-19

maturation of gonads and external genitalia, including production of sperm and ova

5.39 Obj 5-19

physical differences distinguishing males and females after puberty

5.40 Obj 5-19

main class of female-developing hormones

CHAPTER 6
Basic Principles of Learning

INTRODUCTION

This chapter examines basic principles of learning and the classical and instrumental conditioning procedures used to study the process. The chapter is divided into two lessons: Lesson I includes Objectives 1-14, and Lesson II includes Objectives 15-26.

CONCEPT CARDS AND EXERCISES

After you have surveyed and read the text, assemble the concept cards located at the end of this chapter. Use them to learn the important terms, then begin reading the text again, one learning objective at a time, and work through the exercises for each lesson. Answers for questions marked with an asterisk are found at the end of the chapter.

SELF TESTS

Each lesson is followed by a multiple-choice self test. After you are proficient with a lesson's concept cards and exercises, take the self test to see whether you have mastered the material. Review those objectives for questions you answered incorrectly.

INTEGRATING QUESTIONS

To challenge yourself further, answer the integrating questions at the end of the chapter. These questions ask you to apply the information you have learned to consider larger theoretical or real-life issues.

LESSON I: PRINCIPLES OF CLASSICAL AND INSTRUMENTAL CONDITIONING

1. Describe habituation and explain its functional significance. (pp. 234-235)

* 1.1 Your dog is sleeping on a quiet evening when suddenly somewhere in the neighborhood another dog's barking can faintly be heard. Your dog immediately raises its head, perks up its ears, and looks in the direction of the sound. This example illustrates the

_______________ response.

1.2 The neighborhood dog continues to bark faintly in the distance but no other disturbance seems to be developing. What is your dog likely to do? What is the dog's behavior an example of and how does it illustrate a simple type of learning?

1.3 What is the adaptive significance of habituation? Use the preceding example to explain your answer.

1.4 Define a stimulus and identify the stimulus for the orienting response in question 1.1.

1.5 Compare short-term and long-term habituation.

* 1.6 Does the example of the two dogs illustrate short-term or long-term habituation? Explain your answer. How would you change the example to illustrate the other type of habituation?

2. Describe the process of classical conditioning. (pp. 235-237)

* 2.1 A stimulus that elicits a response is called an _______________ _______________ or US.

* 2.2 The response elicited by a US is called an _______________ _______________ or UR.

* 2.3 In an effective classical conditioning procedure, a stimulus presented just before the US is called the _______________ _______________ or CS.

* 2.4 What new response develops to the CS after it has been paired with the US on repeated trials?

3. Explain the biological significance of classical conditioning. (pp. 237-238)

3.1 Define a defensive reflex including under what conditions it is elicited and what functions it serves.

3.2 What is meant by elicitation?

* 3.3 Give examples of some reflexes that may be classically conditioned.

3.4 Give an original example that illustrates how classical conditioning can elicit preparatory behaviors.

3.5 Explain how such preparatory behaviors are adaptive to organisms.

3.6 Discuss the relation between classical conditioning and feelings of emotions. Give some examples of your own.

4. Describe the physiological changes that may be taking place during classical conditioning. (pp. 238-239)

4.1 Describe Hebb's proposal regarding the neurological correlates of learning.

4.2 How is the nictitating membrane used in classical conditioning preparations?

4.3 Describe the possible effect of classical conditioning on heterosynaptic facilitation. Use a diagram to help explain the mechanism involved.

5. Describe how extinction of classically conditioned responses occurs. (pp. 240-241)

* 5.1 If the CS is repeatedly presented by itself, not followed by the US, _____________ is likely to occur. What happens to the strength of the response to the CR and the likelihood of its occurring?

5.2 How is extinction similar to habituation?

* 5.3 After extinction has occurred, what does the organism do if the CS occurs again after a long pause? What is this effect called? Does it last long?

6. Explain how classical conditioning phenomenon can generate unusual behavior. (pp. 241-242)

6.1 Define phobias and fetishes and compare the two.

6.2 Diagram the phobic classical conditioning procedure identifying the CS, US, CR, and UR.

6.3 Describe the apparatus, procedure and results of the study of fetish formation by Rachman and Hodgson.

7. Explain how instrumental conditioning affects behavior. (p. 243)

* 7.1 If an organism's behavior "operates" on the environment and is "instrumental" in producing a change in the environment, the causal relation between the instrumental response and the environmental consequence is known as a _____________.

* 7.2 The presentation of the contingent stimulus may _____________ or _____________ the probability that the organism will make a similar instrumental response under similar conditions in the future.

* 7.3 A situation in which the events that follow a response increase the probability of similar responses under similar conditions in the future is called _____________.

* 7.4 The stimulus object or event which follows behavior in such contingencies is called a _____________.

7.5 How does a reward that is given intentionally differ from a reinforcer?

Note: Reinforcers are operationally defined, rewards are not. Reinforcers must have a strengthening effect on a particular responses. If someone says to you, "That reinforcement didn't work," you should point out that is impossible. If it does not work, it is not a reinforcer.

8. Compare reinforcement and punishment procedures. (pp. 243-246)

8.1 Distinguish between appetitive and aversive stimuli.

* 8.2 Reinforcement usually involves presenting a stimulus that we would tend to approach, enjoy, or work for, generally known as a(n) ______________ stimulus.

* 8.3 When the removal of a stimulus following an instrumental response causes the strength of that response to increase, the procedure is called ______________ ______________. An ______________ ______________ was probably removed.

* 8.4 Punishment is similar to reinforcement because a stimulus change usually occurs ______________ an instrumental response. However, punishment and reinforcement differ in their effects on behavior. Explain this difference.

* 8.5 What type of stimulus is generally associated with punishment?

* 8.6 What term do we use to refer to the effects of removal of an appetitive stimulus after a particular response? What is its effect on instrumental behavior?

9. Describe the research by Logan on the importance of immediacy of reinforcement. (p. 247)

* 9.1 In order for instrumental conditioning to occur, how must the instrumental response and environmental consequence be related in time?

9.2 How did Logan (1965) demonstrate that the immediate consequences of behavior may exert more influence over behavior than the magnitude of the consequences?

10. Compare primary and secondary (conditional) reinforcers and describe their origins. (pp. 247-248)

* 10.1 If an appetitive stimulus is presented every time an animal makes a particular response, it probably will serve as a ______________ reinforcer. If, instead, an aversive stimulus is presented, it will generally serve as a ______________ ______________.

Note: <u>All</u> stimuli can serve either as punishers <u>or</u> reinforcers depending on the circumstances. Food can be a punisher ("I hate lima beans"), and electric shocks can be reinforcing under special conditions. (People who are regularly reinforced by stimuli that most of us consider painful or harmful are called masochists.) It is best not to assume that a particular stimulus is a punisher or a reinforcer before gathering some empirical data. For example, food, water, sex, and sleep will usually be primary reinforcers when the organism has been slightly deprived of them, but not necessarily under other conditions.

* 10.2 Stimuli that are reinforcing for an individual because of its particular history are called _______________ (or _______________) reinforcers. Stimuli that are punishing for an individual because of its particular history are called _______________ (or _______________).

* 10.3 Through what procedure does a conditioned punisher or reinforcer acquire its properties?

* 10.4 How is a CS similar to a conditioned reinforcer or punisher?

* 10.5 For each example decide whether the reinforcing or punishing stimulus is conditioned or primary.

_______________ a) a painting by Picasso

_______________ b) a cup of scalding hot cocoa

_______________ c) the current bestseller

_______________ d) a bite of apple pie in the mouth

_______________ e) an "A" in this course

10.6 What is the biological significance for the organism of each of the these examples?

a) seeing a sign as you drive along saying "Last Gas for 180 Kilometers"

b) seeing a child put down a can with a poison symbol

c) seeing a motorist toss a lit cigarette out his car window while parked at a gas station.

d) hearing a car horn as you step off the curb at a busy intersection

e) noticing a restaurant when you are hungry

11. Describe the Premack principle and explain its importance to instrumental conditioning. (pp. 248-250)

* 11.1 An organism's choice between stimulus/response situations as measured by the amount of time spent in each one is an operational example of _______________.

* 11.2 We can construct a _______________ _______________ by arranging an organism's preference for activities from most reinforcing to least reinforcing.

* 11.3 How did Premack use preference for manipulating a plunger to reinforce consumption of M&M's?

* 11.4 What does the Premack principle suggest about an organism's preferences for various behaviors?

12. Describe the nature and importance of social reinforcers and punishers. (p. 250)

12.1 Give two original examples of social reinforcement from your own experience. Choose an example in which your behavior was reinforced by another person's behavior and an example in which your behavior reinforced the behavior of another person.

12.2 What was the instrumental response in each of your examples?

12.3 Did you specify a reinforcer delivered immediately in each example? If not, do so.

12.4 What is the probability of making similar instrumental responses in similar circumstances in the future in your examples?

13. Explain the process of shaping and its role in reinforcing infrequent or unusual behaviors. (pp. 250-254)

* 13.1 Shaping occurs when a succession of responses that vary in a particular direction are selectively _______________. During shaping the current response is used to produce a _______________ behavior.

* 13.2 A(n) _______________ chamber is an experimental apparatus used in the study of _______________ or instrumental conditioning.

* 13.3 What instrumental behavior is generally measured when a rat is the subject in an operant chamber?

* 13.4 What primary reinforcer is used to shape operant behavior? If this reinforcer is to be effective, how must the daily life of the subject be altered?

* 13.5 What auditory stimulus is paired with the delivery of the primary reinforcer? The auditory stimulus becomes a conditioned reinforcer through _______________ _______________.

* 13.6 Once the "click" becomes an effective CS, what does the rat do when the sound is presented?

* 13.7 How do we establish the response of turning away from the food dispenser after the food has been delivered and eaten by the rat?

13.8 Once the response of turning away from the food dispenser in the direction of the lever has been firmly established, how would you continue to shape lever pressing?

14. Describe the methods used to reinforce chains of responses. (p. 254)

14.1 Describe the behavior of Barnabus the rat who was trained by Pierrel and Sherman at Columbia University.

* 14.2 How was shaping used to establish Barnabus' sequence of responses?

14.3 What is "backward chaining" and how was it used to teach Barnabus?

* 14.4 Explain how each individual response in a chain of responses becomes a reinforcer for the previous response.

LESSON I SELF TEST

1. The townspeople stopped paying attention to the shepherd boy's cries of wolf because no wolf was ever present. This is an example of

   a. inhibition.
   b. regression.
   c. long-term habituation.
   d. intermittent reinforcement.

2. A conditional stimulus is one

   a. to which an organism habituates during operant conditioning.
   b. that must be noticed by the organism for conditioning to occur.
   c. that is neutral with respect to an orienting response.
   d. that is not initially neutral to the unconditional stimulus in the process of instrumental conditioning.

3. The presumed biological significance of classical conditioning is that it

   a. nakes it easier to distinguish pleasant from unpleasant stimuli.
   b. heightens awareness of all physiological functions.
   c. prepares organisms for events that are likely to occur soon.
   d. provides a good explanation of species-typical behavior.

4. Hebb proposed that learning may

   a. occur through a change in the strength of synapses.
   b. be positively correlated with motivation strength.
   c. be accomplished best through modeling.
   d. be enhanced through appropriate reinforcement.

5. When a rat stops pressing a lever to receive food because the response is no longer reinforced with food, we say the behavior has been __________. If, on a later session, the rat resumes begins pressing again, we call this behavior __________.

   a. shaped; the Premack principle
   b. aversive; appetitive
   c. habituated; reinforced

d. extinguished; spontaneous recovery

6. Phobias such as fear of snakes may be the result of

a. classical conditioning early in life.
b. unsuccessful extinction techniques.
c. instrumental conditioning early in life.
d. inappropriate habituation.

7. Most psychologists prefer the term reinforcement to reward when considering instrumental conditioning because

a. not all reinforcers are rewarding.
b. rewards differ in their reinforcement strength.
c. reinforcement is a neutral term.
d. some responses can only be reinforced, not rewarded.

8. Effective rat poisons are difficult to develop because rats do not again eat a food that has made them sick. This behavior

a. has only been demonstrated in the laboratory, not the field.
b. is an exception to the rule that reinforcers must immediately follow a behavior.
c. shows that survival is a stronger drive than hunger.
d. demonstrates that species-typical behaviors can disrupt learned ones.

9. Conditioned reinforcers and conditioned punishers

a. are not influenced by cultural experience.
b. permit organisms to engage in behavior with only long-range benefits.
c. depend on prior instrumental conditioning.
d. frequently perpetuate mechanical, stereotypical responses.

10. Sarah prefers reading novels to writing reports. She allows herself to read a chapter of her book only after she has written a section of her report. Her behavior illustrates

a. response cost.
b. the influence of a conditioned preference
c. the Premack principle.
d. latent inhibition.

10. Judy smiled warmly when Ray held the door for her. Judy's smile was pleasing to Ray. Her smile may serve as a(n) __________ for Ray.

a. primary reinforcer
b. social reinforcer
c. unconditional stimulus
d. elicited response

12. A foreign language teacher differentially praises her students as their pronunciation of new words improves from very poor to excellent. She is probably using

a. negative reinforcement.
b. the method of successive approximations.
c. primary reinforcement.
d. classical conditioning.

LESSON II: AVOIDANCE BEHAVIOR, SCHEDULES OF REINFORCEMENT, DISCRIMINATION, AND GENERALIZATION

15. Compare avoidance and escape behavior and explain why aversive control is often not as effective as positive reinforcement. (pp. 254-256)

* 15.1 An instrumental response that prevents the presentation of an aversive stimulus is called an _______________ _______________.

* 15.2 Responses that serve to remove the organism from contact with an aversive stimulus once the stimulus has been presented are called _______________ _______________.

15.3 Provide original examples of your own experience in both avoiding and escaping from aversive stimuli.

* 15.4 Presentation of aversive stimuli often elicit species-typical _______________ _______________. How do these reactions effect the organism's ability to simultaneously perform instrumental or other kinds of responses?

15.5 Because appetitive stimuli do not generally elicit species-typical defense reactions or other avoidance or escape responses, what does this suggest about the desirability of using reinforcers rather than aversive control procedures to teach new behaviors?

16. Describe how fears can be maintained by negative reinforcement. (p. 256)

16.1 Describe how avoidance responses to conditioned aversive stimuli produce a negative reinforcement procedure. Give an original example to illustrate your answer.

16.2 When a person with a phobia encounters an object he or she fears, walking away from it reduces fear and thus provides negative reinforcement. What implications does this fact have for the likely success of attempts to eliminate phobias through extinction procedures?

16.3 Summarize the processes that maintain phobias to conditional aversive stimuli.

17. Describe how extinction of instrumentally conditioned behavior occurs. (pp. 256-257)

* 17.1 In classical conditioning if a CS is no longer followed by a US, what happens to the response conditioned to the CS?

* 17.2 In instrumental conditioning a similar process may occur if the operant response is no longer followed by the _______________. What is this process called?

* 17.3 What happens to the organism's rate of instrumental responding after the experimenter stops delivering the reinforcers?

* 17.4 What happens to instrumental behavior when an animal is removed from an extinction situation and then put back in that situation at a later time? Is there a similar process in classical conditioning? Explain your answer.

* 17.5 What is the eventual effect on instrumental behavior if an extinction contingency is maintained?

* 17.6 What other behaviors are likely to accompany the initial phase of an extinction condition? (What do people generally do when the soda machine does not reinforce their dropping money into it?)

18. Explain the relation between intermittent reinforcement and resistance to extinction. (pp. 258-259)

* 18.1 What happens to an organism's motivation to respond if it receives a reinforcer each time it makes the operant response? What is such an effect called?

* 18.2 What happens to behavior during an extinction contingency if the response has previously been continuously reinforced? How does this differ from the extinction of behavior that has previously been reinforced on a noncontinuous basis?

18.3 What is intermittent reinforcement?

18.4 Is an extinction contingency more likely to be noticed (discriminated) immediately after a period of continuous reinforcement or intermittent reinforcement? Explain your answer.

18.5 How does this effect the speed with which extinction of behavior occurs?

19. Describe the characteristics and behavioral effects of response-dependent schedules of reinforcement. (pp. 259-260)

19.1 What is the name for rules specifying how often or under what conditions reinforcers will be delivered?

19.2 Name two fundamental categories of reinforcement schedules based on the variables of number of responses and time.

* 19.3 Name the simplest type of ratio schedule (FR-1). In the symbol FR-10, FR stands for

______________ ______________, and 10 stands for 10 ______________ for every one

______________.

* 19.4 If an animal is working on a CRF schedule (FR-1) when suddenly the contingency is switched to FR-500, what is likely to happen to the instrumental response?

* 19.5 What is the best way to train an animal to respond steadily on a FR-500 if it is currently working at a FR-1?

19.6 If an animal is working on an extended FR schedule, such as FR-150, what type of behavior is likely to follow each reinforcer?

19.7 What are variable-ratio (VR) schedules of reinforcement?

19.8 How is instrumental performance on a VR schedule different from that of a FR schedule?

19.9 Explain how VR schedules can make responding highly resistant to extinction. Include an example in your answer.

20. Describe the characteristics and behavioral effects of response-and-time-dependent schedules. (pp. 261-262)

* 20.1 What is the name of a reinforcement schedule in which a period of time must pass before a response will produce a reinforcer?

* 20.2 One such schedule is a fixed-interval schedule in which a ______________ amount of time must pass before the next ______________ is reinforced.

* 20.3 If the animal is not signaled that a fixed interval of time has elapsed, the only way it will know that the interval has ended is when the first response following the interval is reinforced. The sooner it responds after the end of the interval, the sooner it will be ______________ . This condition usually produces ______________ rates of responding just after reinforcement and progressively ______________ rates of responding as time passes.

* 20.4 If the animal is signaled that a fixed interval of time has elapsed, the schedule is called a ______________ FI schedule. How does the animal's behavior on this schedule differ from that on an unsignaled FI schedule?

20.5 How does the arrangement of a variable-interval schedule differ from that of a fixed-interval schedule? How is a VI schedule similar to a VR schedule?

20.6 Describe the typical pattern of response rates on a VI schedule.

21. Describe superstitious behaviors and the conditions that can generate it. (pp. 262-263)

* 21.1 Reinforcement strengthens the probability that an animal will repeat the behavior that occurred immediately before reinforcement. If a potent reinforcer immediately follows a behavior even though the behavior did not cause the reinforcement, what is likely to happen to the probability of the animal repeating that response?

21.2 Describe Skinner's (1948) demonstration of the evolution of superstitious response patterns in pigeons. What situation did he arrange? How did the birds respond?

21.3 Describe an original example of a superstitious behavior that you or someone you know has acquired. Identify the reinforcer and the situation that made its delivery accidental.

22. Explain how interactions between classical and instrumental conditioning can elicit and reinforce species typical behaviors. (pp. 263-265)

22.1 Describe the Brelands' discovery of the phenomenon they named instinctive drift.

22.2 Describe the autoshaping procedures Brown and Jenkins (1968) demonstrated. How did their procedures differ from instrumental conditioning?

* 22.3 If food (grain) is a powerful US for food-deprived pigeons, what UR do they make to the food?

* 22.4 If a disk is always illuminated just before food is delivered, what kind of procedure has been arranged?

* 22.5 What kind of response should the lighted disk elicit? What kind of stimulus function does the disk serve?

22.6 How did Moore (1973) demonstrate that the type of US used in autoshaping controls the type of CR elicited by the illuminated disk?

* 22.7 What have Donahoe et al. (1982) suggested about classical and operant conditioning procedures?

23. Describe observation and imitation and the conditions under which they are likely to occur. (p. 265)

23.1 Describe the procedures of Baer, Peterson, and Sherman (1967) used in their attempt to teach severely retarded children to imitate.

23.2 What was the significant outcome of the study? What general response did the children learn for the verbal stimulus "Do this"?

23.3 What does this study suggest about how reinforcement contributes to learning new social behaviors?

24. Describe discrimination. (pp. 266)

* 24.1 Events or objects that signal to the organism that a particular response is likely to be reinforced are called _______________ _______________.

24.2 At an intersection a green light is a discriminative stimulus for what behavior? A red light is a discriminative stimulus for what behavior?

* 24.3 When appropriate behavioral changes occur in response to changes in the discriminative stimuli, the organism has _______________ between the stimuli.

24.4 What effect do discriminative stimuli have on behavior? Give an original example to illustrate your answer.

24.5 How could discrimination tasks be used to assess the perceptual capabilities of organisms? Give an example of pitch or tone discrimination to illustrate your answer.

25. Describe generalization and explain its relation to concept formation. (pp. 266-270)

25.1 Describe the procedure Honig et al. (1963) used to demonstrate generalization in pigeons to line tilt.

* 25.2 The results of the Honig study show what is called a generalization gradient. Assume that you performed a similar experiment with a rat using auditory tones instead of visual stimuli. If you reinforced the rat's responses to a 1000-Hz tone and later presented it with the following lower pitched tones of 600, 700, 800, and 900 Hz and the following higher pitched tones of 1100, 1200, 1300, and 1400 Hz, how do you think response rate would change as a function of the tone's distance from 1000 Hz? Graph your answer below.

High

response
rate

low

600 700 800 900 1000 1100 1200 1300 1400
test stimuli
(tone values in Hz)

* 25.3 What concept do the following examples illustrate?

a) When a duckling steps on a small panel in the floor of a specially constructed chamber, an opaque wall slides away for ten seconds, providing the duckling with a view of its mother. The duckling continues to step on the panel.

b) A child discovers that all the water in the toilet drains out when he pushes the handle. The child pushes the handle each time the toilet bowl refills.

25.4 Have you ever heard of these particular examples before? Were you, nevertheless, able to answer question 25.5 correctly?

* 25.5 If you correctly answered "reinforcement" to question 25.3 even though you had never heard of these examples, what can be said about your concept of reinforcement?

25.6 Describe the training procedures and identify the concept that Herrnstein and Loveland (1964) taught to pigeons. Explain what their results suggest about the relative abilities of pigeons and humans to identify novel instances of the concept.

26. Compare discrimination and generalization in classical conditioning. (p. 270)

* 26.1 a) If, as a result of classical conditioning, your eyes invariably water at the sight of small yellow onions and if you also notice your eyes watering when you see shallots or garlic, what phenomenon has your response demonstrated?

b) Suppose that when you see a large red onion your eyes do not water. What phenomenon is demonstrated by your lack of response?

26.2 Give an original example of a personal classically conditioned behavior. Identify the CS and CR.

26.3 Give an example of discrimination in classical conditioning using your example in question 26.2. Be sure to indicate how the features of the stimuli differ.

LESSON II SELF TEST

1. Tony is afraid to fly and always has a ready excuse whenever his brother, who lives in Europe, offers him a plane ticket. Tony's excuse is a(n)

 a. species-typical defense reaction.
 b. avoidance response.
 c. escape response.
 d. superstitious behavior.

2. Tony has not flown for many years, yet he still fears flying. Why has his response of making excuses not extinguished?

 a. Because he is exhibiting species-typical defense reactions.
 b. Because of negative reinforcement of his avoidance behavior.
 c. Because of his fear of extinction.
 d. Because an intermittent reinforcement schedule is operating.

3. What will be the response of a rat that has received food each time it pressed a lever if it no longer receives food when it presses the lever? Response rate

 a. will increase steadily with increased hunger
 b. will first increase, then become irregular, and finally stop.
 c. will decrease abruptly then rebound to previous levels.
 d. will taper off in regular decrements and finally stop.

4. How will response rate change if the rat in question 3 had originally received food after every twenty lever presses? Response rate

 a. will be the same.
 b. that is intermittantly reinforced resists extinction.
 c. once extinguished can never be reestablished.
 d. is independent of schedules of reinforcement.

5. An hourly wage is to piece rate as

 a. continuous reinforcement is to intermittent reinforcement.
 b. fixed interval is to fixed ratio.

c. variable ratio is to fixed interval.
d. extinction is to habituation.

6. Variable-ratio schedules of reinforcement

a. produce behavior that is easily extinguished.
b. are associated with low rates of responding.
c. are seen more often than fixed-ratio schedules in life outside the laboratory.
d. are seldom seen in life outside the laboratory.

7. Superstitious behavior occurs when

a. reinforcement is intermittant and not related to behavior.
b. the researcher deliberately establishes a contingency relationship between behavior and reinforcement.
c. aversive stimuli are present.
d. species-typical defense responses are elicited.

8. Autoshaping

a. suggests that instrumental and classical conditioning have different biological roots.
b. occurs if the researcher reinforces behavior on a fixed-ratio schedule.
c. undermines species-typical behaviors.
d. seems to be related to instinctive drift.

9. If an infant is hugged and kissed for imitating the facial expressions of its parents, the infant may develop

a. a general tendency to imitate.
b. autoshaped responses.
c. stereotyped superstitious behaviors.
d. a face fetish as an adult.

10. Rose lives in an apartment with thin walls. When she first moved in she would rush to her telephone when her neighbor's phone would ring. She no longer does that because she has learned

a. to discriminate between the ring of her phone and the neighbor's.
b. to generalize the sound of different phones.
c. avoidance conditioning to the ring of neighbors' phones.
d. autoshaping to the correct ring.

11. Pigeons who learned to peck in response to a slide with a picture of a human being demonstrated

a. negative reinforcement
b. learning of concepts.
c. species-typical defense responses.
d. the power of autoshaping.

12. Which statement is false? Discrimination and generalization

a. involve detection of distinctions and similarities among different stimuli.
b. apply to classical as well as instrumental conditioning.
c. appear to be necessary components of all learning.
d. interfere with classical, but not instrumental, conditioning.

Chapter 6

INTEGRATING QUESTIONS

1. Compare punishment procedures with reinforcement procedures, including a statement of how they are procedurally similar and how their effects on behavior differ. Include a description of negative and positive reinforcement and punishment.

2. Explain why it is useful to switch organisms from continuous reinforcement schedules to intermittent schedules such as VR and VI schedules.

3. Explain, using an original example, how complex human behavior such as verbal behavior or concept formation can be understood in terms of the combined effects of the various basic learning principles covered in this chapter. Select an example that illustrates at least three of the following principles: discrimination, generalization, shaping, chaining, conditioned reinforcement, control by intermittent schedules, etc.

ANSWERS

1.1 orienting
1.6 The example illustrates short-term habituation. For long-term habituation, barking episodes must occur on separate occasions and the initial orienting response must diminish with each succeeding episode.
2.1 unconditional stimulus
2.2 unconditional response
2.3 conditional stimulus
2.4 a CR or conditional response
3.3 Different eliciting stimuli will evoke different reflexes; for example, food elicits salivation, chewing, swallowing, and gastric secretions. Sexual stimuli elicit heart rate increases, pupil dilation and changes in the genitals.
5.1 extinction
5.3 the CR occurs again, spontaneous recovery, the effect is brief—extinction usually follows even more rapidly than it originally did.
7.1 contingency
7.2 increase or decrease
7.3 reinforcement (the <u>process</u> of increasing response strength)
7.4 reinforcer (the <u>stimulus</u> that follows the instrumental response in reinforcement)
8.2 appetitive
8.3 negative reinforcement, aversive stimulus
8.4 contingent upon, following, or after; Positive and negative reinforcement increase response strength; punishment decreases it.
8.5 aversive
8.6 response cost (negative punishment), reduces response strength
9.1 an immediate temporal relation (within several seconds for maximum effectiveness)
10.1 primary, primary punisher
10.2 conditioned or secondary; conditioned or secondary punisher
10.3 classical conditioning
10.4 Conditioned punishers and reinforcers are similar to USs because they first have only a neutral or orienting reflex eliciting effect. Through repeated pairings with primary reinforcers (USs), they acquire their reinforcing or punishing properties.
10.5 a) conditioned b) primary (both heat and flavor) c) conditioned d) primary e) conditioned
11.1 preference
11.2 preference hierarchy
11.3 Premack made access to the plunger contingent on an increase in eating M&M's.
11.4 An individual's preferences for various activities will vary on a continuum from most to least reinforcing. An observer can arrange this as a preference hierarchy.
13.1 reinforced; different, novel, or new

13.2 operant, operant
13.3 lever presses or rate of lever pressing
13.4 food, The rat must be food deprived.
13.5 The "click" of the pellet delivery apparatus becomes a conditioned reinforcer.; classical conditioning
13.6 The rat approaches the food tray when it "clicks."
13.7 The investigator must wait until the rat starts to turn away and then "click" the food pellet delivery apparatus. The rat will go back to eat and then turn away sooner. The "click" and food should be made contingent on turning away sooner or moving further away from the tray each time.
14.2 Before Barnabus could emit the chain of behaviors, each individual skill had to be taught separately. Shaping is used to train him to perform each new behavior.
14.4 Through stimulus pairing, the terminal response becomes a conditioned reinforcer by permitting the organism to engage in the subsequent response, and ultimately obtain the reinforcer. The responses preceding the last response gain some reinforcing value, and so on "backward" through the entire chain of responses. Eventually, each response serves as a conditioned reinforcer for the previous one.
15.1 avoidance response
15.2 escape responses
15.4 defense reactions
17.1 Extinction occurs; the CR decreases and eventually stops.
17.2 reinforcer, extinction
17.3 Responding eventually ceases; extinction occurs.
17.4 Spontaneous recovery of instrumental response rates occurs. In classical conditioning, an extinguished CR will recur following presentation of a CS. This phenomenon is also called spontaneous recovery.
17.5 Both overall response rates and occurrences of spontaneous recovery decrease and eventually end.
17.6 Aggression generally accompanies instrumental extinction. Usually people hit or kick the machine, or want to. (Such aggression often is called "extinction-induced aggression.")
18.1 Motivation decreases as the organism gets its fill of the reinforcer. This phenomenon is called satiation.
18.2 An extinction contingency following CRF leads to very rapid extinction of the response. An extinction contingency following intermittent reinforcement tends to produce persistence (responding for longer times)
19.3 CRF (continuous reinforcement schedule), fixed ratio, responses, reinforcer
19.4 To the animal, the switch will seem the same as extinction and it will probably stop responding before it makes 500 responses.
19.5 By gradually switching the ratio to increasing FR response requirements, say, 1, 3, 6, 12, 24, 36, 60, 90, 120, and so on.
20.1 response-and-time-dependent
20.2 fixed or unvarying, response
20.3 reinforced, low, increasing or higher
20.4 cued; on a cued FI schedule the animal waits until the signal occurs, then responds.
21.1 It will increase.
22.3 pecking and swallowing
22.4 This is a classical conditioning procedure.
22.5 The UR elicited by the US (grain) is pecking. Eventually a similar CR (pecking) should develop in the presence of the light behind the translucent disk (CS).
22.7 Donahoe and his colleagues have suggested that operant conditioning and classical conditioning are different procedures, but nevertheless involve common mechanisms of learning.
24.1 discriminative stimuli
24.3 discriminated

25.2

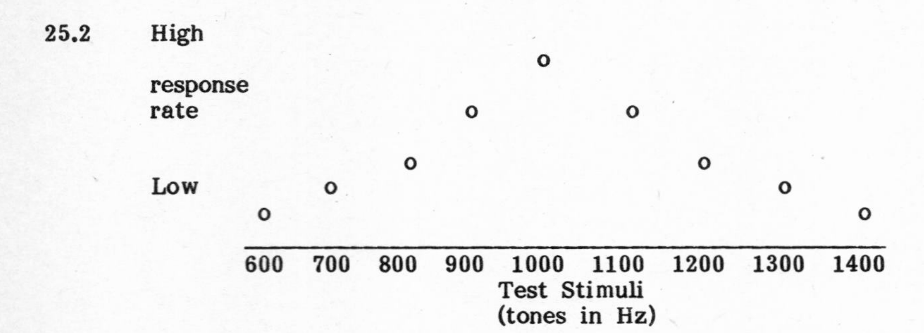

25.3 a) and b) reinforcement
25.5 Your concept of reinforcement can generalize to new samples. (That is, the textbook and study guide have effectively done their job in this instance.)
26.1 a) classical generalization b) classical discrimination

Self Test: Lesson I			Self Test: Lesson II		
1.	c	Obj. 6-1	1.	b	Obj. 6-15
2.	b	Obj. 6-2	2.	b	Obj. 6-16
3.	c	Obj. 6-3	3.	a	Obj. 6-17
4.	a	Obj. 6-4	4.	b	Obj. 6-18
5.	d	Obj. 6-5	5.	b	Obj. 6-19,20
6.	a	Obj. 6-6	6.	c	Obj. 6-19
7.	c	Obj. 6-8	7.	a	Obj. 6-21
8.	b	Obj. 6-9	8.	d	Obj. 6-22
9.	b	Obj. 6-10	9.	a	Obj. 6-23
10.	c	Obj. 6-11	10.	a	Obj. 6-24
11.	b	Obj. 6-12	11.	b	Obj. 6-25
12.	c	Obj. 6-13	12.	a	Obj. 6-26

6.1 OBJ 6-1 LEARNING	6.9 OBJ 6-2 UNCONDITIONAL STIMULUS (US)
6.2 OBJ 6-1 ORGANISM	6.10 OBJ 6-2 UNCONDITIONAL RESPONSE (UR)
6.3 OBJ 6-1 ORIENTING RESPONSE	6.11 OBJ 6-2 CONDITIONAL STIMULUS (CS)
6.4 OBJ 6-1 HABITUATION	6.12 OBJ 6-2 CONDITIONAL RESPONSE (CR)
6.5 OBJ 6-1 STIMULUS	6.13 OBJ 6-4 NICTITATING MEMBRANE
6.6 OBJ 6-1 SHORT-TERM HABITUATION	6.14 OBJ 6-4 HETEROSYNAPTIC FACILITATION
6.7 OBJ 6-1 LONG-TERM HABITUATION	6.15 OBJ 6-5 EXTINCTION (CLASSICAL)
6.8 OBJ 6-2 CLASSICAL CONDITIONING (PAVLOVIAN CONDITIONING)	6.16 OBJ 6-5 SPONTANEOUS RECOVERY

6.9 Obj 6-2

the eliciting stimulus upon which classical conditioning depends; it elicits a response prior to learning

6.10 Obj 6-2

the unlearned response that occurs when a US is presented

6.11 Obj 6-2

a stimulus that initially elicits only an orienting response; if the CS is followed repeatedly by a US the organism learns to respond to the CS

6.12 Obj 6-2

a learned response to a CS that resembles the response elicited by the US

6.13 Obj 6-4

a protective "extra" eyelid that reflexively covers the eye when an irritating stimulus or CS is presented

6.14 Obj 6-4

increasing activity at synapses adjacent to and resulting from the increased activity of another synapse

6.15 Obj 6-5

reduction and eventual cessation of a CR to a CS; results from repeatedly presenting a CS without a US

6.16 Obj 6-5

temporary resumption of an extinguished CR to the presentation of CS following a period of time during which the CS has not been presented

6.1 Obj 6-1

relatively long-lasting changes in an organism's behavior produced by environmental events; an adaptive, interactive process

6.2 Obj 6-1

human and other animals that live and learn in the surrounding physical environment of inorganic, biological, and social events and processes

6.3 Obj 6-1

a behavior elicited by any novel stimulus involving a sudden increase in attention toward the apparent source of the stimulus

6.4 Obj 6-1

simplest form of learning; a decrease in the magnitude of a response to any eliciting stimuli that seem to have no significance for the organism

6.5 Obj 6-1

any physical event that the organism's sense receptors are capable of detecting

6.6 Obj 6-1

a temporary form of habituation to any elicitation procedure repeated over a short period of time

6.7 Obj 6-1

establishment of habituation to an eliciting stimulus across long periods of time during which the stimulus may not be continuously presented

6.8 Obj 6-2

repeated presentation of a "neutral" stimulus (CS) followed by an eliciting stimulus (US), producing a response to the CS like that elicited by the US

6.17 OBJ 6-6

PHOBIA

6.18 OBJ 6-6

FETISH

6.19 OBJ 6-6

PLETHYSMOGRAPH

6.20 OBJ 6-7

CONTINGENCY

6.21 OBJ 6-7

INSTRUMENTAL CONDITIONING

6.22 OBJ 6-8

REINFORCEMENT

6.23 OBJ 6-8

REINFORCING STIMULUS
(REINFORCER)

6.24 OBJ 6-8

APPETITIVE STIMULUS

6.25 OBJ 6-8

AVERSIVE STIMULUS

6.26 OBJ 6-8

NEGATIVE REINFORCEMENT

6.27 OBJ 6-8

POSITIVE REINFORCEMENT
(REINFORCEMENT)

6.28 OBJ 6-8

PUNISHMENT

6.29 OBJ 6-8

RESPONSE COST

6.30 OBJ 6-10

PRIMARY REINFORCERS

6.31 OBJ 6-10

PRIMARY PUNISHERS

6.32 OBJ 6-10

CONDITIONED REINFORCERS
(SECONDARY REINFORCERS)

6.25 Obj 6-8

an object or event that the organism tends to avoid contact with

6.26 Obj 6-8

the termination of a stimulus that follows a response and maintains or increases the likelihood of that response in similar situations

6.27 Obj 6-8

the presentation of a stimulus that follows a response and maintains or increases the likelihood of that response in similar situations

6.28 Obj 6-8

the presentation of a stimulus that follows a response and decreases the likelihood of that response in similar situations

6.29 Obj 6-8

the termination of a stimulus that follows a response and decreases the strength of that response in similar situations

6.30 Obj 6-10

unconditional stimuli whose presentation will increase the strength of the preceding response; usually biological appetitive stimuli

6.31 Obj 6-10

unconditional stimuli whose presentation will decrease the strength of the preceding response; usually noxious (aversive) stimuli

6.32 Obj 6-10

previously nonreinforcing stimuli that have been paired with primary reinforcers, thus becoming reinforcers through classical conditioning

6.17 Obj 6-6

an unreasonable fear reaction to a particular object or situation

6.18 Obj 6-6

abnormal sexual attachment to specific objects

6.19 Obj 6-6

a device for measuring and recording changes in the diameter or volume of a part of the body

6.20 Obj 6-7

a causal relation between two events; a stimulus that occurs only if an animal emits a specific response is said to be contingent on the response

6.21 Obj 6-7

a process in which an organism's response produces an environmental consequence that raises or lowers the likelihood of that responses

6.22 Obj 6-8

a process in which a stimulus follows a response and maintains or increases the likelihood of that response in similar situations

6.23 Obj 6-8

any stimulus change that follows a response and maintains or increases the likelihood of that response in similar situations

6.24 Obj 6-8

an object or event that the organism tends to approach or make contact with

6.33 OBJ 6-10

CONDITIONED PUNISHERS (SECONDARY PUNISHERS)

6.34 OBJ 6-11

PREMACK PRINCIPLE

6.35 OBJ 6-11

PREFERENCE HIERARCHY

6.36 OBJ 6-12

SOCIAL REINFORCERS AND SOCIAL PUNISHERS

6.37 OBJ 6-13

SHAPING

6.38 OBJ 6-13

OPERANT CHAMBER

6.39 OBJ 6-13

OPERANT CONDITIONING

6.40 OBJ 6-14

CHAINING

6.41 OBJ 6-15

ESCAPE RESPONSE

6.42 OBJ 6-15

AVOIDANCE RESPONSE

6.43 OBJ 6-15

SPECIES-TYPICAL DEFENSE REACTIONS

6.44 OBJ 6-17

EXTINCTION (INSTRUMENTAL)

6.45 OBJ 6-18

INTERMITTENT REINFORCEMENT

6.46 OBJ 6-19

SCHEDULES OF REINFORCEMENT

6.47 OBJ 6-19

RESPONSE-DEPENDENT SCHEDULES

6.48 OBJ 6-19

CONTINUOUS REINFORCEMENT (CRF)

6.41 Obj 6-15

behavior that terminates contact with aversive stimuli

6.42 Obj 6-15

behavior that prevents (avoids) contact with an aversive stimulus

6.43 Obj 6-15

protective escape or avoidance response emitted by members of a particular species; elicited by aversive stimuli

6.44 Obj 6-17

gradual elimination of a response by removal of the contingent reinforcer

6.45 Obj 6-18

non-continuous delivery of reinforcer; less than one reinforcer per response

6.46 Obj 6-19

rules specifying the particular contingency between reinforcers and responses

6.47 Obj 6-19

rules specifying the ratio of responses to reinforcers

6.48 Obj 6-19

contingency in which one reinforcer is delivered following each response

6.33 Obj 6-10

previously nonpunishing stimuli that have been paired with primary punishers, thus becoming punishers through classical conditioning

6.34 Obj 6-11

describes reinforcement: lower probability responses are increased by making opportunity for higher probability behaviors contingent on them

6.35 Obj 6-11

description of an individual organism's relative preferences for engaging in any set of behaviors

6.36 Obj 6-12

stimuli provided by the behavior of one organism that serve to weaken (punishers) or strengthen (reinforcers) the response of another organism

6.37 Obj 6-13

reinforcement of a succession of responses that increasingly approximate a particular response; method of successive approximations

6.38 Obj 6-13

experimental apparatus for instrumental condition of laboratory animals

6.39 Obj 6-13

instrumental learning or conditioning

6.40 Obj 6-14

establishment of a novel sequence of behaviors by making the performance of each behavior serve as the reinforcer for the next one

6.49 OBJ 6-19

FIXED-RATIO SCHEDULE (FR)

6.50 OBJ 6-19

POSTREINFORCEMENT PAUSE

6.51 OBJ 6-19

VARIABLE-RATIO SCHEDULE (VR)

6.52 OBJ 6-20

RESPONSE-AND-TIME-DEPENDENT SCHEDULES

6.53 OBJ 6-20

FIXED-INTERVAL SCHEDULE (FI)

6.54 OBJ 6-20

VARIABLE-INTERVAL SCHEDULE (VI)

6.55 OBJ 6-21

SUPERSTITIOUS BEHAVIOR

6.56 OBJ 6-22

INSTINCTIVE DRIFT

6.57 OBJ 6-22

AUTOSHAPING

6.58 OBJ 6-24

DISCRIMINATION

6.59 OBJ 6-24

DISCRIMINATIVE STIMULI

6.60 OBJ 6-25

GENERALIZATION

6.61 OBJ 6-25

CONCEPT FORMATION

6.57 Obj 6-22

development of a behavior pattern resembling an instrumental response but produced by a classical procedure

6.58 Obj 6-24

opposite of generalization; differential responding in the presence of different stimuli; result of prior reinforcement contingencies

6.59 Obj 6-24

stimuli that signal the fact that particular responses will be followed by reinforcers

6.60 Obj 6-25

opposite of discrimination; similar responses caused by stimuli that vary on one or more features, but have some common features

6.61 Obj 6-25

form of generalization involving similar responses to highly variable stimuli that share some common features

6.49 Obj 6-19

contingency in which one reinforcer is delivered following completion of a constant number of responses

6.50 Obj 6-19

a temporary decrease in the rate of responding following an FR delivery of a reinforcer

6.51 Obj 6-19

a contingency in which one reinforcer is delivered following completion of a fluctuating number of responses averaging around a fixed value

6.52 Obj 6-20

rules specifying how much time must pass before a response will be reinforced

6.53 Obj 6-20

contingency in which an invariant specific interval must pass before a response will be reinforced

6.54 Obj 6-20

contingency in which an averaged interval of time must pass before a response will be reinforced

6.55 Obj 6-21

stereotypical response pattern maintained by accidental reinforcement by stimuli that are not contingent on the response

6.56 Obj 6-22

intrusion of species-typical consummatory responses into instrumentally conditioned behavioral sequences

CHAPTER 7
Memory

INTRODUCTION

This chapter examines three stages of memory (Objective 1), sensory memory (Objective 2), short-term memory (Objectives 3-9), and long-term memory (Objectives 10-16). It examines how information is stored in the brain and how it is retrieved. It also reviews the research on forgetting and strategies to improve memory. This chapter is divided into two lessons. Lesson I covers Objectives 1-9; Lesson II, Objectives 10-16.

CONCEPT CARDS AND EXERCISES

After you have surveyed and read the text, assemble the concept cards located at the end of this chapter. Use them to learn the important terms, then begin reading the text again, one learning objective at a time, and work through the exercises for each lesson. Answers for questions marked with an asterisk are found at the end of the chapter.

SELF TESTS

Each lesson is followed by a multiple-choice self test. After you are proficient with a lesson's concept cards and exercises, take the self test to see whether you have mastered the material. Review those objectives for questions you answered incorrectly.

INTEGRATING QUESTIONS

To challenge yourself further, answer the integrating questions at the end of the chapter. These questions ask you to apply the information you have learned to consider larger theoretical or real-life issues.

LESSON I: AN OVERVIEW, SENSORY MEMORY, SHORT-TERM MEMORY

1. Name and briefly describe the three stages of memory. (pp. 275-276)

1.1 For each of the following examples, identify the type of memory that is involved and explain the reasons for your answers.

* _____ a) As a friend is leaving, she tells you her address. You repeat it over to yourself several times while looking for a pen to write it down.

* _____ b) While playing a game of cards your partner flashes a card at you so quickly

that nobody else notices. However, you are able to recognize instantly what the card is.

* _____ c) You are describing to a friend the movie you saw last week.

* _____ d) Someone asks you "How much is six times nine?," and you answer, "Fifty-four."

* _____ e) A horn sounds as a ship enters the harbor. A moment after the sound has stopped, you can still hear it exactly as it sounded originally.

* 1.2 What common finding seems to indicate that short-term and long-term memory are distinct processes?

1.3 A "compartmental" view of memory proposes that short-term and long-term memory are separate but interconnected units. Describe the evidence for this view and for an alternative view.

2. Describe the nature of iconic and echoic memory and the methods used to study them. (pp. 276-279)

* 2.1 Sperling studied visual sensory memory or _______________ memory through the use of _______________ presentations.

2.2 How did Sperling assess the <u>capacity</u> of iconic memory and what did he find?

2.3 Describe Sperling's results regarding the <u>duration</u> of iconic memory. Specify how subjects performed when the tone sounded

a) within a second of the stimulus projection.

b) at a delay of more than one second after the stimulus was projected.

2.4 Describe the study by Eriksen and Collins (1967) in terms of its

a) methods.

b) results.

c) implications for iconic memory.

* 2.5 Echoic memory is another name for _______________ _______________ memory.

* 2.6 In what common human activity does echoic memory appear to play an important role?

2.7 Compare the findings of the studies on echoic memory to those of Sperling on iconic memory.

2.8 Indicate whether or not each of the following is an example of sensory memory (and be able to explain your answers). Also, if an item is an example of sensory memory, note whether it is representative of iconic or echoic memory.

* _____ a) You recall the phone number of your previous address.

* _____ b) You are outside looking at the sky on a very dark night when you see a "shooting star" flash across the sky overhead. The moment it is gone you can still "see"

the path it took.

* _____ c) You read the definition of mammals in your biology text and repeat it over to yourself several times in succession, without looking at the text.

* _____ d) You catch a glimpse of a billboard as you are driving on the expressway and see that the ad portrays a ship in a bottle but you do not catch the name of the liquor that is being promoted.

* _____ e) You ask a friend to repeat what she just said because you did not hear her but before she repeats her message you figure out what she said.

> 3. Describe short-term memory and the process of chunking and identify the role that short-term memory plays in thinking. (pp. 279-282)

* 3.1 In what way(s) do sensory memory and short-term memory differ from each other?

3.2 Consider the following sentence.

EL SUSURRO DE LAS OLAS ME RECORDABA TU VOZ

Explain why the short-term memory for this sentence of a Spanish-speaking person would be much better than that of someone who does not speak Spanish. In what way does the past experience of each of these persons affect their performance?

3.3 On the basis of your answer to 3.2, explain how long-term memory benefits short-term memory.

3.4 Look at the following 36-letter array.

p-e-a-c-h-w-a-t-e-r-p-e-n-c-i-l-b-o-n-e-r-o-s-e-a-m-p-h-i-b-i-a-n-d-o-g

* a) Determine how the letters can be arranged so that they may be recited after only a moment's study.

* b) This arrangement has been referred to by Miller as _______________.

* 3.5 What is the limit for the capacity of short-term memory in terms of "chunks"?

3.6 A friend asserts that chess masters must have incredible memories, far beyond that of the average person. Use research regarding short-term memory to formulate a response to your friend.

3.7 Define working memory and give an example of it.

3.8 In answering 3.7, what parts of your answer required

a) use of your short-term memory (assuming that you just learned about the meaning of "working memory")?

b) use of your long-term memory?

3.9 Is it likely that the performance of any cognitive activity would involve exclusively short-term <u>or</u> long-term memory? Explain your answer, describing why the term working memory is useful.

4. Describe behavioral and physiological evidence regarding sensory-specific representation of information in short-term memory. (pp. 282-286)

* 4.1 What is meant when it is said that short-term memory is compartmentalized?

4.2 Situation I: Suppose you are presented visually with a set of four numbers and then immediately asked to read aloud a list of different numbers.
Situation II: On another occasion, you are presented with a new set of four numbers that are spoken to you and then immediately asked to read aloud a list of other numbers.

* a) Are Situations I or II examples of intramodal or intermodal interference?

* b) In which of the situations would you expect to have done better in recalling the original set of numbers? Why?

4.3 In your own words, describe what the research findings on intermodal and intramodal interference imply about visual and auditory short-term memory.

Note: Be sure to try each of the five self-experiments described in the text using the word "antidisestablishmentarianism" and the song "Happy Birthday." Keep track of your behavior on each and note which parts of the experiments involve intramodal activities and which involve intermodal ones.

* 4.4 Describe conduction aphasia in terms of

a) the abilities and limitations of persons who have this disorder.

b) the parts of the brain that are damaged.

c) the implications of this disorder for a compartmentalized short-term memory.

4.5 Describe the study by Kovner and Stamm (1972), making sure to discuss

a) the hypothesis.

b) the delayed-matching-to-sample task.

c) the different conditions to which the monkeys were exposed.

d) the results.

e) the implications of the results for a compartmentalized short-term memory.

5. Describe research on the exchange of sensory information within short-term memory. (pp. 286-290)

5.1 Examine the following visual stimuli, then look away and try to recall them.

%*@ MIEOW BOP ///... ++)))

a) In recalling the above stimuli, for which one(s) did you "say" the stimulus to yourself?

b) Using the above example, describe the interaction between visual and auditory short-term memory.

c) Relate your answer to the results of Conrad's (1964) study on acoustic coding of visual information in which subjects, who were shown a list of letters and then asked to write them down, made particular kinds of errors.

d) How might long-term memory be involved in the above stimulus examples?

5.2 Posner, Boies, Eichelman, and Taylor (1969) investigated information exchange in short-term memory. Summarize their study by noting their

a) hypothesis.

b) experimental stimulus.

c) two conditions.

d) results.

e) interpretation of their results.

6. Describe the role of subvocal speech in verbal short-term memory and explain the nature and importance of the suffix effect. (pp. 288-290)

6.1 What is(are) the term(s) to describe your behavior when you read Objective 6 and

* a) moved your lips and tongue as you read?

b) did not move your lips and tongue?

6.2 In answering 6.1,

a) what role did articulatory short-term memory play?

b) what parts of your brain were used and what was the relationship of these parts?

* 6.3 What is the suffix effect?

6.4 How was the suffix effect demonstrated in the study by

a) Horton and Mills (1984)?

b) Campbell and Dodd (1980)?

c) Shand and Klima (1981)?

6.5 What does the suffix effect suggest about subvocal articulation and the operation of short-term memory?

Chapter 7

7. Describe the processes that have been suggested as possible reasons for failure of short-term memory. (pp. 290-292)

* 7.1 Define the term <u>decay of information</u>.

7.2 Summarize the study by Peterson and Peterson (1959) to investigate decay of information by

* a) noting the procedures.

b) identifying what happened to the proportion of letters that subjects could recall as the time since they were first presented increased.

* 7.3 Proactive inhibition refers to the deleterious effect of ______________ information on the encoding of ______________ information.

7.4 Which of the following examples illustrates proactive inhibition?

* _____ a) You are repeating to yourself the list of ingredients for a recipe a friend just described to you. Almost immediately she beings to describe a second equally appealing recipe and you begin to rehearse these ingredients. In testing your memory, your friend asks you to recall the ingredients of the second recipe. You begin to list the ingredients of both recipes.

* _____ b) A subject is presented with a set of numbers and is then shown a different set that she rehearses for five seconds. When asked to recall the first set of numbers, she does not do very well.

* _____ c) In a dancing class, the teacher demonstrates two brief series of steps, one after the other. He then asks the students to perform the last series. In doing so, they introduce some movements from the first series, to the dismay of the teacher.

* _____ d) You study for psychology one hour, then you study economics for an hour. You find that you can recall the psychology you studied but do not recall the economics very well.

* 7.5 In what cases are the effects of proactive inhibition particularly noticeable?

7.6 Keppel and Underwood (1962) performed a study that was identical to the Petersons' study, but with one change. What was the change? (Refer to the procedure and results.)

7.7 Summarize Keppel and Underwood's reinterpretation of the results obtained in the Petersons' study, and state the general conclusion that can be made regarding the role of decay and of proactive inhibition in the decline of short-term memory.

* 7.8 Research suggests that the most important cause of proactive inhibition is ______________ with the process of ______________.

* 7.9 Define the term <u>release from proactive inhibition</u>.

7.10 Describe the procedure and results of the study by Wickens (1972).

7.11 How did Gardner, Craik, and Birtwistle (1972) modify the procedure used by Wickens?

7.12 What results did Gardner et al. (1972) obtain?

7.13 What does the research by Wickens (1972) and Gardner, Craik, and Birtwistle (1972) suggest about proactive inhibition and its release?

* 7.14 When new information purges short-term memory of prior information, the phenomenon is referred to as ______________.

* 7.15 Go back to 7.4 and identify the example(s) that illustrate displacement.

8. Describe the consolidation hypothesis, the serial-position curve, and the explanation for the recency effect and the primacy effect. (pp. 292-295)

* 8.1 State the basic premise of consolidation theory.

Note: Perform the self-experiment described in the text using the list of fifteen words. Be sure to read the instructions in the text before looking at the word list.

* 8.2 If you memorize a list of words and then immediately are asked to recall the list, you will probably recall more of the first and last words than those in the middle of the list.

This common finding is often referred to as the ______________.

8.3 a) Draw and label a graph that illustrates the above phenomenon. (See Figure 7.14 in the text to check your work.)

b) Explain what the ordinate (vertical axis) of a serial-position curve represents, and what the abscissa (horizontal axis) represents.

* 8.4 Describe what the recency effect is. Refer to the results of your experiment if necessary.

8.5 Explain how the limited capacity of short-term memory, together with the displacement of information, can account for the recency effect.

8.6 How does preventing rehearsal of the last items in a list affect the recency effect? Refer to the Glanzer and Cunitz (1966) study to support your answer.

* 8.7 The greater probability of recalling the first few items in a list than those in the middle is referred to as the ______________ effect.

* 8.8 Rundus and Atkinson (1970) asked subjects to rehearse a list of words out loud as it was presented to them. Briefly describe what these investigators found.

9. Describe the effects of head injury and electroshock on long-term and short-term memory. (pp. 295-298)

9.1 In your own words, define <u>retrograde amnesia</u>. Provide an original example that illustrates this phenomenon.

* 9.2 What type of memory is affected by retrograde amnesia?

* 9.3 The application of electric shock to the skull induces a brief seizure. This procedure, developed for therapeutic purposes, is known as ________________.

9.4 What are the intended effects of electroshock? What are the unintended side effects?

9.5 Explain what the different effects of electroshock treatment on short-term and long-term memory suggest regarding consolidation and the way in which old and new memories are "stored." Refer to neural firing, rehearsal, and changes in neural structure in your answer.

LESSON I SELF TEST

1. What are the three stages of memory?

   a. sensory memory, short-term memory, long-term memory
   b. tachistoscopic memory, neural memory, structural memory
   c. reconstructive memory, consolidation memory, displaced memory
   d. primacy memory, recency memory, iconic memory

2. You hear a siren of a fire truck before you identify this sound as a fire siren. Hearing a sound before recognizing it illustrates the functioning of

   a. iconic memory.
   b. long-term memory.
   c. sensory memory.
   d. short-term memory.

3. What did Sperling discover about sensory memory when he used the partial-report procedure?

   a. Rehearsal improves recall of information in iconic memory.
   b. Information in iconic memory begins to fade after thirty seconds.
   c. Subjects are able to "see" more information in iconic memory than they are able to report.
   d. The capacity of iconic memory is 7 ± 2 bits of information.

4. Short-term memory is to __________ as sensory memory is to __________.

   a. unpredictability; predictability
   b. chunked; encoded
   c. accuracy; inaccuracy
   d. interpretation; representation

5. Why is short-term memory sometimes referred to as working memory?

   a. It contains information retrieved from long-term memory as well as current information.
   b. It chunks information by independent bits.
   c. It cannot make use of previously learned rules to encode information.
   d. It must combine information from echoic and iconic memory to be effective.

6. In what sense is short-term memory compartmentalized?

   a. It transfers information from iconic memory to long-term memory.
   b. Neurons containing sensory and motor information appear to be located in different parts of the brain.

c. Intermodal interference is more severe that intramodal interference.
d. It sorts information by meaning rather than word length.

7. Which of the following offers the best evidence that short-term memory is divided into sensory-specific components?

a. consolidation
b. electroshock treatment
c. conduction aphasia
d. Korsakoff's syndrome

8. When Conrad (1964) presented letters visually to subjects, what did he observe? Subjects tended to

a. confuse letters that sounded alike.
b. confuse letters that looked alike.
c. make name comparisons more quickly than shape comparisons.
d. perform better when their visual cortex was stimulated electrically.

9. How do Posner, Boies, Eichelman and Taylor (1969) explain their findings that after a one second delay shape comparisons take as long as name comparisons?

a. It takes that long to transfer information from short-term memory to long-term memory.
b. It takes that long to transfer information from iconic memory to short-term memory.
c. Intermodal interference decreases over time.
d. Visual information fades so even shape comparisons require the use of verbally coded information

10. What does the suffix effect suggest about the functioning of memory?

a. Subvocal articulation interferes with the processing of information in short-term memory.
b. Intermodal interference is more pronounced than intramodal interference because of the time involved in transferring information from one form of short-term memory to another.
c. Representation of verbal material in short-term memory may involve the systems used in subvocal articulation.
d. Words presented at the end of a list are recalled better because they have not yet faded from short-term memory.

11. Maura reviewed her French vocabulary words, then studied and tested herself on her Spanish vocabulary words. We could expect that

a. the French vocabulary words would interfere proactively with her recall of the Spanish words.
b. learning the Spanish words would enhance her recall of both the Spanish and French words.
c. all the French words would be masked by the Spanish words and effectively disappear from her memory.
d. learning the French and Spanish words would have no effect upon her recall of either set of words.

12. Keppel and Underwood (1962) replicated and extended Peterson and Peterson's study of the decay of short-term memory. Keppel and Underwood concluded that

a. previously learned material may inhibit the learning of other similar material.
b. information in short-term memory decays rapidly.
c. the recency effect is a function of rehearsal.
d. working memory forms the bridge between sensory and short-term memory.

13. What does consolidation theory hypothesize about short-term memory?

a. It requires structural changes in neural circuits.
b. It codes information by chunks rather than meaning.
c. It loses information by decay rather than displacement or proactive inhibition.
d. It is maintained by short-lived neural activity.

14. The primacy effect seems to be due to

a. intramodal interference.
b. displacement.
c. retroactive interference.
d. rehearsal.

15. Research on the effects of electroshock suggest that

a. short-term and long-term memory are psychologically distinct but not physiologically distinct.
b. information in short-term memory is automatically and instantaneously "dumped" into long-term memory.
c. short-term memories are held by means of neural activity, and long-term memories by "wiring changes."
d. information in short-term memory is coded by meaning and information in long-term memory by acoustics.

LESSON II: LONG-TERM MEMORY

10. Describe research on the concept of depth of processing. (pp. 298-300)

10.1 What aspects of the word <u>car</u> would you consider if you were concerned with

* a) shallow processing.

* b) deep processing.

* c) semantic features.

10.2 Describe how the central processor as conceived by Craik and Lockhart works.

* 10.3 According to the central processor model of memory, what should you do if you really want to remember something?

10.4 Describe the study by Hyde and Jenkins (1969) and explain how it supports the model of memory proposed by Craik and Lockhart.

* 10.5 There is an acronym, KISS, which means keep it simple, stupid. How does this expression fit with the results obtained by Craik and Tulving (1975)?

10.6 How do the results obtained by Craik and Tulving support the depth of processing model proposed by Craik and Lockhart?

11. Describe relational and item-specific processing and their effects on learning. (pp. 300-302)

11.1 An experimenter presented the following list of words to a group of subjects: fly, tree, horse, turtle, turnip. What kind of task would be required of the subjects if they were asked to

* a) concentrate on how the words were alike?

* b) notice how each word differed from the others?

* c) arrange the words alphabetically?

* d) arrange the words in order of their biological complexity?

* 11.2 On the basis of the study by Einstein and Hunt (1980), arrange the tasks in 11.1 in terms of how well each of these tasks would enable subjects to recall the words.

11.3 The more you know about a subject, the easier it is to learn and thus remember more about that subject. Use the research on relational processing to explain why this is true.

11.4 Describe the study by deVilliers (1974) by noting the sample stimuli that were presented to subjects, the results, and the interpretation of those results in terms of relational processing.

11.5 Describe how the results of the study by Stein and Bransford (1079) are similar to those found by Craik and Tulving (1975; see Objective 10).

* 11.6 List two forms of relational processing and give examples of each.

* 11.7 Under which circumstances is item-specific processing better and under which circumstances is relational processing better?

11.8 On the basis of the study by Ritchey and Beal (1980), how could subjects who were asked to perform the task in 11.1b improve their recall?

12. Describe the research on the nature of episodic and semantic long-term memory. (pp. 303-305)

12.1 Identify the kind of long-term memory in each of these examples.

* a) Melody recalled what she ate for breakfast this morning.

* b) Paul can recall what he was doing when he learned that Beatle John Lennon had been murdered.

* c) On the exam Rose was able to state the relationship between long-term and short-term memories.

12.2 Form is less important than substance. How does the study by Sachs (1967) support this statement?

12.3 What is the relationship between thinking and semantic memory?

12.4 Cite an example from your own experience that shows episodic and semantic memory working together.

13. Describe the causes of human anterograde amnesia, its nature, and its implications for the characteristics of episodic and semantic memory. (pp. 305-307)

* 13.1 How would a person who displays Korsakoff's syndrome behave?

* 13.2 What is anterograde amnesia? How does it differ from retrograde amnesia? (See Objective 9.)

13.3 Identify the learning and memory capabilities of a person who has anterograde amnesia. Also, identify the learning and memory tasks that cannot be performed by such a person.

13.4 Describe the study by Johnson, Kim, and Risse (1985) by noting its

a) subjects

b) methods

c) results

d) implications

* 13.5 Julie was able to perform the dance but was unable to describe the steps she had performed. Julie shows _______________ memory and a failure of _______________ memory.

13.6 Describe the location, function, and appearance of the hippocampus.

13.7 What does the clinical evidence regarding Korsakoff's syndrome suggest about the parts of the brain involved in memory?

14. Describe the results and implications of research on anterograde amnesia in laboratory animals. (pp. 307-309)

14.1 Describe the procedure Olton and colleagues devised to measure episodic memory.

14.2 Explain how the performance of the normal, hungry rats in the mazes indicates episodic memory.

14.3 Describe how rats with hippocampal lesions behaved in the eight-arm maze? in the seventeen-arm maze?

14.4 What does the behavior of the rats with the hippocampal lesions suggest about episodic and semantic memories?

15. Describe the role of reconstruction in recalling information from long-term memory. (pp. 309-310)

15.1 What did Bartlett do and what were his results?

15.2 What conclusions did Bartlett derive from his results?

15.3 Summarize Spiro's procedures and results.

15.4 Explain how Spiro's findings extend those of Bartlett.

* 15.5 What are the implications of the study by Loftus and Zanni (1975) for lawyers questioning people on the witness stand?

15.6 What are the benefits of reconstruction? the disadvantages? the implications for the storage and retrieval of memories?

16. Describe the nature and uses of the mnemonic systems, including the method of loci and narrative stories. (pp. 310-313)

16.1 What is a mnemonic system and how does it work?

16.2 What is the relationship between mnemonic systems and deep processing? (See Objective 10.)

* 16.3 Two examples of mnemonic systems are ______________ and ______________.

16.4 Describe the method of loci and identify the characteristics of mnemonic systems that it possesses.

16.5 Describe narrative stories and identify the characteristics of mnemonic systems that it possesses.

LESSON II SELF TEST

1. Which of the following is an example of deep processing?

   a. Suzie looks at the length and shape of the word.
   b. Jeremy recalls the first time he drove a car.
   c. Maureen reflects upon the meaning of Dave's comments.
   d. Frank examined the words to see how they differed.

2. What have the studies by Craik and colleagues on depth of processing shown?

   a. Because surface processing is less complex, it facilitates recall more effectively than does deep processing.
   b. Deep processing often leads to better retention than surface processing does.
   c. Subjects show better recall using deep processing than shallow processing only when they know in advance that they will be tested on the material.

d. Longer sentences are better handled by surface processing than deep processing.

3. Relational processing is most concerned with

a. connections.
b. episodes.
c. distinctions.
d. surface structures.

4. Which of the following is more likely to be remembered?

a. the sentence, "A store contained a row of wooden cages."
b. looking for similarities among the following words: daisy, tulip, rose, chrysanthemum, orchid, begonia, dandelion
c. the sentence, "The fat man read the sign warning of thin ice."
d. looking for differences among the following words: horse, armchair, slacks, pencil, metronome, cough medicine

5. When Nelson smells a certain perfume, he smiles and thinks fondly of his wife who also wears this scent. This example suggests that long-term memory

a. connects sensory memory and short-term memory.
b. changes sensations to perceptions.
c. can encode information in terms of sense modality.
d. stores information by meaning rather than by sensory modality.

6. Which of the following is most likely to contain products of thinking about what we already have learned?

a. semantic memory
b. echoic memory
c. episodic memory
d. anterograde memory

7. Ned cannot remember anything that has occurred since he developed brain damage. It is likely that he is suffering from

a. retrograde amnesia.
b. conduction aphasia.
c. anterograde amnesia.
d. mnemonic memory.

8. What part of the brain seems to be involved in anterograde amnesia?

a. amygdala
b. corpus callosum
c. Wernicke's area
d. hippocampus

9. What kind of memory did Olton and colleagues study when they compared the behavior of normal rats and rats with hippocampal lesions on an eight-arm maze?

a. reconstructive
b. deep
c. semantic
d. episodic

10. In a party game a story is whispered from person to person. Studies of memory suggest that the stories told by each person will vary because

a. memory is a creative process.
b. these stories are stored in episodic rather than semantic memory.
c. accurate memory depends upon maintenance rehearsal.
d. these stories offer few retrieval cues.

11. Studies on the reconstructive aspect of memory suggest that

a. use of a definite article may lead people to recall something that did not happen.
b. a person's confidence in the accuracy of a particular memory is a good indication that the memory is correct.
c. people are more likely to recall correctly the inconsistencies of a story.
d. the storage and retrieval of information in long-term memory is a passive process.

12. Mnemonic systems

a. work best if there is not much to learn.
b. make information more elaborate.
c. compact information into smaller bits.
d. establish new categories to classify material stored in long-term memory.

13. Fifth grade Dennis used the word HOMES to recall the names of the Great Lakes: Huron, Ontario, Michigan, Erie, Superior. Dennis used

a. the method of loci.
b. a mnemonic technique.
c. a narrative story.
d. the flower-pot technique.

INTEGRATING QUESTIONS

1. Draw up a list of suggestions on how to study based on the current theory and research on memory.

2. What would happen to a computer internally and externally if it had a memory like a human being?

3. Recall your first memory. Identify the types of memory involved in this memory. Describe the processes involved in storing, maintaining and retrieving this memory. Speculate on why you recall this event rather than other events. Offer suggestions about what your recall of this event rather than of other events suggests about memory. Estimate the accuracy of this memory and offer reasons for your estimate.

4. Memory, we take it for granted so often yet it is a complex process vital to our existence. Describe the physiology of memory, noting how each memory system functions and how sensory information is received, manipulated, retained, and reconstructed.

ANSWERS

1.1 a) short-term memory, b) sensory memory, c) long-term memory, d) long-term memory, e) sensory memory
1.2 limited ability to recall more than the seven independents bits of information that has just been memorized
2.1 iconic; tachistoscopic
2.5 auditory sensory
2.6 understanding speech
2.8 a) no; b) yes, iconic; c) no; d) yes, iconic; e) echoic

Chapter 7

3.1 In contrast to sensory memory, short-term memory has greater duration and capacity but more importantly it codes information by meaning.
3.4 a) peach; water; pencil; bone; rose; amphibian; dog. b) chunking
3.5 5 to 9 (seven plus or minus two)
4.1 There appear to be distinct short-term memories for each sensory modality.
4.2 a) Intramodal interference occurred during Situation I. b) You probably would have recalled the original numbers more accurately in the first situation.
4.4 a) Can speak and understand others but cannot recall information verbatim. b) left parietal lobe. c) Because the patient can recall information presented visually but not acoustically, this suggests that there are separate short-term memories for vision and hearing.
6.1 a) subvocal articulation
6.3 reduction in short-term memory caused by experimenter signaling the end of a list with the word, end
7.1 loss of information in short-term memory due to failure to rehearse
7.2 a) Subjects were presented with a set of three consonants, then given a verbal task to prevent rehearsal.
7.3 old (prior), new
7.4 a) yes, b) no, c) yes, d) yes
7.5 when new information is similar to what has just been learned
7.8 interference, retrieval
7.9 improvement in short-term memory due to change in type of information
7.14 displacement
7.15 Example b) illustrates displacement.
8.1 transferring information from short-term memory where memories are retained by neural activity to long-term memory requires structural changes in neuronal circuits.
8.2 serial-position effect
8.4 better recall of words presented at the end of a list
8.7 primacy
8.8 Subjects rehearsed words presented at beginning of list more than other words.
9.2 short-term memory
9.3 electroshock treatment
10.1 a) surface features of a word such as its length, the color and shape of the letters of a word; b) analysis of the meaning of the word car; c) the meaning of the word
10.3 engage in deep processing by attending to the item's meaning
10.5 The opposite is true. Medium to high complex sentences were recalled better than simple ones because they provided greater imagery, which facilitated recall.
11.1 a) relational processing. b) item-specific processing; c) shallow item-specific processing. d) deep relational processing
11.2 d, a, b, c
11.6 categorizing words by meaning, establishing cause-and-effect relations
11.7 when items are similar; when they are unrelated
12.1 a) episodic, b) episodic, c) semantic
13.1 able to remember situations before the disorder developed but not those that occurred after the disorder developed
13.2 Anterograde amnesia causes inability to store new information in long-term memory while retrograde amnesia disrupts recall of information that occurred before the amnesia developed.
13.5 semantic; episodic
15.5 If they or the opposing attorney use the definite article in questions to witnesses, they may bias the witnesses' responses.
16.3 method of loci, narrative stories

Self Test: Lesson I

1. a Obj. 7-1
2. c Obj. 7-2
3. c Obj. 7-2
4. d Obj. 7-3
5. a Obj. 7-3
6. b Obj. 7-4
7. c Obj. 7-4
8. a Obj. 7-5
9. d Obj. 7-5
10. c Obj. 7-6
11. a Obj. 7-7
12. a Obj. 7-7
13. d Obj. 7-8
14. d Obj. 7-8
15. c Obj. 7-9

Self Test: Lesson II

1. c Obj. 7-10
2. b Obj. 7-10
3. a Obj. 7-11
4. c Obj. 7-11
5. d Obj. 7-12
6. a Obj. 7-12
7. c Obj. 7-13
8. d Obj. 7-13
9. d Obj. 7-14
10. a Obj. 7-15
11. a Obj. 7-15
12. b Obj. 7-16
13. b Obj. 7-16

7.1 OBJ 7-1

SENSORY MEMORY

7.2 OBJ 7-1

SHORT-TERM MEMORY
(STM)

7.3 OBJ 7-1

LONG-TERM MEMORY
(STM)

7.4 OBJ 7-2

ICONIC MEMORY

7.5 OBJ 7-2

TACHISTOSCOPE

7.6 OBJ 7-2

ECHOIC MEMORY

7.7 OBJ 7-3

CHUNKING

7.8 OBJ 7-3

WORKING MEMORY

7.9 OBJ 7-4

INTRAMODAL INTERFERENCE

7.10 OBJ 7-4

INTERMODAL INTERFERENCE

7.11 OBJ 7-4

CONDUCTION APHASIA

7.12 OBJ 7-6

SUBVOCAL ARTICULATION

7.13 OBJ 7-7

DECAY OF INFORMATION

7.14 OBJ 7-7

PROACTIVE INTERFERENCE

7.15 OBJ 7-7

RELEASE FROM
PROACTIVE INHIBITION

7.16 OBJ 7-7

DISPLACEMENT

7.9 Obj 7-4

disruption of STM as a result of new information within the same sense modality as the material to be remembered

7.10 Obj 7-4

disruption of STM as a result of new information within a different sense modality as the material to be remembered

7.11 Obj 7-4

memory disorder, usually caused by damage to left parietal lobe; inability to repeat words verbatim

7.12 Obj 7-6

talking to oneself without actually speaking

7.13 Obj 7-7

fading of information in STM due to the passage of time and lack of rehearsal

7.14 Obj 7-7

deleterious effect of previously learned information on retention of new material

7.15 Obj 7-7

improvement in recall from STM due to change in type of stimulus to be learned

7.16 Obj 7-7

interference of previous STM by presentation of new material

7.1 Obj 7-1

type of memory in which the original stimuli are represented quite accurately; occurs almost simultaneously with perceiving

7.2 Obj 7-1

immediate, conscious storage of recently perceived information; has a limited capacity

7.3 Obj 7-1

type of memory in which an apparently unlimited amount of information can be stored and recalled after long periods of time

7.4 Obj 7-2

visual sensory memory

7.5 Obj 7-2

experimental device used for the presentation of brief visual stimuli

7.6 Obj 7-2

auditory sensory memory

7.7 Obj 7-3

organization of information into units according to previously learned rules; in STM

7.8 Obj 7-3

concurrent use of STM and LTM; activity which requires use of both

7.17 OBJ 7-8

CONSOLIDATION

7.18 OBJ 7-8

SERIAL-POSITION CURVE

7.19 OBJ 7-8

RECENCY EFFECT

7.20 OBJ 7-8

PRIMACY EFFECT

7.21 OBJ 7-9

RETROGRADE AMNESIA

7.22 OBJ 7-9

ELECTROSHOCK TREATMENT

7.23 OBJ 7-10

CENTRAL PROCESSOR

7.24 OBJ 7-10

SHALLOW PROCESSING

7.25 OBJ 7-10

DEEP PROCESSING

7.26 OBJ 7-11

ITEM SPECIFIC PROCESSING

7.27 OBJ 7-11

RELATIONAL PROCESSING

7.28 OBJ 7-12

EPISODIC MEMORY

7.29 OBJ 7-12

SEMANTIC MEMORY

7.30 OBJ 7-13

ANTEROGRADE AMNESIA

7.31 OBJ 7-16

MNEMONIC SYSTEM

7.32 OBJ 7-16

METHOD OF LOCI

7.25 Obj 7-10

memory analysis based on meaning of stimulus

7.26 Obj 7-11

analysis based on differences among stimuli

7.27 Obj 7-11

analysis based on how items fit together

7.28 Obj 7-12

type of LTM for specific times and experiences; proposed by Tulving (1972)

7.29 Obj 7-12

type of LTM for meaningful information, abstract rules, and concepts, etc.; proposed by Tulving (1972)

7.30 Obj 7-13

failure to recall information that has occurred since brain damage

7.31 Obj 7-16

procedures or strategies for facilitating recall of new information by use of LTM, elaboration, and organization

7.32 Obj 7-16

mnemonic system; remember items by associating them with specific locations

7.17 Obj 7-8

transfer of information from STM to LTM

7.18 Obj 7-8

graph representing the mean percent of items remembered from a list according to the position of the items; illustrates recency and primacy effects

7.19 Obj 7-8

greater probability of recalling the last few items in a list than those in the middle

7.20 Obj 7-8

better recall of first few items in a list than those in the middle, due to rehearsal

7.21 Obj 7-9

forgetting of events that occurred immediately before head injury or electroshock treatment

7.22 Obj 7-9

application of an electric shock to the skull; first used for therapeutic purposes and later for memory research

7.23 Obj 7-10

Craik and Lockhart's model of memory; states because memory has limited capacity it analyzes information at given level, depending on person's focus

7.24 Obj 7-10

memory analysis based on surface features of stimulus

CHAPTER 8
Language

INTRODUCTION

Our study of language will be divided into two lessons. Lesson I, covering Objectives 1-13, reviews the functions of verbal and written communication, the ways speakers and listeners perform these functions, and what can happen to communication after a person's brain has been damaged. Lesson II, covering Objectives 14-22, examines both the acquisition of language by human infants and attempts by humans to teach communication skills to nonhuman primates.

CONCEPT CARDS AND EXERCISES

After you have surveyed and read the text, assemble the concept cards located at the end of this chapter. Use them to learn the important terms, then begin reading the text again, one learning objective at a time, and work through the exercises for each lesson. Answers for questions marked with an asterisk are found at the end of the chapter.

SELF TESTS

Each lesson is followed by a multiple-choice self test. After you are proficient with a lesson's concept cards and exercises, take the self test to see whether you have mastered the material. Review those objectives for questions you answered incorrectly.

INTEGRATING QUESTIONS

To challenge yourself further, answer the integrating questions at the end of the chapter. These questions ask you to apply the information you have learned to consider larger theoretical or real-life issues.

LESSON I: VERBAL BEHAVIOR

1. Describe the basic functions of spoken and written verbal behavior. (p. 318)

* 1.1 What are some of the advantages humans enjoy because we can engage in verbal behavior?

* 1.2 List three major functions of verbal communication. Provide an example to illustrate each function.

Chapter 8

2. Describe the nature of the task of providing information verbally, the role of the given-new contract, and some features that speakers use to distinguish new from old information. (pp. 318-320)

* 2.1 The usefulness of the information a speaker gives to a listener depends on the nature of the listener's _______________ schemes.

* 2.2 A speaker can help the listener to retrieve previously stored information by placing new information in the correct context. In the following examples, what information does the speaker expect the listener to recall?

    1. The surprise birthday party was a real success.

    2. Jonathan didn't suspect a thing until he walked into the room.

    3. The Browns were able to come after all.

* 2.3 Speakers and listeners as well as writers use the _______________-_______________ _______________ to organize information in verbal communication.

* 2.4 Why do writers have to be more careful than speakers about observing the given-new contract?

* 2.5 Name two techniques that speakers frequently use to help identify old and new information for their listener.

* 2.6 Underline the word that the speaker should stress.

    a) The ripe tomatoes should be picked. (There are also some green ones on the vine.)

    b) The ripe tomatoes should be picked. (There are also some ripe cucumbers in the garden.)

* 2.7 The articles used in these two sentences indicate old and new information. Identify them and the new and old information they indicate in each sentence.

    a) The boy will bring a chair.

    b) A boy will bring the chair.

3. Describe the features of requests for information and for behavior. (pp. 320-322)

* 3.1 What two kinds of questions do speakers use when they request information?

3.2 Explain what a directive is and discuss the protocols we observe in using them correctly.

4. Explain how the auditory system performs phoneme discriminations. (pp. 322-325)

* 4.1 What is a phoneme? Write down the individual phonemes in the word truck.

4.2 a) Briefly describe the subjects and methods that Miller and Nicely (1955) used to study the perception of consonants.

b) List the five distinguishing features that they discovered.

c) How did Miller and Nicely further test their hypothesis of consonant perception?

4.3 Now look at Table 8.1 in your text and explain how /t/ differ and how /d/ and /t/ and /v/ differ. Which of the following words are English-speaking listeners likely to confuse?

tent vs. dent or tent vs. vent

4.4 Lisker and Abramson asked subjects to listen to computer generated sounds of a puff followed by ah.

a) What two phonemes did the subjects report they heard?

b) What basis did the subjects use to distinguish between phonemes?

c) Explain the results. Be sure to use the term voice-onset time.

* 4.5 Name two other factors that affect our recognition of phonemes.

5. Describe the role of learning in recognition of phoneme sequences. (pp. 325-326)

* 5.1 What is a phonological constraint? Provide an example.

5.2 a) Briefly describe the subjects and methods used by Day (1968, 1970).

b) Which word did the subjects say they heard when Day simultaneously presented /blanket/ and /lanket/ or /sin/ and /pin/? Why?

c) What do Day's results indicate about the role of learning for all listeners regardless of the language they speak?

6. Describe the importance of contextual cues in recognizing words in continuous speech. (pp. 326-328)

* 6.1 Explain why the subjects tested by Pollack and Pickett (1964) said the correct word less than half the time.

* 6.2 Consider research conducted by the Warrens (1970) and answer the following questions.

a) What words are imaginary subjects likely to report in the following situations if a cough replaces the *?

The ball is *ound.

The lost ball was finally *ound.

It was lying on the *ound.

b) Why were you and the imaginary subjects able to supply the correct missing letter?

6.3 List some of the nonverbal contextual cues listeners use in determining meaning.

7. Describe the basic features of syntactic analysis. (pp. 328-330)

* 7.1 We use ________________ ________________ to form sentences and to analyze the meaning of new sentences.

* 7.2 Consider the following sentence.

The man that she asked was unable to answer.

a) Using parentheses, break the sentence into the smallest groups of words that seem to go together.

b) What name do we give to these word groups?

c) Define <u>function word</u> and <u>content word</u>.

d) Use a <u>f</u> or a <u>c</u> to label function words and content words in the examples.

e) What kind of word marks the beginning of a constituent part?

8. Describe the basic features of semantic analysis. (pp. 330-331)

* 8.1 Define <u>semantics</u>.

8.2 Consider this ambiguous sentence.

Johnny tripped shoelace hurt knee sidewalk.

a) Carefully describe how you know what this sentence really means. Refer to syntax, function words, content words, semantics and your knowledge of the world in your answer.

8.3 Fillenbaum asked subjects to paraphrase sentences with peculiar meanings. How did they respond?

a) When the experimenter asked the subjects to look at the sentences again, what did they say about the meaning of the sentence and their response?

b) What can you say about their responses and the interaction of semantics and syntax?

9. Explain how syntax and semantics interact in verbal behavior. (pp. 331-332)

* 9.1 According to Chomsky, what is the deep structure and the surface structure of a sentence?

9.2 The woman with conduction aphasia and the speaker who said "Rosa always date shranks" make the point that there is more than one way to say something. Explain this statement in terms of the way the brain transforms deep structure to surface structure.

* 9.3 A speaker transforms ______________ ______________ to ______________ ______________, and the listener reverses the process by transforming ______________ ______________ to ______________ ______________.

10. Describe Wernicke's aphasia and what it indicates about speech comprehension. (pp. 332-334)

* 10.1 What does <u>aphasia</u> mean?

10.2 a) What is Wernicke's aphasia? What area of the brain has been damaged?

b) Look at Figure 8.4 in your text and use words or a quick sketch to locate Wernicke's area.

c) Describe the speech of patients with Wernicke's aphasia.

d) What do most investigators believe the primary deficit of Wernicke's aphasia to be?

10.3 a) Patients with pure word deafness can recognize the sound of a ringing telephone, but they cannot communicate using a telephone. Why? b) How do they communicate with other people?

10.4 Review the differences between Wernicke's aphasia and pure word deafness and state in your own words the importance of Wernicke's area in speech production and communication.

11. Describe Broca's aphasia and what it indicates about speech production. (pp. 334-335)

11.1 a) What is Broca's aphasia? What area of the brain has been damaged?

b) Look at Figure 8.4 and use words or a quick sketch to locate Broca's area.

c) Describe the speech of patients with Broca's aphasia.

d) Now contrast it with the speech of patients with Wernicke's aphasia.

e) What do most investigators believe the primary deficit of Broca's aphasia to be?

* 11.2 Damage to Broca's area often produces another speech deficit. What is it?

11.3 How successful were agrammatic patients at matching pictures with sentences or describing what was happening in a picture? What do their responses reveal about the effects of damage to Broca's area on speech production?

12. Compare phonological and surface dyslexia and describe phonetic and whole-word reading. (pp. 335-337)

12.1 Describe phonetic reading and whole-word reading.

* 12.2 What kind of reading difficulties do people with phonological dyslexia and surface dyslexia have?

12.3 What is developmental dyslexia? At what age is this disorder usually noticed? What have researchers tentatively identified as the cause?

13. Describe the evidence for two phases of whole-word reading. (pp. 337-338)

* 13.1 What are the two phases of whole-word reading?

13.2 When Margolin, Marcel, and Carlson studied the woman who had suffered brain damage in an automobile accident

a) what did they notice about her speech?

b) what did they conclude about her ability to read?

c) what happened to make them change their conclusion?

d) what did they learn about the relationship between the two phases of whole-word reading?

LESSON I SELF TEST

1. The three major functions of speech are

   a. asking questions, exchanging information, and entertaining.
   b. initiating behavior, directing behavior, and stopping behavior.
   c. making statements, persuading, and asking for information.
   d. providing information, requesting information, and requesting a behavior.

2. When a speaker includes both familiar and unfamiliar information in his communication with a listener, the speaker

   a. is using the given-new contract.
   b. is helping the listener to break the information into its constituent parts.
   c. is observing a rule of speech etiquette.

d. can always be certain that the listener understands and can ignore any nonverbal signs the listener makes.

3. Writers must be more careful than speakers to provide enough familiar information for their readers because

   a. readers are not as attentive as listeners are.
   b. writers cannot benefit from the verbal and nonverbal signs of understanding or confusion that their readers make.
   c. writers cannot use hand gestures and facial expressions to help them communicate.
   d. readers must often try to ignore competing stimuli such as background music, nearby conversation, and street noise.

4. "Turn down the stereo." is an example of

   a. auditory discrimination.
   b. a constituent phrase.
   c. a directive.
   d. voicing.

5. What are the smallest units of sound that contribute to the meaning of a word?

   a. phonemes
   b. letters
   c. consonants
   d. syllables

6. Identify the five features found by Miller and Nicely (1955) that permit listeners to discriminate between consonants.

   a. intensity, breathing, gutterality, diction, and verbalization.
   b. intensity, voicing, tonality, duration, and place of articulation
   c. place of articulation, frequency, pitch, stress, and phonetics.
   d. stridency, duration, nasality, place of articulation, and voicing.

7. English-speaking subjects who heard the stimuli <u>blanket</u> and <u>lanket</u> simultaneously always reported they heard the word <u>blanket</u> and never <u>lanket</u>. Why?

   a. The perception of sound follows phonological constraints and we tend to hear sequences of sounds found in our native language.
   b. The delay in voicing that permits us to distinguish between the <u>b</u> in <u>blanket</u> and the <u>l</u> in <u>lanket</u> was too brief.
   c. Consonant discrimination is difficult without contextual cues.
   d. Phoneme recognition strategies do not apply to nonsense words such as <u>lanket</u>.

8. To recognize the meaning of words in continuous speech as opposed to isolated words, we rely on

   a. the five distinguishing features identified by Miller and Nicely.
   b. frequent use of the given-new contract.
   c. important cues from speech context.
   d. cadence to break speech into meaningful parts.

9. Content words help us to determine the __________ of a sentence and function words help us determine its __________.

   a. meaning, syntax.
   b. structure, semantics.
   c. clarity, intent.

d. meaning, value.

10. Chomsky suggests that communication involves the transformation of _________ into _________.

a. intent; action
b. symbolic meaning; concrete meaning
c. deep structure; surface structure
d. experience; speech

11. Most investigators believe the primary deficit of Wernicke's aphasia is

a. loss of speech comprehension.
b. an inability to speak fluently.
c. pure word deafness.
d. loss of whole word reading skills.

12. If the subject looked at a picture of a bird building a nest and described it by saying, "Bird . . . builds . . . twigs and eggs . . . builds . . . eggs hatch," what condition does this subject most likely suffer from?

a. Broca's aphasia
b. pure word deafness
c. phonological dyslexia
d. Wernicke's aphasia

13. Lisa can read words such as church and nonsense words such as rugly, but she has difficulty reading irregularly spelled words such as yacht. Lisa condition is most likely

a. phonological dyslexia and uses the whole-word reading method.
b. surface dyslexia and must reads phonetically.
c. phonological dyslexia and must read phonetically.
d. surface dyslexia and uses the whole-word reading method.

14. What is developmental dyslexia?

a. A learning disability, frequently seen when children are taught a second language too young, that makes learning to read very difficult
b. A learning disability that occurs when reading and spelling skills differ by more than one grade level.
c. A learning disability, usually noticed during development, when children with otherwise normal intelligence have great difficulty learning to read.
d. A learning disability, usually noticed during development, that disappears with the onset of puberty.

15. What did Margolin, Marcel, and Carlson (1985) learn when they studied a woman who had suffered brain damage in an automobile accident?

a. Pronunciation strongly influences spelling skills.
b. Word recognition skills and spelling skills are virtually the same.
c. Pronunciation and word recognition are separate phases of whole-word reading.
d. Word recognition skills are not a good predictor of spelling skills.

LESSON II: ACQUISITION OF LANGUAGE

14. Describe current procedures and findings in infant speech perception. (pp. 339-340)

* 14.1 What is the response of

a) newborns in the delivery room to a sound in the room?

b) infants a few weeks old to the sound of a voice and nonspeech sounds?

c) infants a few months old when they hear a pleasant voice and an angry one?

d) What is your response to the question, "How well developed is the human infant's auditory system?"

14.2 Psychologists use a special technique to study what kinds of sounds very young infants can perceive. How does it work?

14.3 When Trehub (1976) used this technique to study how well infants discriminated between sounds, what happened to sucking rate when the

a) infant first heard the sound <u>zah</u>?

b) novelty of <u>zah</u> wore off? Use a formal term you learned earlier to describe the response.

c) auditory stimulus changed to <u>rah</u>

d) What did this research demonstrate?

15. Describe the four stages of infant vocalization and the two-word stage of linguistic development. (pp. 340-343)

* 15.1 Name the four stages of early vocalization in infants, noting the approximate age of infants at each stage and the kind of sounds they are able to make.

15.2 Is it just a coincidence that the names infants and children all over the world use to address their parents usually begin with <u>m</u>, <u>p</u>, or <u>b</u>? Explain.

* 15.3 What is the most important feature of children's grammar in the two-word stage? Is your answer also true for the grammar of deaf children?

15.4 What are some of the reasons children have different rules of grammar than adults?

15.5 What did Weiman observe about the use of stress in two-word speech?

* 15.6 List the seven categories that Weiman developed to classify examples two-word speech.

* 15.7 Look at this list and underline the word a child would stress to convey the meaning in parenthesis. Indicate the category (from 15.6) to which each word belongs.

Daddy shirt (That is daddy's shirt.)

Daddy shirt (Daddy is putting on his shirt.)

Terry car (Terry is in the car.)

Terry car (That is Terry's car.)

15.8 What is the importance of Weiman's work?

15.9 What are some of the problems researchers have had trying to discover the rules of grammar that children use?

16. Describe the acquisition of adult rules for grammatical verbal behavior. (pp. 343-344)

* 16.1 If you look at Table 8.3 in your text and conclude that because children learn to use ing correctly before they learn to use the 's, using ing must be an easier concept, what error are you making?

16.2 Briefly describe the orderly acquisition of adult grammar rules by children when they move past the two-word stage.

16.3 Give several original examples to illustrate how children overgeneralize the use of adding ed to form the past tense.

17. Explain how words become meaningful. (pp. 344-345)

17.1 Paul and his mother always sat in a large overstuffed chair just before he went to bed. At first his mother would say, "Come and sit in the chair with Mommy." Later he would say to his mother "Paul chair." when he had his pajamas on. His mother was surprised when on a trip to a furniture store, he looked at a sofa and said, "Chair."

a) What error did Paul make when he saw the sofa in the furniture store?

b) When the new dining room chairs that his parents had bought were delivered, Paul did not know what to call them. Why?

c) Paul's mother explained to him, "Mommy and Daddy bought these chairs for Paul's house." Why didn't his mother (and other adults as well) simply say, "We bought these for our house."?

d) Why will Paul's mother have more difficulty teaching him what the words ideally or knowledge mean?

18. Explain the arguments for and against language acquisition as an innate ability. (pp. 345-346)

* 18.1 How did Chomsky describe the grammatical structure of everyday adult speech?

18.2 Outline the position taken by McNeil (1970) and others that language acquisition is an innate ability. Refer to Chomsky's description of adult speech, language acquisition device, language universals, and critical period in your answer.

18.3 How do some psychologists refute this argument?

19. Describe the nature of adult speech to children. (pp.347-348)

19.1 After reviewing the research on how adults speak to children, the deVilliers (1978) identified several characteristics of adult speech to children. What are they? Can you think of some examples of these characteristics from your own experiences with young children?

19.2 What effect does the age of the child an adult is speaking to have on adult speech? What about conversations between children?

* 19.3 How does an adult's speech differ in the presence or absence of a child?

20. Explain how a child's behavior affects the speech patterns of adults. (pp. 348)

* 20.1 An adult's speech with a child is influenced by the age and presence of the child. What particular characteristic of the child controls the adult's speech?

20.2 If you want a child to pay attention to what you are saying, how complex should your speech be?

20.3 How does complexity influence learning? Have you ever made use of this relationship?

21. Explain how reinforcement processes may be important in shaping effective verbal behavior. (pp. 348-351)

21.1 State the main points of the position that reinforcement does not play an important role in language acquisition.

21.2 State the main points of the position that reinforcement plays an important role in language acquisition. Who is the best-known proponent of this position?

21.3 What essential feature of reinforcement do his critics miss?

21.4 According to your text, what are the two roles reinforcement plays in language acquisition?

21.5 What ethical consideration will constrain research on this topic?

22. Describe the findings regarding the acquisition of verbal behavior by nonhuman primates. (pp. 351-354)

* 22.1 Why did attempts to teach nonhuman primates speech before the Gardners fail?

22.2 Describe Project Washoe noting

a) why the Gardners chose Ameslan.

b) Washoe's progress compared to human children.

c) the influence this research has had on people's conceptions of the nature of language.

22.3 What are some of the language and cognitive skills that Premack and his colleagues have demonstrated with Sarah?

22.4 Compare Washoe's "parental" attempts to teach Loulis sign language with those of human parents who are teaching their children to speak.

22.5 What has work with nonhuman primates such as Washoe and Sarah taught us about verbal ability as a social behavior?

LESSON II SELF TEST

1. What is not true about an infant's auditory system?

   a. two- or three-week-old infants can distinguish the human voice from other nonspeech sounds.
   b. it is remarkably well developed.
   c. two-month-old infants can tell an angry voice from a pleasant one.
   d. newborns turn away from sound sources.

2. What is the first sound a baby makes?

   a. babbling
   b. gurgling
   c. cooing
   d. crying

3. Babbling in infants

   a. gradually replaces crying when infants are about six months of age.
   b. contains all the sounds that occur in all languages around the world.
   c. is the speech stage that occurs just before patterned speech emerges.
   d. is inhibited by the presence of adults.

4. Two-word speech

   a. is characterized by random groupings of words by children.
   b. is often the result of brain damage from disease or injury.
   c. does not follow adult grammar rules, but has its own rules for forming sentences.
   d. is unambiguous.

5. Children learn adult rules of grammar

a. automatically.
b. in response to a perceived need.
c. in an orderly way starting with the simplest rules and moving onto the more complex ones.
d. only if an adult carefully explains what the rule is and how to use it properly.

6. The first words children learn to use tend to be

a. present tense verbs.
b. content words.
c. function words.
d. exclamations

7. Jenny stood at her bedroom window looking up at the moon and said, "Look at the big ball in the sky." Jenny's comment is an example of

a. syntactic irregularity.
b. undergeneralization.
c. overgeneralization.
d. abstraction.

8. Which of the following is an argument made by critics of the hypothesis that children's ability to learn language is innate?

a. No language acquisition area has been found in the brain.
b. Adults speak more carefully and grammatically to young children than to other adults.
c. Children learn a language more easily than adults.
d. Language is complex yet almost all children learn to use it correctly.

9. When adults speak to children they

a. usually use the present tense and avoid abstract words.
b. explain the syntactical rules they are using.
c. sometimes rephrase what the child has said more simply.
d. rarely make allowances for the age of the child they are speaking to.

10. When children speak to children

a. the younger child must work very hard to hold the attention of the older child.
b. the older child takes the age of the younger child into account.
c. the older child frequently uses function words that the younger child cannot understand.
d. the younger child frequently uses too many content words.

11. What is the most important factor controlling adults' speech to children?

a. child's attentiveness
b. child's age
c. adult's relationship to the child
d. syntactic rules

12. What appears to be the optimum strategy for learning a language?

a. constant repetition.
b. interaction with someone who is slightly more competent.
c. read, recite, and review
d. learning through more than one sensory modality

13. According to your text, when considering the role of reinforcement in language acquisition it is important to remember that reinforcement

a. cannot occur without the deliberate intervention of another person.
b. is not especially effective in teaching grammar.
c. is not synonymous with reward.
d. in the form of future promises is not satisfying.

14. What is Project Washoe?

a. a research effort to locate the language acquisition area of the brain
b. a largely successful attempt to teach a manual language to nonhuman primates
c. a research project, headed by Noam Chomsky, to study the transformation of deep structure into surface structure
d. a scientific symposium to determine the role of reinforcement in language acquisition

15. The Gardners chose to teach Ameslan because

a. it had already been used successfully in early pioneering research.
b. they were already highly skilled with it and would not lose valuable research time.
c. it is a manual language and chimps' hand and finger dexterity is almost as good as ours
d. hundreds of signs can be taught in a few months and communication between humans and chimps can be established quickly.

INTEGRATING QUESTIONS

1. If you have studied a foreign language then you know that it is difficult to understand what is being said and even more difficult to make yourself understood. It is difficult enough in class, but it is much worse when you must try to make a telephone call in a foreign country. Carefully consider what we would lose and what we would gain if everyone spoke the same language.

2. Project Washoe and other attempts to teach nonhuman primates is especially interesting to we humans and has received much attention. Research into the ways that other nonhuman animals communicate is also progressing. Learn something about current research on the note patterns of songbirds or porpoise sounds.

3. Educating deaf children to live as normally as possible in a hearing world is especially difficult. Educators are divided as to whether it is better to teach deaf children only speech, only sign language, or some combination. What is your own position?

ANSWERS

1.1 profit from the experiences of others living and dead, share our own experiences, request helpful information and behaviors, use language as a tool in our own remembering and thinking, think about abstract and complex issues
1.2 provide information, request information, request a behavior
2.1 classification
2.2 1. There was going to be a surprise birthday party. 2. It was Jonathan's birthday. 3. The Browns were not sure they would be able to attend.
2.3 given-new contract
2.4 Writers do not have access to verbal and nonverbal signs of understanding and puzzlement from their readers.
2.5 stress, choice of article
2.6 a) ripe b) tomatoes
2.7 a) old: "the boy" implies we already know who he is
new: "a chair" implies we did not know he will bring a chair
b) old: "the chair" implies we already knew someone was bringing a chair
new: "a boy" implies we did not know who will bring the chair

3.1 wh- questions and yes/no questions
4.1 the smallest elements of sound that contribute to the meaning of a word; /t/ + /r/ + /u/ + /k/
4.5 effects of a speaker's accent and speech peculiarities
5.1 restrictions on the kinds of sounds we are likely to perceive
6.1 They could not use the context of the original conversation to help them identify the word.
6.2 a) round, found, ground b) The human auditory system can "fill-in" missing speech sounds when they are obscured by a noise. It appears to be a largely automatic process we are are often unaware of.
7.1 syntactical rules
7.2 a) (The man that she asked)(was unable to answer.)
((The man)(that she asked))((was unable)(to answer.))
b) constituent parts c) Function words such as prepositions and determiners help express the relations between content words. Content words such as nouns, adjectives, verbs, and adverbs express meaning. d) Functions words are the, that, was, to. Content words are man, she, unable, answer. e) function words
8.1 Semantics is the study of the meanings represented by words.
9.1 Deep structure represents the essence of what a person intended to say. Deep structure must be translated into surface structure or the particular form that the sentence takes.
9.3 deep structure, surface structure, surface structure, deep structure.
10.1 Aphasia is the loss of the ability to produce meaningful speech caused by brain damage.
11.2 agrammatism; Agrammatism is the loss of the ability to comprehend or produce speech that uses complex syntactical rules.
12.2 People with phonological dyslexia have difficulty with phonetic reading. People with surface dyslexia have difficulty using the whole-word method.
13.1 recognition and pronunciation
14.1 a) Infants turn their head toward the source of sound. b) Infants at this age can already discriminate between the sound of a voice and other nonspeech sounds. c) The infant cries at the sound of an angry voice and smiles and coos at the sound of a pleasant one. d) It is remarkably well developed.
15.1 Stage 1: Crying, from birth onward, crying; Stage 2: Other Vocalizations and Cooing, about one month, other sounds in addition to crying, cooing; Stage 3: Babbling, about six months, sounds that resemble speech; Stage 4: Patterned Speech, about one year, begins to produce words beginning with "p," "b," and "m."
15.3 Children's grammar at this stage appears to be the same throughout the world as well as for deaf children.
15.6 1. new or contrasting information, 2. location, 3. possession, 4. noun object, 5. action, 6. pronoun object, and 7. agent that performs some action
15.7 Daddy shirt (possession, noun object)
Daddy shirt (agent that performs some action, noun object)
Terry car (noun object, location)
Terry car (possession, noun object)
16.1 The simplest rules of grammar are the first to be learned, which may not be the case.
18.1 defective and degenerate
19.3 When a woman pretended to speak to a child her speech was simpler than if she was speaking to an adult. If the child was present, her speech was simpler still.
20.1 the child's attentiveness
22.1 Early researchers attempted to teach chimps human language. Chimps lack the control of tongue, lips, palate, and vocal cords to reproduce human voice sounds.

Chapter 8

Self Test: Lesson I

1.	d	Obj.	8-1
2.	a	Obj.	8-2
3.	b	Obj.	8-2
4.	c	Obj.	8-3
5.	a	Obj.	8-4
6.	d	Obj.	8-5
7.	a	Obj.	8-5
8.	c	Obj.	8-6
9.	a	Obj.	8-7
10.	c	Obj.	8-9
11.	a	Obj.	8-10
12.	b	Obj.	8-11
13.	a	Obj.	8-12
14.	c	Obj.	8-12
15.	c	Obj.	8-13

Self Test: Lesson II

1.	d	Obj.	8-14
2.	d	Obj.	8-15
3.	c	Obj.	8-15
4.	c	Obj.	8-15
5.	b	Obj.	8-16
6.	b	Obj.	8-16
7.	c	Obj.	8-17
8.	b	Obj.	8-18
9.	a	Obj.	8-19
10.	b	Obj.	8-19
11.	a	Obj.	8-20
12.	b	Obj.	8-20
13.	c	Obj.	8-21
14.	b	Obj.	8-22
15.	c	Obj.	8-22

8.1 OBJ 8-1

VERBAL BEHAVIOR

8.2 OBJ 8-1

PSYCHOLINGUISTICS

8.3 OBJ 8-2

GIVEN-NEW CONTRACT

8.4 OBJ 8-2

STRESS

8.5 OBJ 8-4

PHONEME

8.6 OBJ 8-5

PHONOLOGICAL CONSTRAINTS

8.7 OBJ 8-7

SYNTAX

8.8 OBJ 8-7

SYNTACTICAL RULES

8.9 OBJ 8-7

CONSTITUENT PARTS

8.10 OBJ 8-7

FUNCTION WORD

8.11 OBJ 8-7

CONTENT WORD

8-12 OBJ 8-8

SEMANTICS

8-13 OBJ 8-9

DEEP STRUCTURE

8-14 OBJ 8-9

SURFACE STRUCTURE

8-15 OBJ 8-10

APHASIA

8-16 OBJ 8-10

WERNICKE'S AREA

8.9 Obj 8-7

smallest group of words in a sentence that appear to form a unit

8.10 Obj 8-7

words that express relation among content words; usually mark beginning of constituent part; e.g., to, in, through, the

8.11 Obj 8-7

words that express meaning: nouns, verbs, adjectives, adverbs

8.12 Obj 8-8

study of meaning of verbal stimuli

8.13 Obj 8-9

according to Chomsky, essence of what a person intended to say

8.14 Obj 8-9

the particular form a speaker's sentence takes

8.15 Obj 8-10

loss of ability to produce meaningful speech caused by brain damage; not caused by simple deficits such as paralysis of the vocal muscles

8.16 Obj 8-10

region of auditory association cortex in upper part of temporal lobe on left side of brain; first described by Wernicke

8.1 Obj 8-1

acts of speaking, listening, writing, and reading; emphasizes use of language is a behavior that can be studied like other behaviors

8.2 Obj 8-1

branch of psychology; principal interest is human cognition, not rules that describe language

8.3 Obj 8-2

speaker/listener cooperation; speaker makes "old" and "new" information explicit, listener signals comprehension

8.4 Obj 8-2

in speech, emphasis on a syllable or word

8.5 Obj 8-4

smallest unit of speech sound that contributes to meaning of word

8.6 Obj 8-5

tendency of listeners to perceive speech sounds in ways most similar to sounds in their native language

8.7 Obj 8-7

the grammatical structure of spoken or written sentences

8.8 Obj 8-7

rules describing the ways that people combine words to form sentences

8-17 OBJ 8-10

WERNICKE'S APHASIA

8-18 OBJ 8-10

PURE WORD DEAFNESS

8-19 OBJ 8-11

BROCA'S AREA

8-20 OBJ 8-11

BROCA'S APHASIA

8-21 OBJ 8-11

AGRAMMATISM

8-22 OBJ 8-12

PHONETIC READING

8-23 OBJ 8-12

WHOLE-WORD READING

8-24 OBJ 8-12

PHONOLOGICAL DYSLEXIA

8-25 OBJ 8-12

SURFACE DYSLEXIA

8-26 OBJ 8-12

DEVELOPMENTAL DYSLEXIA

8-27 OBJ 8-15

TWO-WORD STAGE

8-28 OBJ 8-15

INFLECTIONS

8-29 OBJ 8-17

OVEREXTENSION

8-30 OBJ 8-17

UNDEREXTENSION

8-31 OBJ 8-18

LANGUAGE UNIVERSALS

8-32 OBJ 8-22

PROJECT WASHOE

8.25 Obj 8-12

brain damage marked by difficulty in recognizing whole words, but not reading them phonetically

8.26 Obj 8-12

learning disability in children with normal intelligence marked by great difficulty in learning to read

8.27 Obj 8-15

two word sentences first spoken at 18-20 months; follows universal grammar rules different from adult rules

8.28 Obj 8-15

suffixes added to words to indicate syntax or change their meaning; e.g., -ed, -ing, 's

8.29 Obj 8-17

speech characteristic of children; one word used incorrectly to describe all objects with similar attribute

8.30 Obj 8-17

speech characteristic of children; failure to recognize that a word can describe other similar objects

8.31 Obj 8-18

characteristics of all languages; e.g., noun phrases, syntactical categories

8.32 Obj 8-22

attempt by the Gardners to teach a manual language (Ameslan) to a chimp named Washoe

8.17 Obj 8-10

speech disorder marked by poor speech comprehension, fluent, meaningless speech; caused by damage to Wernicke's area

8.18 Obj 8-10

speech disorder marked by inability to understand speech; ability to understand nonspeech sounds is unimpaired; can read, write, and speak normally

8.19 Obj 8-11

region of left frontal cortex just in front of the base of the primary motor cortex; first described by Broca

8.20 Obj 8-11

speech disorder marked by labored, ungrammatical, but meaningful speech; caused by damaged to Broca's area

8.21 Obj 8-11

speech disorder marked by inability to understand or produce speech using syntactical rules such as word order; Broca's area damaged

8.22 Obj 8-12

reading technique in which words broken into letters or small groups of letters, then pronounced

8.23 Obj 8-12

reading technique in which a word is recognized as a whole

8.24 Obj 8-12

brain damage marked by difficulty in reading phonetically,
but no difficulty in recognizing whole words

CHAPTER 9
Intelligence

INTRODUCTION

What is intelligence? What does an IQ test really measure? These are some of the questions that this chapter explores. Specifically, this chapter considers intelligence testing (Objectives 1-8), the differential (Objectives 9-10) and information-processing (Objectives 11-15) approaches to intelligence, and the roles of heredity and environment in shaping intelligence (Objectives 16-22). Lesson I covers Objectives 1-10 and Lesson II, Objectives 11-22.

CONCEPT CARDS AND EXERCISES

After you have surveyed and read the text, assemble the concept cards located at the end of this chapter. Use them to learn the important terms, then begin reading the text again, one learning objective at a time, and work through the exercises for each lesson. Answers for questions marked with an asterisk are found at the end of the chapter.

SELF TESTS

Each lesson is followed by a multiple-choice self test. After you are proficient with a lesson's concept cards and exercises, take the self test to see whether you have mastered the material. Review those objectives for questions you answered incorrectly.

INTEGRATING QUESTIONS

To challenge yourself further, answer the integrating questions at the end of the chapter. These questions ask you to apply the information you have learned to consider larger theoretical or real-life issues.

LESSON I: INTELLIGENCE TESTING AND THE DIFFERENTIAL APPROACH

1. Identify and briefly describe the three major approaches to intelligence. (pp. 359-360)

1.1 Identify the approach to intelligence illustrated in these examples, and explain how these examples are representative of the approaches to intelligence.

* a) Psychologists studied children to ascertain the ages most children are able to comprehend directional concepts such as up and down, left and right.

* b) The psychologist developed a test of musical aptitude to assess people's abilities to

coordinate their sense of hearing with intellectual processes.

* c) The psychologists directed subjects to memorize a list and to report the steps they followed in memorizing the list.

* 1.2 Wechsler developed several tests of intelligence; he, therefore, worked in the field of psychology known as ______________.

2. Describe the contributions Galton made to the study of intelligence. (p. 360)

* 2.1 Sir Francis Galton was influenced by a theory developed by his cousin. Identify his cousin, his cousin's theory, and the features of this theory that gave Galton reason to generalize it to human intelligence.

* 2.2 What measurement did Galton use to assess human intelligence and what was the fate of this measure?

* 2.3 Identify and describe Galton's major contributions to the study of intelligence.

Note: For objectives 3, and 4, you may want to review the meaning of <u>reliability</u>, <u>validity</u>, and <u>standard deviation</u> in Chapter 2 of the text.

3. Describe Binet's definition of intelligence and the development and nature of the Binet-Simon and Stanford-Binet scales. (pp. 360-362)

3.1 Compare the views of Binet and Galton regarding the types of tests necessary to measure intelligence. Which of these views do you think has more validity?

3.2 State the purpose of the original Binet-Simon Scale and the 1905 revision.

3.3 What did Binet and Simon do to enable their test of intelligence to be used by other investigators to assess the abilities of other children?

3.4 In each of the following examples of scores on the revised Binet-Simon Scale indicate the mental age of the individual and identify what this measure indicates.

* _____ a) A six-year-old child scores as well as most other six-year-olds.

* _____ b) The average score obtained by five-year-old children is earned by an eight-year-old child.

* _____ c) A twelve-year-old child obtains a score usually obtained by fourteen-year-olds.

3.5 How does the Binet-Simon scale come to be known in the United States as the Stanford-Binet scale?

* 3.6 Specify the formula for the ratio IQ, define each term in this formula, and apply the formula to calculate the ratio IQ for each child in question 3.4 above.

3.7 Assuming the mean is 100, and the standard deviation is 16, calculate the deviation IQ for the following.

* a) a score two standard deviations above the mean

* b) a score 1.5 standard deviations below the mean

4. Describe the nature of validity and reliability of intelligence tests. (p. 362)

* 4.1 The adequacy of a measure of intelligence is determined by its ______________ and ________________.

4.2 Explain how psychologists assess the reliability and validity of intelligence tests and note the level of reliability and validity of intelligence tests.

5. Describe the Wechsler Adult Intelligence Scale. (p. 363)

5.1 Distinguish between the two general categories of behavior tested by the WAIS and list four tests from each category.

5.2 Describe why the WAIS is useful to neuropsychologists.

5.3 Explain why the WAIS may be useful for assessing the potential of individuals with educationally-deprived backgrounds.

6. Describe the Kaufman Assessment Battery for Children. (pp. 363-366)

* 6.1 The Kaufman Assessment Battery for Children (K-ABC) attempts to measure ______________ and ________________ processing, tasks associated with the ______________ ________________ of the brain. Give an example of tasks illustrating each of these processes.

6.2 What scores are provided by the K-ABC and how are they derived?

6.3 Identify an advantage of the K-ABC over some intelligence tests.

7. Describe the issue of cultural bias in intelligence tests and the controversy over the use of intelligence tests to assess and predict children's academic ability. (pp. 366-369)

* 7.1 Describe the problem of cultural bias inherent in the design of intelligence tests.

7.2 What does the example of the Kpelle man suggest about the cultural bias of intelligence tests?

* 7.3 Intelligence tests are good predictors of what?

* 7.4 Identify three potential problems associated with the use of intelligence tests in schools.

7.5 Identify some student populations that may benefit by diagnostic use of intelligence test scores when they are used in accordance with Binet's original intentions.

8. Name and describe the degrees of mental retardation. (pp. 369-370)

* 8.1 What was the original use of the term <u>mental retardation</u>?

8.2 Identify the four degrees of mental retardation and describe the abilities and limitations of people at each of these degrees.

9. Describe Spearman's two-factor theory of intelligence. (pp. 370-372)

* 9.1 Spearman proposed that intelligence is composed of two factors, a <u>g</u> or ______________

factor and an <u>s</u> or ______________ factor. Explain what each of these factors represent.

9.2 Estimate whether people's scores on the questions in the groups below would be likely to be correlated.

* _____ a) Explain the principles of the internal combustion engine; name and identify plants of the northeastern United States; name some recently enacted state laws.

* _____ b) Identify correct usage of English grammar, sentence structure, and vocabulary words.

* _____ c) Explain the principle of natural selection; name the major life forms of the Jurassic period; describe the ecological niche of the snail darter.

9.3 Assume that for group c) in 9.2, the correlation coefficient (r) between test scores was about .50 for most individuals.

* a) Calculate r^2 for these scores.

b) In general, what does r^2 measure?

c) What does r^2 suggest in this particular case?

9.4 What would Spearman's assumption have been about the source of the common variance measures you calculated? Would such assumptions be consistent with the data?

10. Summarize the evidence from factor analytic studies on the nature of intelligence. (pp. 372-375)

* 10.1 To assess whether correlations between tests are attributable to s or g factors,

_______________ analysis must be used.

10.2 A friend asks you to help him to understand a psychology article. The article reports a factor analysis of a group of intelligence tests. Explain to your friend what factor analysis is by noting its a) purpose, b) general method, c) limitations, and d) the meaning of the term factor loading.

10.3 What aspects of intelligence are being measured when a psychologist asks a person to

* a) say what the word breakfast means.

* b) arrange a set of blocks to match a particular design.

10.4 Identify the views of a) Cattell and b) Horn regarding the relationships among fluid intelligence, crystallized intelligence, heredity, and learning.

10.5 Your friend gave her two-year-old an "intelligence" test found in a popular magazine and was upset that her child had an IQ of 90. Help your friend to evaluate this score in light of what is known about validity, reliability, standardization, norms, and stability of IQ.

LESSON I SELF TEST

1. Which branch of psychology is most concerned with the development of tests of ability and personality?

   a. developmental psychology
   b. psychometrics
   c. differential psychology
   d. informational-processing psychology

2. Which of the following is one of Galton's lasting contributions to the development of intelligence testing?

   a. He conducted the first extensive study of twins.
   b. He supported the creationist theory in opposition to Darwin's theory of evolution.
   c. His observation that human traits are normally distributed became the foundation for many tests of statistical significance.
   d. He developed the first valid standardized test of intelligence.

3. Unlike Galton, Binet believed that intelligence should be determined by

   a. inference from the salaries and wealth people earned and accumulated.
   b. measuring psychological abilities such as attention and imagination.
   c. measuring sensory abilities.
   d. examining the bumps on people's heads.

4. The original purpose of the Binet-Simon Scale was to

a. identify children who were unable to profit from normal classroom instruction.
b. assess the intellectual abilities of normal children.
c. determine students' IQs.
d. evaluate the effectiveness of classroom instruction.

5. Calculate a ratio IQ for a twelve-year-old child who has a mental age of sixteen. The standard deviation of the test is sixteen.

a. 116
b. 84
c. 120
d. 133

6. In one school system scores on the Stanford-Binet were positively correlated with the children's grades. This finding suggests that the Stanford-Binet

a. is a reliable test.
b. has some validity.
c. is a poor predictor of grades.
d. should be restandardized for this population.

7. What advantage does the WAIS offer neuropsychologists?

a. It allows them to assess both the verbal and performance abilities of brain damaged people.
b. It allows them to calculate the more useful and understandable ratio IQ.
c. It has been standardized for normal and retarded children.
d. It presents tests in order of difficulty so as not to frustrate patients with various brain disorders.

8. The Kaufman Assessment Battery for Children provides scales on which of the following?

a. verbal, performance, and derivation IQ
b. fluid, crystallized, general and specific
c. culture-specific, culture-free, and interactional
d. simultaneous, sequential, achievement, and mental processing

9. One researcher argues that IQ tests prove the superiority of some races. One of the problems with this conclusion is that IQ tests in the past

a. had not been standardized.
b. measured aptitude rather than achievement.
c. had been biased culturally.
d. measured sensory abilities rather than intellectual abilities.

10. Which of the following is a legitimate application of tests of intellectual abilities?

a. Students who score poorly are evaluated for special educational programs.
b. Students who score better than their class performance would suggest are evaluated for learning disabilities.
c. Students' scores are analyzed to evaluate the effectiveness of the new curriculum.
d. all of the above.

11. What is the degree of mental retardation of an adult who has a mental age of 48 and lives in a group home?

a. profound
b. severe
c. moderate

d. mild

12. According to Spearman, if various tests of intellectual ability are correlated but not perfectly so, they

    a. are measuring a g factor and a s factor.
    b. are measuring two or more overlapping abilities.
    c. are inadequate measures of intelligence.
    d. may be reliable but they lack validity.

13. Which of the following is true of factor analysis?

    a. Factor analysis can reveal important skills in addition to the ones measured by the tests upon which the factor analysis was based.
    b. Factor analysis can only give hints about the nature of intelligence.
    c. Factor analysis is limited to identifying broad, uncorrelated factors.
    d. Factor analysis clearly distinguishes g and s factors.

14. Cattell performed a second factor analysis of factors derived from a first factor analysis. He found

    a. a g and many s factors in support of Spearman's hypothesis.
    b. that a second factor analysis reverses the effects of the first factor analysis.
    c. that intelligence could be conceptualized as a three- dimensional structure.
    d. two factors, fluid intelligence and crystallized intelligence, that accounted for most of the variability.

15. Your friend is distressed. She gave her six-month-old an intelligence test she found in the Sunday supplement of the newspaper and the baby had an IQ of 85. What advice would you offer your friend?

    a. Explain to your friend that the relation between IQ scores at infancy and eighteen years of age is negligible.
    b. Advise her to take the baby to a neuropsychologist for a complete battery of tests.
    c. Encourage her to place less demands upon the baby, who obviously cannot handle too much stimulation.
    d. Advise her to have the baby's IQ recalculated by using more recent norms.

LESSON II: THE INFORMATION-PROCESSING APPROACH AND THE ROLE OF HEREDITY AND ENVIRONMENT

11. Describe the information-processing approach to intelligence and the relation of reading ability to verbal ability in general. (pp. 375-376)

11.1 What are the relationships among the following terms: information-processing approach, cognitive psychology, computers, and artificial intelligence?

* 11.2 If a psychologist could only use a test of a single ability to predict school success, what test should be used? Offer reasons for your answer.

12. Describe research on the four major component processes that make up reading ability. (pp. 376-379)

* 12.1 Complete the following chart and define the terms you use.

______________ Processes of Reading Comprehension

Component	Correlates with	Why?
1. ____________		
a. ____________	____________	____________
b. ____________	____________	____________
2. ____________	____________	____________
a. ____________	____________	____________
3. ____________	____________	____________
a. ____________		
b. ____________		
4. ____________		

12.2 Explain why Hunt's analysis of reading is an example of the information-processing approach to intelligence.

13. Describe research on an information-processing analysis of deductive reasoning. (pp. 379-381)

* 13.1 The sentence below is a ______________ and measures ______________ reasoning.

All the entrepreneurs are rich.
All the economists are rich.
Therefore, all the entrepreneurs are economists; True or False.

13.2 Explain why syllogistic reasoning is much more highly correlated with spatial ability than verbal ability.

14. Describe and evaluate Sternberg's triarchic theory of intelligence. (pp. 381-383)

* 14.1 Identify the aspect of intelligence illustrated by the people below and describe the abilities each of these people are likely to have

a) Rose is "book smart."

b) Nancy has "street smarts."

c) Pat is creative.

* 14.2 Write an outline of Sternberg's ______________ theory of intelligence and define the terms you use.

14.3 Cite clinical evidence that supports Sternberg's model of intelligence.

15. Describe and evaluate Gardner's neuropsychological theory of intelligence. (pp. 383-386)

* 15.1 According to Gardner, what are the six categories of intelligence?

* 15.2 Explain the a) derivation and b) advantages of Gardner's theory of intelligence.

16. Explain the meaning of heritability. (pp. 386-387)

16.1 Some have turned the study of the roles of heredity and environment on intelligence into a debate. Identify the arguments and fears on both sides of this debate.

* 16.2 What is the relationship between heritability and variability?

* 16.3 If all changes in a particular trait of members of a population were demonstrated to be determined strictly by genetic variation, what heritability coefficient would be assigned to this trait?

16.4 If any environmentally produced variability in a trait is demonstrated how is the measure of heritability changed? Will it still be 1.0? Explain your answer.

17. Describe how the interaction between heredity and environment can affect intelligence. (pp. 387-388)

17.1 Apply the formula OV = GV + EV + interaction to the study by Cooper and Zubek (1958) to identify the experimental conditions, results, and implications.

18. Discuss the prenatal and postnatal factors that can affect intelligence. (pp. 388-389)

* 18.1 How can we say that prenatal factors affect the intelligence of a newborn infant when

the fetus does not yet possess intellectual abilities?

18.2 Summarize the types of genetic and environmental factors that influence potential intelligence at each of the following stages of development: a) conception, b) prenatal development, c) birth, d) infancy, and e) later life.

19. List three major considerations that researchers must take into account in evaluating the relative importance of genetic or environmental factors in intelligence. (pp. 389-390)

19.1 Describe the heritability of intelligence in genetically heterogenous and genetically homogeneous groups of people.

* 19.2 If environmental differences could be eliminated, what would be the expected effect of genetic contributions to variability in intelligence?

19.3 Describe how the interaction of genetic and environmental factors can affect a person's intellectual abilities.

20. Describe the methods, results, and limitations of the twin studies and family-of-twin studies of intelligence. (pp. 390-392)

20.1 What is the logic behind

a) studies of monozygotic twins separated at birth?

b) comparisons between monozygotic and dizygotic twins?

* 20.2 Identify three problems that limit the utility of the monozygotic twin studies.

20.3 Describe the a) method, b) results, and c) implications of the studies by Rose et al. (1979) that used the family-of-twins design.

20.4 Review the table by Henderson (1982) and comment on what these figures suggest about the roles of heredity and environment in intelligence.

21. Describe the difficulties in defining racial groups and the implications of these difficulties in assessing the relation of race to intelligence. (pp. 392-393)

* 21.1 What is the biological meaning of "race"? Explain the difficulty of applying this term to the human species.

21.2 Describe the evolutionary reasons for differences in skin pigmentation.

21.3 Explain why skin pigmentation is a poor criterion to use to distinguish human races.

* 21.4 Identify the crucial obstacle in an investigation of the effects of different environments

on inherited intellectual capacity.

22. Discuss the role of environmental differences in the relation of race to intelligence. (pp. 393-395)

* 22.1 What are the average scores of blacks and whites on IQ tests?

22.2 Identify at least four specific ways in which the treatment of blacks in this country may contribute to the observed differences in test scores.

22.3 Describe the Scarr and Weinberg (1976) study. Explain what they recorded and what it suggests about cultural factors in the development of intelligence.

LESSON II SELF TEST

1. Which of the following offers the best quick estimate of a person's intelligence?

   a. a syllogism test
   b. a test of memory span
   c. a test of verbal ability
   d. a test of arithmetic skills

2. According to Hunt, which of the following is a primary component of lexical access?

   a. comprehending isolated sentences
   b. vocabulary size
   c. knowledge of scripts
   d. selective attention

3. Which of the following did Johnson-Laird observe to be more highly correlated with syllogistic reasoning?

   a. spatial ability
   b. vocabulary size
   c. iconic memory
   d. allocation of attention

4. Who among the following has devised a theory of intelligence that derives from the information-processing approach?

   a. Spearman
   b. Sternberg
   c. Wechsler
   d. Binet

5. According to Sternberg's triarchic theory, componential intelligence is to contextual intelligence as

   a. metacomponents are to experiential intelligence.
   b. knowledge-acquisition is to shaping.
   c. selection is to adaptation.
   d. metacomponents are to performance components.

6. One advantage of Gardner's model of intelligence is that it

   a. presents a triarchic view of intelligence.
   b. is readily measured by paper-and-pencil tests.
   c. is based on the factor analytic research on intelligence.
   d. accommodates the views of intelligence of both Western and non-Western cultures.

7. Which of the following statements reflects the debate over the nature of human intelligence?

   a. It seems to me you think intelligence is innate. I believe it is learned.
   b. Gardner believes there are seven kinds of intelligence, but I prefer to consider intelligence as a global trait.
   c. Because everything that is learned comes through the senses, I believe intelligence should be inferred by measuring sensory ability, rather than these so-called psychological abilities.
   d. I have concluded that verbal intelligence is associated with the left hemisphere of the brain and performance with the right hemisphere.

8. Which of the following is a correct description of the heritability of intelligence?

   a. Because there is a wide-spread variability in IQ, the heritability of intelligence is zero.
   b. Because both genetic and environmental factors affect a person's intelligence, the heritability of intelligence is less than 1.0 but more than zero.
   c. Heritability of intelligence is about fifty percent, which means that about half of our intelligence is attributable to biological factors, and half to environmental factors.
   d. The amount of the heritability of intelligence is less than 1.0 but is independent of environmental factors.

9. What implication does the study of maze-bright and maze-dull rats by Cooper and Zubek (1958) have for the understanding of human intelligence?

   a. The effects of a strong heredity mask the effects of a strong environment.
   b. Only impoverished environments are strong enough to mask the effect of a strong heredity.
   c. People, regardless of heredity, can do reasonably well if placed in optimal environments.
   d. No implications can be drawn from this study because rats are not people.

10. What is known about familial mental retardation?

    a. It is by definition caused by hereditary.
    b. It accounts for 25 percent of the observed cases of mental retardation.
    c. It may be caused by environmental factors as well as genetic ones.
    d. It affects potential intelligence more than actual intelligence.

11. In which of the following cases would the heritability of IQ be most likely to be greatest?

    a. in cases where GV is responsible for the interaction term
    b. in cases where people are tested in their natural environments
    c. in a North American culture
    d. in an isolated culture

12. The early studies of separated twins must be interpreted with care because

    a. some of the studies failed to take into account the similarity of the households in which the separated twins were raised.
    b. the variability among adopted children during the 1920s and 1930s was greater than that in the general population.
    c. many of the early researchers expressed prejudice toward certain ethnic and racial groups.
    d. the logic underlying twin studies is spurious.

13. What have Rose et al. in their family-of-twin studies found the heritability of IQ to be?

a. .4 to .28
b. .25 to .40
c. .40 to .58
d. .69 to .80

14. An instructor glances through students' files. One of the files notes that Jim Jones is black. What else might the instructor legitimately assume about Jim Jones?

    a. He will have a lower IQ score than his white classmates.
    b. He lives in a home that offers little intellectual stimulation.
    c. He is a member of the Negroid race.
    d. He was identified by someone as black.

15. A study by Scarr and Weinberg of black children adopted by educated, affluent, white families suggests that

    a. blacks as a race are culturally and biologically inferior to whites.
    b. black children because of genetic limitations do not respond as well as white children to an enriched environment.
    c. optimal environments are associated with higher intelligence scores.
    d. differences in IQs between blacks and whites are exclusively due to environmental factors.

INTEGRATING QUESTIONS

1. There is a good correlation between IQ scores and school success but the correlation between IQ scores and career success is lower. Offer reasons for these correlations. (Hint: Use the newer theories of intelligence based on the information-processing approach as well as what you know about statistics, test construction, and IQ tests.)

2. College entrance examinations such as the SAT's and the ACT's are intended to predict how well a student will perform in college. Use your knowledge of test construction and the issues surrounding the roles of heredity and environment in intelligence to describe the factors about which the publishers and users of these examinations must be concerned.

3. Describe an environment that is likely to promote the achievement of an individual's intelligence. Be sure to consider the interaction of genetic and environmental factors, the stability of IQ scores, and the definition and measurements of intelligence as you formulate your answer.

ANSWERS

1.1 a) developmental, b) differential, c) information-processing
1.2 psychometrics
2.1 Charles Darwin, evolution and natural selection; Galton observed family differences in ability and hypothesized that intelligence must be heritable.
2.2 measures of sensory discrimination, abandoned in favor of more psychological measures
2.3 statistics (logic for correlations observation re. normal curve, model of systematic evaluation of large numbers of people, methods of population statistics) and research ideas (logic for twin and adoptive parents studies)
3.4 a) six, b) five, c) fourteen
3.6 IQ=MA/CA x 100; MA=mental age; CA=chronological age; a) 6/6 x 100=100, b) 5/8 x 100=62.5 (63), c) 14/12 x 100=116.7 (117)
3.7 a) 132, b) 76
4.1 reliability, validity
6.1 sequential, simultaneous, two hemispheres; sequential—e.g. apply rules of grammar,

simultaneous—e.g. interpret maps
7.1 distinguishing between person's potential to learn and the learning that occurred or not because of the culture (environment)
7.3 academic success
7.4 deleterious effects of labeling for child's self-concept and for treatment (e.g. educational opportunities he or she receives), teaching the test
8.1 severe learning problems demonstrated by seriously lagging behind other children
9.1 g=general, s-specific
9.2 a) no, b) yes, c) yes
9.3 a) .25,
10.1 factor
10.3 a) crystallized intelligence, b) fluid intelligence
11.2 verbal ability
12.1 Hunt's; 1. lexical access, a. vocabulary size, verbal ability; b. speed of access, verbal ability; 2. comprehension isolated sentences, verbal comprehension; a working memory, verbal ability; 3. comprehension of connected discourse, a. scripts, b. recognize script being use; 4. allocation of attention
13.1 syllogism, deductive
14.1 a) componential, b) contextual, c) experiential
14.2 triarchic, I. Componential, a. metacomponents, b. knowledge acquisition components, c. performance acquisition components; II. Experiential, a. novel situations (fluid), b. automatic (crystallized); III. Contextual, a. adaptation, b. selection, c. shaping
15.1 linguistic, musical, logical-mathematical, spatial, bodily-kinesthetic, personal
15.2 a) way brain organized; b) current neuropsychological research; accommodation of non-Western as well as Western views of intelligence
16.2 heritability assesses variability of trait in population in terms of contributions of differences in genetic factors relative to contributions of differences in environmental factors
16.3 1
18.1 affects potential of infant to learn
19.2 GV would determine the OV of intelligence
20.2 assumption that environments will be different; tendency to place bright children with educated, more economically advantaged homes; age of adoptive parents
21.1 population that has reproductive isolation from other groups of the species
21.4 not possible to measure inherited intellectual ability
22.1 blacks 85, whites 100

Self Test: Lesson I

1. b Obj 9-1
2. c Obj 9-2
3. b Obj 9-3
4. a Obj 9-3
5. d Obj 9-3
6. b Obj 9-4
7. a Obj 9-5
8. d Obj 9-6
9. c Obj 9-7
10. d Obj 9-7
11. c Obj 9-8
12. a Obj 9-9
13. b Obj 9-10
14. d Obj 9-10
15. a Obj 9-10

Self Test: Lesson II

1. c Obj 9-11
2. b Obj 9-12
3. a Obj 9-13
4. b Obj 9-14
5. b Obj 9-14
6. d Obj 9-15
7. a Obj 9-16
8. b Obj 9-16
9. c Obj 9-17
10. c Obj 9-18
11. c Obj 9-19
12. a Obj 9-20
13. c Obj 9-20
14. d Obj 9-21
15. c Obj 9-22

9.1 OBJ 9-1

DIFFERENTIAL APPROACH

9.2 OBJ 9-1

PSYCHOMETRICS

9.3 OBJ 9-1

DEVELOPMENTAL APPROACH

9.4 OBJ 9-1

INFORMATION-PROCESSING APPROACH

9.5 OBJ 9-2

INTELLIGENCE

9.6 OBJ 9-2

CORRELATION

9.7 OBJ 9-3

BINET-SIMON SCALE

9.8 OBJ 9-3

NORMS

9.9 OBJ 9-3

MENTAL AGE

9.10 OBJ 9-3

STANFORD-BINET SCALE

9.11 OBJ 9-3

INTELLIGENCE QUOTIENT

9.12 OBJ 9-3

RATIO IQ

9.13 OBJ 9-3

DEVIATION IQ

9.14 OBJ 9-5

CRITERION

9.15 OBJ 9-5

WECHSLER ADULT INTELLIGENCE SCALE (WAIS)

9.16 OBJ 9-6

KAUFMAN ASSESSMENT BATTERY FOR CHILDREN (K-ABC)

9.9 Obj 9-3

expected average level of intellectual achievement for a particular age

9.10 Obj 9-3

translated and revised version of Binet test for the United States; revised over the years

9.11 Obj 9-3

score reflecting person's performance on measure of intelligence relative to other people

9.12 Obj 9-3

intelligence quotient based on the ratio of a person's mental age to his or her chronological age, multiplied by 100 to eliminate fractions

9.13 Obj 9-3

IQ expressed as number of standard deviations above or below mean; mean = 100, usually one standard deviation = 16

9.14 Obj 9-5

comparison measure used to assess validity of a test; if both yield similar results, test presumed to be valid

9.15 Obj 9-5

test divided into performance and verbal tasks; designed by Wechsler to measure intelligence of adults

9.16 Obj 9-6

intelligence measure that assesses sequential and simultaneous processing, skills associated with left and right brain respectively

9.1 Obj 9-1

study of intelligence that designs tests to identify and measure individual differences to discover factors underlying intelligence

9.2 Obj 9-1

branch of psychology concerned with development of tests of ability and personality

9.3 Obj 9-1

study of intelligence through observation of ways children learn to perceive, manipulate and think about the world

9.4 Obj 9-1

cognitive psychological approach to study of intelligence; analyzes processes of intelligent behavior

9.5 Obj 9-2

term revived by Spenser and Galton in nineteenth century to indicate individual's ability to perceive, comprehend and act upon the world

9.6 Obj 9-2

degree to which variability in one measure is related to variability in another; logic for which outlined by Galton

9.7 Obj 9-3

first comprehensive intelligence test, 1905; items arranged in increasing difficulty, provides norms for deriving mental age

9.8 Obj 9-3

data from comparison groups that permit individual's score to be assessed relative to his or her peers'

9.17 OBJ 9-8

MENTAL RETARDATION

9.18 OBJ 9-9

G FACTOR

9.19 OBJ 9-9

S FACTOR

9.20 OBJ 9-9

APPREHENSION OF EXPERIENCE

9.21 OBJ 9-9

EDUCTION OF RELATIONS

9.22 OBJ 9-9

EDUCTION OF CORRELATES

9.23 OBJ 9-10

FACTOR ANALYSIS

9.24 OBJ 9-10

FLUID INTELLIGENCE (G_F)

9.25 OBJ 9-10

CRYSTALLIZED INTELLIGENCE (G_C)

9.26 OBJ 9-11

ARTIFICIAL INTELLIGENCE

9.27 OBJ 9-12

LEXICAL ACCESS

9.28 OBJ 9-12

COMPREHENSION OF ISOLATED SENTENCES AND EXPRESSIONS

9.29 OBJ 9-12

SENTENCE VERIFICATION TASK

9.30 OBJ 9-12

COMPREHENSION OF CONNECTED DISCOURSE

9.31 OBJ 9-12

SCRIPT

9.32 OBJ 9-12

ALLOCATION OF ATTENTION

9.25 Obj 9-10

one of two general factors identified by Cattell and Horn; defined by tasks that require people to have learned information from their culture, e.g., vocabulary

9.26 Obj 9-11

information-processing study of intelligence; develops computer programs that simulate human abilities

9.27 Obj 9-12

one of Hunt's four components of reading comprehension; ability to "get at" vocabulary item; involves size and speed of access of vocabulary

9.28 Obj 9-12

one of Hunt's four components of reading comprehension; involves holding and manipulating information in working memory

9.29 Obj 9-12

measures comprehension of isolated sentences by having subjects read sentence and quickly identify display illustrating sentence

9.30 Obj 9-12

one of Hunt's four components of reading comprehension; involves knowledge of scripts and ability to recognize which script is being referenced

9.31 Obj 9-12

knowledge of particular kind of event or interaction that enables person to fill in details of the situation

9.32 Obj 9-12

Hunt's fourth component of reading comprehension; involves control of attention to and analysis of task depending on task requirements

9.17 Obj 9-8

term used to designate people with severe learning problems

9.18 Obj 9-9

general intelligence factor postulated by Spearman in his two-factor theory

9.19 Obj 9-9

specific intelligence factor postulated by Spearman in his two-factor theory

9.20 Obj 9-9

part of *g* factor, concerned with perception and comprehension of experience

9.21 Obj 9-9

part of *g* factor, concerned with ability to perceive relationships between concepts

9.22 Obj 9-9

part of *g* factor, concerned with ability to apply rule inferred from one case to a similar case

9.23 Obj 9-10

mathematical procedure developed by Spearman and Pearson to identify common factors or source of variability among tests

9.24 Obj 9-10

one of two general factors identified by Horn and Cattell; concerned with relatively culture-free tasks

9.33 OBJ 9-13

SYLLOGISTIC REASONING

9.34 OBJ 9-14

TRIARCHIC

9.35 OBJ 9-14

COMPONENTIAL INTELLIGENCE

9.36 OBJ 9-14

METACOMPONENTS

9.37 OBJ 9-14

PERFORMANCE COMPONENTS

9.38 OBJ 9-14

KNOWLEDGE-ACQUISITION COMPONENTS

9.39 OBJ 9-14

EXPERIENTIAL INTELLIGENCE

9.40 OBJ 9-14

CONTEXTUAL INTELLIGENCE

9.41 OBJ 9-14

ADAPTATION

9.42 OBJ 9-14

SELECTION

9.43 OBJ 9-14

SHAPING

9.44 OBJ 9-15

APRAXIA

9.45 OBJ 9-16

HERITABILITY

9.46 OBJ 9-17

INTERACTION

9.47 OBJ 9-18

FAMILIAL MENTAL RETARDATION

9.48 OBJ 9-20

FAMILY-OF-TWINS DESIGN

9.41 Obj 9-14

Sternberg: part of contextual intelligence; fit self into environment

9.42 Obj 9-14

Sternberg: part of contextual intelligence, find niche in environment

9.43 Obj 9-14

Sternberg: part of contextual intelligence, tailor environment to fit self

9.44 Obj 9-15

inability to perform sequence of voluntary skilled movements; associated with damage to left parietal lobe

9.45 Obj 9-16

proportion of observed variability in physical or behavioral trait caused by genetic variability; ranges from 0 to 1.0

9.46 Obj 9-17

events whose effects influence each other, such as influence of genetic and environmental effects upon each other

9.47 Obj 9-18

retardation in members of family; caused by genetic or environmental factors or both

9.48 Obj 9-20

study of adult monozygotic twins, and both their spouses and offspring, to assess heritability of intelligence

9.33 Obj 9-13

deduction presenting major and minor premises presumed to be true and a conclusion that may or may not be true

9.34 Obj 9-14

literally ruled by three, such as Sternberg's three component theory of intelligence

9.35 Obj 9-14

Sternberg: component of intelligence involving mental mechanisms to plan and execute tasks

9.36 Obj 9-14

Sternberg: part of componential intelligence; process by which person decides nature of task, strategy to solve it, and application of resources

9.37 Obj 9-14

Sternberg: part of componential intelligence, involves processes used to perform task

9.38 Obj 9-14

Sternberg: part of componential intelligence; process used to gain new knowledge by sifting out relevant knowledge and integrating it with existing knowledge

9.39 Obj 9-14

Sternberg: component of intelligence involving ability to deal with novel situations, and to treat these automatically when they become more familiar

9.40 Obj 9-14

Sternberg: component of intelligence involving ability to adapt, select, and shape one's environment

CHAPTER 10
Consciousness

INTRODUCTION

This chapter considers consciousness as a social behavior (Objective 1), attention (Objective 2), consciousness and the brain (Objective 3), hypnosis (Objectives 4-8), the control of consciousness (Objective 9), and sleep and sleep disorders (Objectives 10-17). Lesson I covers Objectives 1-8, and Lesson II, Objectives 9-17.

CONCEPT CARDS AND EXERCISES

After you have surveyed and read the text, assemble the concept cards located at the end of this chapter. Use them to learn the important terms, then begin reading the text again, one learning objective at a time, and work through the exercises for each lesson. Answers for questions marked with an asterisk are found at the end of the chapter.

SELF TESTS

Each lesson is followed by a multiple-choice self test. After you are proficient with a lesson's concept cards and exercises, take the self test to see whether you have mastered the material. Review those objectives for questions you answered incorrectly.

INTEGRATING QUESTIONS

To challenge yourself further, answer the integrating questions at the end of the chapter. These questions ask you to apply the information you have learned to consider larger theoretical or real-life issues.

LESSON I: CONSCIOUSNESS AS A SOCIAL BEHAVIOR, ATTENTION, CONSCIOUSNESS AND THE BRAIN, AND HYPNOSIS

1. Define consciousness and explain how it is a social behavior. (pp. 403-407)

* 1.1 a) Identify and b) explain the two prerequisites necessary for communication to be effective.

1.2 Do the following examples illustrate verbal access or verbal control? Explain your choice.

* __________ a) telling ourselves that our leg hurts

* __________ b) crying for help

* __________ c) saying we are sleepy

* __________ d) asking someone to pass us the bread

* __________ e) telling someone their answer is wrong

* __________ f) telling ourselves we will visit a friend

1.3 Explain how communication may or may not be conscious. Give an example of

a) animal nonconscious communication.

b) human nonconscious communication.

c) human conscious communication.

* 1.4 All conscious communication is verbal. True _____ False _____. Explain the reasons for your answer.

1.5 What are the benefits of communication?

* 1.6 Subtle or complex activities such as formulating rules, logical analysis, and reasoning are examples of _______________ behavior.

1.7 Are the following activities likely to be verbally mediated?

* _____ a) preparing for the long jump in a track meet

* _____ b) learning to operate a film projector

* _____ c) learning to draw the human body

* _____ d) embroidering a pattern

* _____ e) learning to carry out an experiment

* _____ f) learning to ski

2. Describe selective attention, its importance, and the factors that affect it. (pp. 407-411)

* 2.1 The ability to attend to only some aspects of the environment that surrounds us is referred to as _______________.

2.2 Suppose you are studying at your desk next to the window. A friend stops by and comments that it is snowing. Looking out the window, you see that the ground is covered with snow. Your friend tells you that it has been snowing for half an hour. You are amazed that you had not noticed until now. At this point, you also notice that your back hurts from sitting in the same position for so long.

Use the above example to

a) explain selective attention.

b) explain how attention is related to verbal access.

2.3 a) Describe the shadowing task that subjects performed in the study by Cherry (1953).

b) Describe the subjects' performance on this task and their recall of what they had heard from the unattended ear.

c) What do these results suggest regarding attention to auditory input?

2.4 Cite some evidence that suggests that some stimuli may become conscious even though they are not attended to at the time they are presented by referring to

a) von Wright et al.'s (1975) study with aversively conditioned auditory stimuli.

b) McKay's (1973) study of sentence recall.

c) Treisman's (1960) study on switching messages from ear to ear.

d) Neisser and Becklen's (1975) study with a videotape containing two different actions, presented one on top of the other.

e) Neisser's (1969) study using text printed in red and black.

3. Describe the significance of the symptoms of isolation aphasia, a case of visual agnosia, and the split-brain syndrome to our understanding of consciousness. (pp. 411-415)

3.1 Summarize the case of the woman with isolation aphasia by a) noting the brain damage she suffered, b) the abilities that she lost, c) the abilities that she maintained, and d) the implications of this case for the relationships among consciousness, the brain's speech mechanisms, and memory.

3.2 a) Explain whether the motor movements of the patient with visual agnosia while he looked at visual stimuli were "conscious."

b) What does this case suggest about consciousness and verbal systems?

* 3.3 The largest bundle of association fibers that connects the cortex of the two hemispheres of the brain is the ______________. The surgery that severs these fibers in order to reduce ______________ is known as the ______________ operation.

3.4 Describe the performance of people who have undergone split-brain operations and have been studied by Gazzaniga and his colleagues on the following tasks.

* a) smelling a perfume through the left nostril only and having to say what the odor is.

* b) smelling an odor through the right nostril only and then choosing the object that corresponds to the odor with the left hand.

* c) building a tower with blocks using the right hand.

3.5 Explain what the performance of patients who have undergone split-brain operations suggests about the unity of consciousness.

4. Describe the history of hypnosis, its induction, and its characteristics. (pp. 415-418)

* 4.1 Hypnosis is a form of ________________. Another name for hypnosis is ________________.

4.2 In order for a person to be hypnotized, an object must be moved at a constant pace in front of the person's face and a low, grave voice must repeatedly say, "You are getting tired."

* a) True _____ False _____

b) Explain the reason for your answer and

* c) identify the <u>one</u> critical feature that must be present in order for hypnosis to be induced.

* 4.3 When a hypnotized person sees things that are not present, we call this ________________; when this person acts as though he or she cannot perceive events that are present, we call this ________________. When returned to a nonhypnotized state and this person follows the hypnotist's instructions, we call this ________________, and when this person cannot recall what occurred while he or she was hypnotized, we call this ________________.

4.4 Does hypnosis change people's sensory experiences or merely their report of them? Review the studies by Pattie (1937) and Miller, Hennessy and Leibowitz (1973) to answer that question.

4.5 Describe Barber's (1961) conclusion regarding whether people may be induced to commit antisocial behavior under hypnosis.

4.6 What are the implications of the studies by Milgram (1963, 1974) for studies of hypnotically-induced antisocial behavior?

5. Describe Hilgard's neodissociation theory of hypnosis. (pp. 418-419)

5.1 Give two examples of dissociation induced by hypnosis.

5.2 Offer an example of the phenomenon of the hidden observer and explain how this phenomenon fits into Hilgard's theory of hypnosis.

6. Describe Barber's social role theory of hypnosis and his explanation of Hilgard's "hidden observer." (pp. 419-421)

6.1 Briefly state Barber's argument regarding the relation between hypnosis and day-to-day behavior.

6.2 a) How is behavior under hypnosis similar to participating in a story or a movie?

* b) __________ is the ability to understand the feelings, thoughts, and motives of another person.

c) Explain how this ability is related to hypnosis.

6.3 What does the study by Spanos, Gwynn, and Stam (1983) suggest about Hilgard's notion of the hidden observer?

7. Describe the characteristics of people who are susceptible to hypnosis and relate these characteristics to theories of hypnosis. (p. 421)

* 7.1 Personality type and susceptibility to hypnosis appear to be related. True _____ False _____ Explain the reasons for your answer.

7.2 What aspects of personality seems to be related to susceptibility to hypnosis?

7.3 What are the current speculations regarding the hemispheres of the brain and hypnosis?

8. Describe the uses and limitations of hypnosis. (pp. 422-423)

* 8.1 List some of the applications of hypnosis to research and therapy.

8.2 Describe the uses and limitations of the television technique.

8.3 What does the study by Laurence and Perry (1983) suggest about the use of hypnosis as an aid to recall?

LESSON I SELF TEST

1. It is foolish to tell a one-year-old child to brush his teeth because

   a. we do not have verbal access to a child.
   b. the child does not have verbal access to teeth brushing.
   c. teeth brushing for this child is not under verbal control.
   d. the child is not aware of himself as a person.

2. Which of the following is most likely a conscious communication?

   a. Judy automatically cries during a sad movie.
   b. Although Michelle is attractive and wants to meet men, her body language tells them to stay away.
   c. Joe signaled to Renee to be quiet by raising his index finger to his lips.
   d. The infant cried when she wet.

3. Which of the following tasks is most likely to benefit from verbal mediation?

   a. learning how to cook
   b. learning how to ice skate
   c. learning how to ride a bicycle
   d. learning how to jump rope

4. Jonathan is a brilliant scholar who has earned the label, absent-minded professor. Jonathan's apparent forgetfulness regarding the more mundane tasks of daily life is due to

   a. dissociation.
   b. the split-brain syndrome.
   c. dichotic listening.
   d. selective attention.

5. You are trying to listen to the conversation on your left ear and ignore the one that is taking place on your right. This is an instance of

   a. shadowing.
   b. cross-conversation.
   c. dichotic listening.
   d. cross-modal transfer of information.

6. What is most clearly suggested by the case of the woman who had isolation aphasia?

   a. Consciousness is simply an activity of the brain's speech mechanism.
   b. Consciousness is synonymous with a person's ability to talk about his or her perceptions or memories.
   c. Consciousness involves the brain speech mechanisms as well as information received from other parts of the brain concerning memories or presently occurring events.
   d. Consciousness and self-awareness are two different phenomena.

7. Studies of individuals who have had the corpus callosum severed suggest that

   a. unless various brain structures can communicate with each other, consciousness cannot be unified.
   b. consciousness is located in the right hemisphere, and the unconscious is located in the left hemisphere.
   c. the corpus callosum controls the verbal mediation of consciousness.
   d. the human species has two brains, the old instinctive animal brain and the new cognitive brain.

8. Another name for hypnosis is

   a. psychological magnetism.
   b. sleep induction.
   c. meditation.
   d. mesmerism.

9. In order for a person to be hypnotized, he or she must

   a. be completely relaxed.
   b. fixate his or her eyes on a bright, moving object.
   c. become sleepy as he or she listens to the hypnotist's voice.
   d. understand that he or she is to be hypnotized.

10. During hypnosis a subject is told that he will forget the number four. When he returns to a nonhypnotized state, he is asked to count from one to five. He counts "One, two, three, five." This is an example of

a. posthypnotic suggestibility.
b. positive hallucination.
c. negative hallucination.
d. posthypnotic agnosia.

11. Most studies on the extent to which hypnotized subjects will follow suggestions to perform antisocial acts have been flawed. One problem with these studies is that they

 a. do not operationally define antisocial acts.
 b. rely upon subjects who expect to be hypnotized.
 c. do not measure the degree to which subjects are hypnotized.
 d. fail to use control groups to determine the limits of an unhypnotized person's behavior.

12. Hilgard regards the hidden observer as a function of

 a. the split-brain phenomenon.
 b. dissociation.
 c. role playing.
 d. selective attention.

13. Which of the following appears responsible for hypnosis if hypnosis involves participation in a story?

 a. visual agnosia
 b. attention withdrawal
 c. empathy
 d. sleep induction

14. Which characteristic is most clearly associated with susceptibility to hypnosis?

 a. imagination
 b. neurosis
 c. weak will
 d. humor

15. Research has demonstrated that hypnosis

 a. can induce people to recall events that never happened.
 b. can induce people to commit antisocial acts that they would never perform if nonhypnotized.
 c. is less effective than tranquilizers in producing analgesia.
 d. is more closely associated with the left hemisphere of the brain.

LESSON II: CONTROL OF CONSCIOUSNESS AND SLEEP

9. Describe and compare the techniques for withdrawing attention with those for increasing or dishabituating consciousness. (pp. 423-427)

* 9.1 What feature is common to all methods of producing changes in consciousness and how is this feature illustrated in meditation?

9.2 If you have used a method to alter your own consciousness, describe it and identify how it changed your attention to various stimuli.

* 9.3 a) What are the effects of repetitive stimuli on consciousness and b) what are their effects upon a person's EEG?

* 9.4 Identify the two general goals of withdrawal of attention.

* 9.5 What fundamental learning process describes the general tuning down to most of our daily stimulus surroundings? Explain why we might wish to reverse this process.

* 9.6 Identify four ways of reducing habituation.

10. Name and describe the stages of sleep and describe the methods used to measure these stages. (pp. 427-430)

10.1 Describe the arrangements for subjects in a sleep laboratory, the recording apparatus, and the four common measures gathered by sleep researchers.

* 10.2 Identify the names and describe the characteristics of the EEG activity records for each of the following states.

    a) the alert or waking state

    b) the state of drowsy relaxation just before sleep

* 10.3 As sleep begins and moves from stage 1 to stage 4, what corresponding changes occur on the EEG recording?

* 10.4 What name is given to EEG activity during stage 4 sleep? What name is given to EEG activity during stages 2-4?

* 10.5 As sleep progresses from stage 1 to stage 4, how do the effects of environmental stimuli on a person change?

10.6 How long does it take to reach stage 4? Describe what next occurs to

    a) the sleeper's respiration and heart rate.

    b) the sleeper's eye muscles.

    c) the sleeper's mental activity.

11. Describe the dreams that occur during slow-wave sleep and REM sleep and discuss the nature of symbolism in dreams. (p. 430-433)

* 11.1 What do people who are awakened during REM sleep report?

* 11.2 How do reports of REM dreams differ from reports of dreams during slow-wave sleep?

* 11.3 Distinguish between the latent and manifest content of a dream.

11.4 If a person has dreams that are sometimes about mundane or prosaic events and sometimes explicitly erotic, what does this suggest about the assertion that prosaic dreams invariably contain repressed or hidden sexual symbolic content?

11.5 What evidence is there that whatever symbolic content may be contained in dreams is readily available in most cases to the person having the dream? What does this suggest about the need for a trained psychotherapist to interpret dreams for the average person?

12. Describe the hypothesis that the function of sleep is to repair, and discuss relevant evidence. (p. 433-435)

12.1 What evidence is there that strenuous physical exercise increases the need for sleep and lack of exercise reduces the need for sleep?

12.2 What conclusion can be drawn about the hypothesis that the function of sleep is to repair the body?

* 12.3 What appears to be the primary effect of sleep deprivation?

12.4 What happens when a person who has been deprived of sleep is allowed to fall asleep?

12.5 What do the cases of total sleep deprivation suggest about the hypothesis that sleep serves necessary physiological functions?

12.6 Describe how human subjects in a sleep laboratory can be deprived of only REM sleep, and how such selective REM sleep deprivation can be arranged for in nonhuman laboratory subjects.

* 12.7 What two things happen to an organism's REM sleep following a period of selective REM sleep deprivation?

13. Describe the hypothesis that sleep serves as a useful instinctual response, and discuss relevant evidence. (pp. 435-436)

13.1 Describe the view proposed by Webb (1975) regarding the origins and adaptive functions of sleep as a biological activity.

13.2 Describe the procedure used by Magni et al. (1959) to demonstrate that certain areas of the brain regulate sleep onset and termination.

13.3 What seems to be the relation between a species' normal amount of sleep and evolutionary development? Be sure to mention the species' housing, metabolism, and eating habits.

14. Describe the nature and treatment of the various types of insomnia. (pp. 436-437)

* 14.1 Explain why insomnia is often an iatrogenic disorder.

14.2 Describe the effects of sleeping medications on a person's slow-wave and REM sleeping.

14.3 Some people believe themselves to have insomnia when they do not. Offer reasons as to how this can be.

14.4 Describe sleep apnea, and identify those most likely to experience it.

* 14.5 What has been suggested as a cause of sudden infant death?

14.6 If you have a night (or a few nights) of insomnia, what behavioral strategies will increase your probability of returning to a night of restful sleep?

15. Describe the nature and treatment of sleep disorders associated with REM sleep. (pp. 437-438)

* 15.1 Identify two response features common to normal REM sleep.

15.2 Describe cataplexy, its causes, and associated behaviors.

15.3 Describe hypnagogic hallucinations.

15.4 Describe the treatment for cataplexy. What do the effects of this treatment suggest about the effects of LSD and mescaline?

15.6 Describe narcolepsy and its relationship to sleep attacks.

16. Describe the nature and treatment of sleep disorders associated with slow-wave sleep. (pp. 438-440)

16.1 Name the four kinds of slow-wave disorders, including the stage of sleeping in which they occur and the population that is most affected.

* 16.2 What are two common myths about sleepwalking?

* 16.3 What behavioral features of sleeptalking make it similar to a waking state?

* 16.4 How do night terrors differ from nightmares?

* 16.5 When children exhibit enuresis what conclusions are justified about their psychological adjustment?

16.6 Describe the behavioral procedure for eliminating enuresis.

LESSON II SELF TEST

1. Which purpose is shared by withdrawing attention and increasing consciousness?

   a. reduction of verbal control over nonverbal functions of the brain
   b. heightening of awareness
   c. increased delta wave activity
   d. reduction of social inhibition

2. One of the benefits of travel to new and different places is

   a. increasing consciousness during the trip and habituation after the trip.
   b. increasing attention withdrawal during the trip and consciousness after the trip.
   c. decreasing habituation during the trip and increasing routines after the trip.
   d. increasing consciousness during and after the trip.

3. What kind of electrical signal measures the rapid eye movement associated with paradoxical sleep?

   a. polygraph
   b. electro-oculogram
   c. electroencephalogram
   d. electromyogram

4. Janet is asleep. Her brain waves show delta activity. What kind of sleep is Janet experiencing?

   a. drug-induced sleep
   b. REM sleep
   c. slow-wave sleep
   d. stage 1 sleep

5. Frank claims that he does not dream. It is likely that Frank

   a. has sleep that is limited to slow-wave activity.
   b. has an impoverished fantasy life.
   c. has sleep that is desynchronized.
   d. does not wake up during his dreams.

6. Current research on dreams suggests that symbols in dreams

   a. are the private property of the dreamer.
   b. reflect unconscious connections with our forebears.
   c. can only be understood by a person with special training.
   d. form the latent content of dreams.

7. Which of the following situations is likely to produce a decrease in REM sleep and an increase in slow-wave sleep?

   a. sleep deprivation
   b. stimulation of the pons
   c. night terrors
   d. intense physical activity

8. Caroline has not slept in five days. This lack of sleep is likely to

   a. precipitate a psychosis.
   b. make Caroline very sleepy, especially during the night time.
   c. cause a disruption of the synthesis of brain proteins.
   d. intensify Caroline's anxiety and other emotional reactions.

9. The neural mechanisms for sleep may have evolved to ensure

   a. facilitation of memory storage.
   b. emotional assimilation.
   c. synthesis of protein in the brain.
   d. safety and energy conservation.

10. The principal cause of insomnia is

    a. sleep medications.
    b. sleep apnea.
    c. narcoleptic sleep attacks during the day.
    d. cataplexy.

11. Which of the following has been implicated as a cause of sudden infant death?

    a. enuresis
    b. night terrors
    c. sleep apnea
    d. REM-sleep deprivation

12. Individuals who have narcolepsy may put themselves and others in danger because they

    a. can be overcome by a sleep attack at any time.
    b. may become cataplectic especially during emotional situations.
    c. are likely to hallucinate and see things that are not there.
    d. experience uncontrollable bouts of sleep apnea.

13. What is the relationship between hallucinations produced by LSD and dreams?

    a. Both cease during states of cataplexy.
    b. Both occur during slow-wave sleep.
    c. Serotonin-stimulating drugs reduce them.
    d. Both are iatrogenic.

14. Which of the following is a disorder associated with slow- wave sleep?

    a. hypnagogic hallucinations
    b. night terrors
    c. sleep attacks
    d. cataplexy

15. Although asleep, Yvonne would get out of bed and walk to the school that was next door. Which of the following statements is supported by research on sleepwalking?

    a. Yvonne is acting out a deep-seated emotional problem related to school.
    b. Sleep paralysis during REM sleep has been inhibited, probably by damage to some parts of the brain.
    c. When Yvonne is awakened from this stage 4 sleep, she will be confused and disoriented.
    d. If her parents locked the outside door when Yvonne goes to bed, Yvonne will become frustrated and experience night terror if she cannot leave the house.

INTEGRATING QUESTIONS

1. The layperson sometimes thinks that hypnosis is a form of sleep. Compare and contrast hypnosis and sleep in terms of their function and physiological and behavioral effects in order to answer the question, "Is hypnosis a form of sleep?"

2. Define consciousness and explain how the brain maintains consciousness.

3. List as many different ways of altering consciousness as you can. Offer hypotheses as to how three of these methods alter consciousness and as to the evolutionary (functional) purposes of the alteration of consciousness.

ANSWERS

1.1 b) verbal access, verbal control
1.2 verbal access: a, c, f; verbal control: b, d, e
1.4 False
1.6 verbally mediated
1.7 a) no, b) yes, c) no, d) no, e) yes, f) no
2.1 selective attention
3.3 corpus callosum, epilepsy, split-brain
3.4 a) The person will identify the odor correctly because olfactory inputs do not cross to the opposite hemisphere. b) The person will pick the appropriate object because the right hemisphere controls the left hand and olfactory stimuli entering the right nostril go to the right hemisphere. c) The person will be clumsy at this task because the left hemisphere, which controls the right hand, is not very good at perceptual and artistic activities.
4.1 mesmerism
4.2 a) False, c) understanding that one is to be hypnotized
4.3 positive hallucination, negative hallucination, posthypnotic suggestion, posthypnotic amnesia
6.2 b) empathy
7.1 False
8.1 as analgesia, in therapy as aid to breaking bad habits or recalling painful memories, as tool for research into consciousness
9.1 All methods include changes in <u>attention</u> to stimuli. Meditation changes consciousness by either withdrawal of attention or by increasing dishabituation.
9.3 a) learn to ignore other stimuli, hence sharpen focus; b) EEG pattern shows brain processing very little information
9.4 reduce verbal control over nonverbal functions, produce rebound phenomenon
9.5 habituation, increase appreciation of our environment
9.6 encounter new stimuli, do things differently, do something dangerous, withdraw attention from world
10.2 a) high frequency/low amplitude waves, beta activity; b) medium frequency/medium amplitude waves, alpha activity
10.3 EEG records show an increase of lower frequency/higher amplitude waves.
10.4 slow-wave sleep, delta activity
10.5 Low intensity stimuli are less effective in eliciting waking (sensitivity decreases).
11.1 If awakened during REM sleep, people report having a dream.
11.2 REM sleep dreams are narrative stories; slow-wave dreams are situations, usually unpleasant
11.3 latent-underlying meaning of dream; manifest-surface content of dream
12.3 sleepiness, feeling tired and grouchy, Both are correct.
12.7 affect retention of newly learned tasks and assimilation of events that produced strong emotions
14.1 Sleep medications exacerbate the problems associated with insomnia; for example, they disrupt REM sleep
14.5 sleep apnea
15.1 paralysis, dreaming
16.2 acting out dream; indicative of emotional problem
16.3 able to carry on conversation and to be suggestible
16.4 not a dream as such, not occur during REM sleep
16.5 None of these disorders implies that anything is psychologically wrong with the child who displays them.

Chapter 10

Self Test: Lesson I			Self Test: Lesson II		
1.	c	Obj 10-1	1.	b	Obj 10-9
2.	c	Obj 10-1	2.	d	Obj 10-9
3.	a	Obj 10-1	3.	b	Obj 10-10
4.	d	Obj 10-2	4.	c	Obj 10-10
5.	a	Obj 10-2	5.	d	Obj 10-11
6.	c	Obj 10-3	6.	a	Obj 10-11
7.	a	Obj 10-3	7.	d	Obj 10-12
8.	d	Obj 10-4	8.	b	Obj 10-12
9.	d	Obj 10-4	9.	d	Obj 10-13
10.	a	Obj 10-4	10.	a	Obj 10-14
11.	d	Obj 10-4	11.	c	Obj 10-14
12.	b	Obj 10-5	12.	b	Obj 10-15
13.	c	Obj 10-6	13.	c	Obj 10-15
14.	a	Obj 10-7	14.	b	Obj 10-16
15.	a	Obj 10-8	15.	c	Obj 10-16

10.1 OBJ. 10-1

VERBAL ACCESS

10.2 OBJ 10-1

VERBAL CONTROL

10.3 OBJ 10-1

VERBALLY MEDIATED BEHAVIORS

10.4 OBJ 10-2

SELECTIVE ATTENTION

10.5 OBJ 10-2

DICHOTIC LISTENING

10.6 OBJ 10-2

SHADOWING

10.7 OBJ 10-3

ISOLATION APHASIA

10.8 OBJ 10-3

VISUAL AGNOSIA

10.9 OBJ 10-3

CORPUS CALLOSUM

10.10 OBJ 10-3

SPLIT BRAIN OPERATION

10.11 OBJ 10-4

MESMERISM

10.12 OBJ 10-4

POSITIVE HALLUCINATION

10.13 OBJ 10-4

NEGATIVE HALLUCINATION

10.14 OBJ 10-4

POSTHYPNOTIC SUGGESTIBILITY

10.15 OBJ 10-4

POSTHYPNOTIC AMNESIA

10.16 OBJ 10-4

PONZO ILLUSION

10.9 Obj 10-3

largest bundle of association fibers; connects corresponding parts of cortex between both hemispheres of the brain

10.10 Obj 10-3

surgical procedure; cut corpus callosum to reduce severe epileptic seizures

10.11 Obj 10-4

another name for hypnosis, an altered state of consciousness; named after its discoverer Mesmer

10.12 Obj 10-4

perceiving something that is not there; can be produced through hypnosis

10.13 Obj 10-4

not perceiving something that is present; can be produced through hypnosis

10.14 Obj 10-4

tendency to follow instructions given under hypnosis after the hypnotic session has ended

10.15 Obj 10-4

lack of recall for events that occurred during a hypnotic session

10.16 Obj 10-4

belief that one of two parallel horizontal lines of equal length is longer due to slanted lines that form side boundaries

10.1 Obj 10-1

ability to tell ourselves or someone else about the conditions that are affecting us (e.g., "I'm thirsty.")

10.2 Obj 10-1

effect speaking or writing has on behavior of others

10.3 Obj 10-1

complex activities people can perform due to ability to think in words about what they are doing

10.4 Obj 10-2

attending to only some of the features of our environment at a particular time

10.5 Obj 10-2

listening to two auditory stimuli presented simultaneously to each ear

10.6 Obj 10-2

repeating verbal auditory stimuli as they are being presented

10.7 Obj 10-3

caused by brain damage that isolates brain's speech mechanisms from rest of brain; cannot comprehend or produce meaningful speech but can repeat and learn sequences of words

10.8 Obj 10-3

inability to visually recognize object in a person who is not blind; usually caused by brain damage

10.17 OBJ 10-5

NEODISSOCIATION

10.18 OBJ 10-5

HIDDEN OBSERVER

10.19 OBJ 10-6

EMPATHY

10.20 OBJ 10-8

TELEVISION TECHNIQUE

10.21 OBJ 10-10

POLYGRAPH

10.22 OBJ 10-10

ELECTROENCEPHALOGRAM (EEG)

10.23 OBJ 10-10

ELECTROMYOGRAM (EMG)

10.24 OBJ 10-10

ELECTROCARDIOGRAM (EKG)

10.25 OBJ 10-10

ELECTRO-OCULOGRAM (EOG)

10.26 OBJ 10-10

BETA ACTIVITY

10.27 OBJ 10-10

ALPHA ACTIVITY

10.28 OBJ 10-10

DELTA ACTIVITY

10.29 OBJ 10-10

SLOW-WAVE SLEEP

10.30 OBJ 10-10

RAPID EYE MOVEMENT SLEEP (REM SLEEP)

10.31 OBJ 10-11

LATENT CONTENT

10.32 OBJ 10-11

MANIFEST CONTENT

10.25 Obj 10-10

record produced by polygraph of electrical activity of eye movements

10.26 Obj 10-10

high frequency, low amplitude EEG activity; characteristic of awake, alert state

10.27 Obj 10-10

medium frequency, medium amplitude EEG activity; characteristic of calm, relaxed state

10.28 Obj 10-10

low frequency, high amplitude EEG activity; characteristic of deep (Stage 4) sleep

10.29 Obj 10-10

stages 2-4 of sleep, characterized by low frequency EEG activity

10.30 Obj 10-10

paradoxical, active, or desynchronized sleep, characterized by dreams, activation, muscular paralysis

10.31 Obj 10-11

in Freud's view, the actual, hidden subject matter of a dream, expressing unresolved, repressed sexual conflicts or desires

10.32 Obj 10-11

in Freud's view, the plot or story line of a dream; actually a symbolic representation of the latent content expressed in nonsexual events

10.17 Obj 10-5

Hilgard's theory that hypnosis divides consciousness into separate channels of mental activity

10.18 Obj 10-5

part of hypnotized person's consciousness that has become dissociated from the rest

10.19 Obj 10-6

imagining ourselves in someone else's situation; according to Barber, related to ability to be hypnotized

10.20 Obj 10-8

hypnotic technique used in criminal investigation to help witnesses recall details of the crime

10.21 Obj 10-10

apparatus for measuring and recording various physiological responses; used in sleep research and as "lie detector"

10.22 Obj 10-10

record produced by polygraph of brain's electrical activity

10.23 Obj 10-10

record produced by polygraph of the electrical activity of muscles

10.24 Obj 10-10

record produced by polygraph of the electrical activity of the heart

10.33 OBJ 10-12

FLOWERPOT TECHNIQUE

10.34 OBJ 10-14

IATROGENIC DISORDER

10.35 OBJ 10-14

SLEEP APNEA

10.36 OBJ 10-14

SUDDEN INFANT DEATH SYNDROME

10.37 OBJ 10-15

CATAPLEXY

10.38 OBJ 10-15

HYPNAGOGIC HALLUCINATION

10.39 OBJ 10-15

NARCOLEPSY

10.40 OBJ 10-15

SLEEP ATTACK

10.41 OBJ 10-16

SLEEPWALKING

10.42 OBJ 10-16

SLEEPTALKING

10.43 OBJ 10-16

NIGHT TERRORS

10.44 OBJ 10-16

ENURESIS

10.41 Obj 10-16

walking during deepest (Stage 4) sleep; not symptomatic of emotional problem nor acting out dream; children usually outgrow this

10.42 Obj 10-16

talking during sleep, usually during non-REM sleep; person suggestible at this time

10.43 Obj 10-16

child awakens in great fear; apparently caused by sudden awakenings from Stage 4 sleep; not a nightmare

10.44 Obj 10-16

bedwetting; disorder associated with slow-wave sleep; can be cured by conditioning procedure

10.33 Obj 10-12

experimental procedure to study REM-sleep deprivation in rats

10.34 Obj 10-14

disorder produced by attempts to treat a symptom, e.g. insomnia caused by sleeping pills

10.35 Obj 10-14

sleep disorder in which people become unable to breathe while asleep

10.36 Obj 10-14

crib death; infants mysteriously die during sleep; may be caused by sleep apnea

10.37 Obj 10-15

attack in which the victim remains conscious but paralyzed; caused by REM sleep mechanisms

10.38 Obj 10-15

dreamlike imagery preceding sleep; accompanied by paralysis

10.39 Obj 10-15

"numbness seizure"; general term for a disorder that includes sleep attacks, cataplexy, and hypnagogic hallucinations

10.40 Obj 10-15

uncontrollable, sudden wave of irresistible sleepiness; person awakens feeling refreshed

CHAPTER 11
Motivation

INTRODUCTION

The study of motivation is divided into two parts. The first is a consideration of the nature of motivation and reinforcement and control of eating (Lesson I Objectives 1-10). The second focuses on the motivated behaviors of sex and aggression (Lesson II Objectives 11-19).

CONCEPT CARDS AND EXERCISES

After you have surveyed and read the text, assemble the concept cards located at the end of this chapter. Use them to learn the important terms, then begin reading the text again, one learning objective at a time, and work through the exercises for each lesson. Answers for questions marked with an asterisk are found at the end of the chapter.

SELF TESTS

Each lesson is followed by a multiple-choice self test. After you are proficient with a lesson's concept cards and exercises, take the self test to see whether you have mastered the material. Review those objectives for questions you answered incorrectly.

INTEGRATING QUESTIONS

To challenge yourself further, answer the integrating questions at the end of the chapter. These questions ask you to apply the information you have learned to consider larger theoretical or real-life issues.

LESSON I: THE NATURE OF MOTIVATION AND REINFORCEMENT AND CONTROL OF EATING

1. Describe drives and explain the drive reduction theories of Hull and Spence. (pp. 446-447)

* 1.1 What is a drive? Be sure to include more than examples in your answer. Look at your examples, are all drives based on biological needs?

* 1.2 a) Who devised the most important theory of motivation and reinforcement based on drive and drive reduction?

b) According to this theory, what is the role of drive?

c) Identify what directs behavior.

d) State the formula for determining the relationship between drive strength, habit strength, and the excitatory potential of a response.

* 1.3 a) Who extended the drive-reduction theory?

* b) What new concept was added?

c) Explain this new concept and list a few examples.

* 1.4 Your afternoon chemistry lab was going slowly and you were beginning to get hungry. You went into the hall and purchased a bag of potato chips from a vending machine.

a) Identify the drive that motivated your behavior.

b) Explain your behavior of operating the vending machine in terms of the drive-reduction hypothesis of motivation.

c) If you had never seen a vending machine before, what would be the excitatory potential of making the response of operating it, according to the formula in 1.2 d? Why?

1.5 What two serious problems are confronted by theories of motivation and reinforcement that depend on the concept of drive?

2. Describe the problems with drive-reduction theories and explain the alternative optimum arousal hypothesis. (pp. 447-451)

2.1 Why do observations that some reinforcing events actually increase drive pose a problem for the drive-reduction theory?

2.2 Describe the classic research of

a) Sheffield, Wulff, and Backer (1951) with male rats and sexually receptive females.

b) Olds and Milner with rats and the effects of electrical brain stimulation.

c) How do these results contradict the drive-reduction theory?

* 2.3 What new theory was proposed to explain the positive and negative aspects of reinforcement?

* 2.4 According to this theory, when arousal level is too ______________, less stimulation is sought; and when arousal level is too low, ______________ stimulation is reinforcing.

3. Explain the features of expectancy theory that may help to explain human motivation. (pp. 451-453)

3.1 In general, what do expectancy theories attempt to explain?

* 3.2 a) Name the four variables that influence a person's motivation to perform a particular behavior, as suggested by the theory of achievement motivation.

b) The relation of these variables is expressed in a formula that permits an experimenter to predict a person's ______________ ______________.

3.3 How would you describe a high school senior who applies to some colleges and universities that are extremely selective and some that are nonselective, but does not apply to schools in the middle range. Explain this behavior in terms of the four factors named in 3.2.

3.4 For the Thematic Apperception Test (TAT), explain

a) the testing procedure.

b) what the results apparently measure.

* 3.5 Can you think of some tasks that a person with a high motivation to avoid failure would approach or avoid? If you had access to some people who would volunteer as experimental subjects, could you test whether or not you were correct? The fact that you probably could illustrates what positive feature of expectancy theory?

3.6 What is a drawback to the expectancy theory?

4. Describe the motivating roles of intermittent and conditioned reinforcers. (pp. 453-454)

* 4.1 Why does a fisherman who catches fish occasionally continue to try on a day when he is completely unsuccessful?

4.2 Working with very young rats, what did Chen and Amsel (1980a) demonstrate about the effects of intermittent reinforcement?

4.3 Helen has worked as the assistant bookkeeper in a small business for five years. She takes pride in the fact that the accounts she handles always balance. Her supervisor has sometimes commented on her accuracy. Although she has still not been promoted to head bookkeeper, she continues to work carefully. Explain Helen's motivation in terms of conditioned reinforcement and satisfaction.

5. Describe how reinforcement can affect intrinsic motivation and relate this influence to preference for free-choice situations. (pp.454-458)

* 5.1 What is intrinsic motivation? Explain what is intrinsically motivating about Helen's bookkeeping job.

* 5.2 What is extrinsic reinforcement?

5.3 Lepper, Greene, and Nisbett (1973) studied the relationship between intrinsic motivation and extrinsic reinforcement with nursery school children.

a) Briefly describe the experiment, including the treatment of the three groups.

b) Consult Figure 11.5 and summarize what the researchers observed a few days later.

c) Explain the results in terms of effect of the extrinsic reinforcer on intrinsic motivation.

5.4 Discuss the most important characteristic of an extrinsic reinforcer that influences its effect on intrinsic motivation. Cite research by Deci (1971, 1975) in your answer.

5.5 Because we believe that we are free to choose, scientists study the consequences of this belief. For research on this topic by Swann and Pittman (1977)

a) describe both experimental groups of school children.

b) what did children in each group prefer to play with when they actually were free to choose?

c) discuss the results in terms of what appears to influence preference for free choice.

5.6 How did Catania and Sagvolden (1980) investigate free choice in pigeons?

6. Describe learned helplessness and the conditions that lead to it. (pp. 458-459)

* 6.1 Describe learned helplessness. How does this phenomena differ from other examples of learning that you have studied in this chapter?

6.2 Describe the basic research of Overmeier and Seligman (1967) on learned helplessness.

6.3 How does Seligman interpret the results of this study?

6.4 What alternative explanation of learned helplessness did McReynolds advance?

* 6.5 Phil was mistreated by the teachers running the day-care center he attended while his parents were at work. They ridiculed him in front of the other children, and sometimes abused him physically. At first he tried to defend himself, but he was no match for them, and eventually he became passive. His parents noticed that his behavior changed at home. He seemed to have lost his initiative.

What predictions would Seligman and McReynolds make about Phil's future behavior?

7. Summarize the role of physiological mechanisms of reinforcement and describe the reinforcing effects of opiates. (pp. 459-463)

7.1 Consult Figure 11.9 as you answer this question. If the lateral hypothalamus is electrically stimulated

a) what kinds of behaviors are elicited?

b) and a behavior is reinforced, neural mechanisms of reinforcement must somehow be connected to what?

c) what substance do the terminal buttons of neurons there release?

d) the activity of neurons in what nearby region of the brain are altered?

e) what is the effect on behavior?

7.2 Now consult Figure 11.10 in your text as you answer this question. Concerning research by Rolls and his colleagues, (Rolls, 1982)

a) What neural pathway did they trace?

b) What class of stimuli did they find activated neurons in a portion of visual association cortex on the temporal lobe?

c) Name one of the regions of the brain that these neurons send axons to.

d) What kinds of stimuli did neurons in the amygdala respond to and under what conditions did they respond?

e) Name one region of the brain that neurons in the amygdala project to.

f) What kinds of stimuli did neurons in the lateral hypothalamus respond to and under what conditions?

g) What substance is released into the nucleus accumbens?

h) In general, what happens to behavior when this substance is released in the nucleus accumbens?

* 7.3 How do stimulant drugs such as cocaine affect the re-uptake of dopamine in the brain?

* 7.4 Describe the principal effects of opiates in the brain.

7.5 Summarize the way stimulant drugs and opiates are thought to influence reinforcement.

8. Describe the physiological mechanisms and learning processes that initiate eating. (pp. 463-467)

* 8.1 a) What one word can you use to describe an important influence on what we eat and when we eat? b) How does the presence of others affect our eating?

8.2 Turning to the role of physiological factors that initiating eating, how did Cannon explain hunger? Cite research that has disproved his theory.

8.3 Outline the glucostatic hypothesis proposed by Jean Mayer.

* 8.4 Who demonstrated where glucose detectors are located?

8.5 What did Russek observe that caused him to look for glucose receptors outside the brain?

8.6 Describe Russek's research pinpointing the site.

9. Describe the physiological mechanisms and learning processes that bring a meal to its end. (pp. 467-468)

* 9.1 Now consider the physiological factors that stop eating. What common sense observation suggests that the stomach must contain receptors to stop eating? Cite supporting research.

9.2 What happened when researchers removed some of the food from the stomachs of rats that had just eaten?

9.3 Rats who received milk injections in their stomachs stopped eating sooner than rats who had received a dilute salt solution. Why?

9.4 For research conducted by Booth, Mather, and Fuller (1982

a) What was their hypothesis?

* b) What was the independent variable?

* c) What was the dependent variable?

d) What were the results?

e) What do the results suggest about the role of learning and food intake?

10. Describe the factors that may produce obesity. (pp. 469-472)

10.1 How does habit influence how much we eat?

10.2 What is an "efficient metabolism" and how does it affect body weight?

10.3 a) When nonobese volunteers began to consume up to 8000 calories a day, what happened to their weight?

b) Later, when they were allowed to choose their own diet, what happened to their weight?

c) How does their experience with weight loss differ from the experience of obese people?

10.4 Describe research that supports the notion that differences in metabolism appear to have a hereditary basis.

* 10.5 a) Will overweight children "outgrow" their obesity?

b) Offer one explanation why obese juveniles become obese adults.

10.6 Cite human and animal research on the role of prenatal malnutrition and obesity. How does this research help us explain why obesity is seen more often in people of lower socioeconomic status?

10.7 After studying a group of Indian men, what did Mayer conclude about the relationship between physical activity and food intake?

LESSON I SELF TEST

1. Which of these is a drive?

   a. eating three meals a day
   b. hunger
   c. eating chicken and fish, but not red meat
   d. habit

2. According to the drive-reduction theory of motivation

   a. drive energize an organism's behavior and reinforcement reduces drive.
   b. both drive and reinforcement energize an organism's behavior
   c. drive energizes an organism's behavior and habit inhibits drive reduction
   d. drive and habit are synonymous.

3. Research on the effects of electrical brain stimulation suggests that stimulation of certain areas of the brain

   a. reduces drive.
   b. results in learned helplessness.
   c. increases drive.
   d. impairs natural feedback.

4. According to the achievement motivation theory, the four factors that effect motivation to perform a particular task are

   a. expectation of success, need to achieve, peer pressure, and previous experience.
   b. drive strength, habit formation, incentive value, and need to achieve.
   c. drive strength, perceived value of task, previous experience, peer pressure
   d. expectation of success, perceived value of task, need to achieve, and motivation to avoid failure.

5. Chris is studying Spanish. She was very pleased with herself when she was able to read and understand a notice in Spanish about kindergarten registration printed in the local newspaper. Chris will most likely continue to study Spanish

   a. diligently to obtain a good grade.
   b. because she has learned to obtain satisfaction from small successes.
   c. because her small successes with the language have lowered her motivation to avoid failure.
   d. diligently because her success with the language has been reinforced continuously.

6. If an extrinsic reinforcer is not to cause undermining of intrinsic reinforcement, it should

   a. correlate positively with the intrinsic reinforcer.
   b. be able to be manipulated experimentally.
   c. be based on a person's performance.
   d. remain constant.

7. One group of school children was told to draw with felt-tipped pens and another group was told they could choose a toy, but were actually subtly persuaded to play with the pens. The "free-choice" group chose the pens more often than the other group did when they could pick any toy to play with because

a. we value activities that we are allowed to choose more highly than those that are chosen for us.
b. habit can be reinforced easily.
c. felt-tipped pens were still new at that time and novelty is an important component of free choice.
d. we value activities that are part of a scientific experiment.

8. Learned helplessness involves learning that an aversive event cannot be avoided

a. only postponed.
b. or escaped.
c. but can be predicted.
d. only modified.

9. What chemical is released when the lateral hypothalamus is stimulated?

a. serotonin
b. RNA
c. dopamine
d. lithium

10. How do stimulant drugs such as amphetamines and cocaine produce their reinforcing effects?

a. by facilitating the release of transmitter substances
b. by closing the post-synaptic gap
c. by preventing dopamine from being released
d. by slowing the re-uptake of dopamine by the terminal buttons

11. If you miss a meal, you will

a. notice that your stomach churns until you eat again.
b. jeopardize your body's homeostasis.
c. find that your hunger decreases about the time the meal you missed would have ended.
d. feel tired until you eat again.

12. The empty stomach hypothesis was

a. undermined by research that found a relationship between hunger pangs and stomach contractions.
b. challenged by evidence that hunger occurs even after the stomach is surgically removed.
c. supported by evidence that the stomach empties more quickly during vigorous physical activity.
d. invalidated by pioneering research that located the glucostat.

13. The detectors for satiety are located in the

a. liver
b. stomach walls
c. villi of the intestines
d. lymph nodes

14. Research on obesity suggests that

a. drinking two glasses of water before a meal will curb the appetite.
b. people with an "efficient metabolism" must consume more calories than normal people in order to maintain their body weight.
c. eating three meals a day is largely a matter of custom.
d. as people grow older the effect that activity has on maintaining body weight decreases.

15. Obese children do not

   a. suffer some social stigma.
   b. become obese adults.
   c. have the same number of fat cells that normal weight children have.
   d. have success with adult diets because they are based on the adult metabolism.

LESSON II: SEXUAL BEHAVIOR AND AGGRESSION

11. Compare the responses of males and females to erotic imagery. (pp.472-473)

11.1 Compare the responses of men and women to picture of couples in a) romantic situations and b) explicit sexual situations.

11.2 According to Masters and Johnson, how do men and women respond to an erotic picture of an attractive woman or an attractive man?

11.3 In what way does sexual orientation influence a person's sexual fantasies?

12. Describe the role of androgens in sexual responses. (pp. 473-475)

* 12.1 Describe the organizational effects of androgens on prenatal development?

* 12.2 Describe the activational effects of androgens on sexual response. Cite supporting research with laboratory animals.

12.3 How did men whose testes failed to secrete normal amounts of androgens respond to monthly injections of testosterone? of a placebo?

12.4 What are the effects of castration on sex drive in the human males? What may account for this progression? What medical treatment is effective?

* 12.5 How does the anticipation of sexual activity affect testosterone production?

* 12.6 Does testosterone effect sexual preference?

12.7 Cite research that defines the effect of androgens on sex drive and sexual desire in women.

13. Describe the role of progesterone and estrogen in sexual responses. (pp. 475-478)

* 13.1 In most species of mammals, the hormones _______________ and _______________ have strong effects on female sexual behavior. The levels of these hormones _______________

during the ______________ ______________ of primates and the ______________

______________ of other female mammals.

13.2 a) Describe the sexual response of a female laboratory rat when her blood levels of estradiol and progesterone are high.

b) When blood levels of these hormones drop, perhaps as a result of surgery to remove the ovaries, how is her sexual response affected?

13.3 Contrast the sexual receptivity of human females and female rats throughout their respective cycles. What is the most important difference in the receptivity of human females and female rats? How may this difference foster the formation of monogamous relationships in humans?

* 13.4 During the menstrual cycle

a) which hormone peaks at midcycle?

b) which hormone dominates in the second half of the cycle?

c) what happens to levels of both hormones near the end of the cycle?

13.5 Describe female sexual desire throughout the menstrual cycle noting the peak periods and accompanying sexual desires.

13.6 How does menopause effect a woman's sex drive?

14. Compare transvestism and transsexualism. (pp. 477-479)

* 14.1 Transvestism is an example of a(n) ______________.

* 14.2 Are men or women most likely to develop paraphilias? Why?

14.3 List some of the explanations for the occurrence of paraphilias.

14.4 For both transvestism and transexualism

a) define the term.

b) are people with these conditions most likely to be men or women?

c) compare the reasons why each group dresses in clothes of the opposite sex.

14.5 What do experts speculate about the causes of transsexualism?

15. Describe the adaptive significance of aggression and the nature and value of ritualized aggression. (pp. 480-481)

* 15.1 Define <u>intraspecific aggression</u>.

15.2 List two biological advantages of intraspecific aggression for animals. Are there any apparent advantages for humans?

15.3 Give an example of a threat gesture and an appeasement gesture.

15.4 What is the survival value of these ritualized displays of aggression?

16. Describe the evidence for the role of brain mechanisms and hormones in aggression. (pp. 481-482)

16.1 What are the effects of electrical stimulation of the hypothalamus and other parts of the limbic system on aggression in animals? Compare these effects with the effects on aggression when certain brain structure are destroyed.

16.2 What appears to be the role of the limbic system in aggression?

* 16.3 What is psychosurgery? What is the essential difference between psychosurgery and the neurosurgery described in this section?

* 16.4 Why is it difficult to evaluate the success of psychosurgery in controlling aggression?

16.5 Cite research on the organization and activational effects of testosterone on aggression in laboratory rats. What preliminary research suggests this hormone may also affect aggression by human males?

17. Describe the effects of imitation on aggression. (pp. 482-484)

17.1 Name the two important models of aggression for children cited in your text. Can you think of others?

17.2 Describe research that supports and challenges the conclusion that television violence promotes human violence.

18. Describe the relation of frustration to aggression. (pp. 484-485)

18.1 Briefly summarize the frustration-aggression hypothesis proposed by Dollard et al. (1939). Pay special attention to their definition of frustration, the invariable result of frustration and the kinds of aggression this hypothesis attempts to explain.

* 18.2 What important conclusion of this hypothesis did Berkowitz (1978) dispute?

* 18.3 Give several examples of aggressive behaviors that are not caused by frustration.

18.4 How did Berkowitz test the possibility that frustration may invariably increase an organism's tendency to behave aggressively?

* 18.5 What modification of the frustration-aggression hypothesis has Berkowitz suggested?

18.6 Explain the evolutionary significance for a species of animal whose members have learned to continue fighting while in pain.

18.7 Describe research (Berkowitz and Frodi, 1977) on pain and aggressive behavior in humans.

19. Describe experimental evaluation of the role of catharsis in suppressing aggression. (pp. 485-486)

* 19.1 Define and give an example of catharsis in daily life.

19.2 Review the research of Geen, Stonner, and Shope (1975) and answer these questions.

a) Some subjects were given the opportunity to punish the confederate twice and others only once. According to the catharsis hypothesis of aggressive behavior, which subjects should show less anger? Why?

b) Did blood-pressure readings confirm the catharsis hypothesis?

c) What behavioral effects did punishing the confederate have on each group of subjects? Why?

d) In view of this research, how satisfactory is the catharsis theory?

LESSON II SELF TEST

1. Research indicates that women

a. find pictures of couples in romantic situations sexually arousing.
b. are not aroused by pictures of couples in explicitly sexual situations.
c. find that romantic novels are not as sexually arousing as pictures of romantic situations.
d. prefer to read romantic novels toward the end of their menstrual cycle.

2. The organizational effects of testosterone on male sexual development are

a. are also an important determinant of intelligence.
b. alter the organization of the sex organs and the brain.
c. are completely reversed by socialization.
d. occur during puberty.

3. The activational effects of testosterone on male sexual development are

a. to delay the onset of puberty.
b. frequently associated with low sperm production.
c. to initiate responses in sex organs and brain circuits that have already developed.
d. to increase preference for athletics.

4. If a man who has been castrated is given testosterone supplements, his ability to have intercourse will

a. be fully restored.
b. decline, only more slowly than if he did not receive testosterone.
c. be restored, but he will have to take ever increasing amounts to maintain his potency.
d. always be unpredictable.

5. Female laboratory rats

   a. form life-long pair bonds.
   b. permit copulation throughout the estrous cycle.
   c. have never been observed to initiate sexual activity.
   d. mate only when their blood levels of estradiol and progesterone are high.

6. Maura reports that her interest in sexual activity has been very high for the last few days. It is likely that

   a. her testosterone level is low.
   b. her progesterone level is high.
   c. she is in midcycle.
   d. she is taking birth control pills.

7. Some investigators have suggested human monogamous relationships are possible because

   a. humans are the only primates capable of experiencing love.
   b. of sophisticated birth control techniques.
   c. women are potentially willing to engage in sex throughout the reproductive cycle.
   d. of the selective advantage conferred by a tightly organized social structure.

8. Paraphilias are

   a. seen only in Western cultures.
   b. practiced by more women than men.
   c. now understood by social psychologists.
   d. abnormal sexual practices.

9. Which of the following is a biological advantage of intraspecific aggression?

   a. provides all animals with an opportunity to mate, which prevents the gene pool from shrinking
   b. deters members of the species from roaming and exposing themselves to danger from other predators
   c. maintains the feeding hierarchy assuring the oldest and weakest animals the first share of the kill
   d. tends to disperse the population into new areas where new environmental conditions may increase flexibility of the species

10. A recent nature series filmed a male wolf intruding into the territory of another. The owner of the territory growled, bared his teeth, and raised the fur on the back of his neck. Suddenly the intruder lowered his head and put his tail between his legs. The intruder forestalled intraspecific aggression by exhibiting a(n)

    a. threat gesture
    b. subversive gesture
    c. appeasement gesture
    d. ambivalent gesture

11. Considering research on the biology of aggression, psychosurgery appears to be

    a. the treatment of choice for highly aggressive individuals.
    b. an experimental procedure whose effects have not been evaluated carefully.
    c. most effective when combined with behavior modification therapy.
    d. an appropriate treatment for adults, but not children.

12. Field studies on the effects of long-term television viewing on violence in children suggest that

a. children readily recognize fact and fantasy.
b. boys are not more likely that girls to be influenced by violent television shows.
c. long-term viewing of violence may cause children to be more violent, but definite evidence is lacking.
d. any negative effects of viewing violent shows can be mitigated if the child watches with a parent or caregiver.

13. Dollard et al. (1939) hypothesized that

a. frustration causes all forms of aggression.
b. different brain regions mediate different forms of aggression.
c. acceptable forms of aggression are culturally influenced.
d. aggressive behavior is intrinsically rewarding.

14. Berkowitz and Frodi (1977) demonstrated that pain

a. can be reduced or eliminated by psychosurgery.
b. produced in the laboratory is different from pain experienced in real life.
c. can elicit aggressive behavior.
d. is a highly individualized response.

15. Freudians suggest that acting out aggression leads to __________.

a. catharsis
b. frustration
c. intraspecific aggression
d. heightened drive

INTEGRATING QUESTIONS

1. It's hard to miss ads for local diet centers, weight control workshops, and diet counselors. You may have read about the Scarsdale Diet, the Grapefruit Diet or the Calories Don't Count Diet. In spite of all these efforts, why haven't we found the perfect diet?

2. If research on the effects of television violence on juvenile violence is still uncertain when you have children, what kinds of television shows do you think you will permit them to watch?

3. What kind of motivational strategies can you use to help you persevere and study for a difficult and uninteresting course that is required?

ANSWERS

1.1 Drive is an unpleasant state that energizes an organism's behavior. Examples include those based on physiological needs, such as the need for food, water, and warmth, and those not based on physiological needs, such as sexual drive.
1.2 a) Hull b) energizes, but does not give direction to behavior c) habit d) E = D x H (excitatory potential = drive x habit strength)
1.3 a) Spence b) incentive
1.4 a) Hunger was the drive that caused you to operate the vending machine. b) Operating the vending machine is a habit—that is, a learned behavior that was previously reinforced by drive reduction in the presence of particular stimuli and now gives direction to behavior. c) zero, because habit strength would be zero
2.3 optimum level hypothesis

2.4 high; more
3.2 a) expectation of succeeding at a task, perceived value of the goal, need to achieve (success motivation), motivation to avoid failure b) resultant motivation
3.5 If you can think of some specific examples in which people with a high motivation to avoid failure chose either very easy or very difficult tasks, you have demonstrated that the theory makes specific predictions that can be tested experimentally.
4.1 The behavior has been intermittently reinforced.
5.1 The notion that performance of a task can be its own reward. Helen finds making her accounts balance satisfying (intrinsically motivating).
5.2 Reinforcers delivered to a subject after performing a task that are not related to the level of the person's performance on the task.
6.1 Learning that an aversive event cannot be avoided or escaped no matter what the organism does. Previous examples were of cases in which organisms learned about the consequences of their behavior (instrumental conditioning) or the relation between stimuli (classical conditioning).
6.5 According to Seligman, Phil has learned that his behavior has no effect on escaping or avoiding aversive stimuli. He will generalize what he has learned, and will become more passive. According to McReynolds, Phil has not yet learned that he is powerless only in some situations. In future situations, if he learns to recognize that the schedule of reinforcement has changed, he will begin to try again. The more similar a new situation is to the ones in which he was mistreated, the less likely he will recognize the change.
7.3 They slow re-uptake.
7.4 mimic effects of endorphins—brain's natural reinforcers that are released at times of stress and arousal
8.1 a) habit b) We are more likely to feel hungry and consume more food in the presence of others who are eating.
8.4 Russek
9.1 We fill our stomach with food when we eat, but we stop eating well before appreciable amounts of nutrients are absorbed from the intestine into the bloodstream. Hunger can be abolished by injecting food directly into an animal's stomach.
9.4 b) nutritional value of soup c) number of sandwiches eaten
10.5 a) Although more research needs to be done, the answer appears to be probably not. b) Juvenile obesity may predispose these children to adult obesity because of an increase in the number of fat cells in their bodies.
12.1 causes male sex organs to develop and affects brain development
12.2 activates sex organs and brain circuits that have already developed; 1) if the organizational effects of androgens on brain development are prevented, the animal later fails to exhibit male sexual behavior 2) the ability of males to have intercourse depends on presence of testosterone in adulthood.
12.5 increases
12.6 No. It will only increase desire for the object of preference that was determined by some other mechanism.
13.1 progesterone, estrogen, fluctuate, menstrual cycle, estrous cycle
13.4 a) estradiol b) progesterone c) Both fall.
14.1 paraphilia
14.2 No. Male sexuality appears to be more easily disrupted.
15.1 attack by one animal upon another member of the same species
16.3 Psychosurgery is the removal of brain tissue to alter a person's behavior without direct evidence of tissue abnormality. The woman thrown from the horse had clear evidence of brain damage.
16.4 Preoperative and postoperative evaluations have not been carefully performed.
18.2 That all aggressive acts are caused by frustration
18.3 attack by trained dogs, assassination by hired killers, aggressive behavior caused by pain
18.5 restructure hypothesis to account for other aversive stimuli like pain
19.1 Catharsis is a decline in the aggressive drive following an actual or symbolic act of aggression. Getting rid of your aggressive feelings by yelling at your spouse in the morning, then being cheerful and pleasant the rest of the day.

Chapter 11

Self Test: Lesson I			Self Test: Lesson II		
1.	b	Obj. 11-1	1.	a	Obj. 11-11
2.	a	Obj. 11-2	2.	b	Obj. 11-12
3.	a	Obj. 11-2	3.	c	Obj. 11-12
4.	d	Obj. 11-3	4.	a	Obj. 11-12
5.	b	Obj. 11-4	5.	d	Obj. 11-13
6.	c	Obj. 11-5	6.	c	Obj. 11-13
7.	a	Obj. 11-5	7.	c	Obj. 11-13
8.	b	Obj. 11-6	8.	d	Obj. 11-14
9.	c	Obj. 11-7	9.	d	Obj. 11-15
10.	d	Obj. 11-7	10.	c	Obj. 11-15
11.	c	Obj. 11-8	11.	b	Obj. 11-16
12.	b	Obj. 11-8	12.	c	Obj. 11-17
13.	b	Obj. 11-9	13.	a	Obj. 11-18
14.	c	Obj. 11-10	14.	c	Obj. 11-18
15.	c	Obj. 11-10	15.	a	Obj. 11-19

11.1 OBJ 11-1

MOTIVATION

11.2 OBJ 11-1

DRIVE

11.3 OBJ 11-1

DRIVE-REDUCTION HYPOTHESIS

11.4 OBJ 11-1

HABIT

11.5 OBJ 11-1

INCENTIVE

11.6 OBJ 11-2

OPTIMUM LEVEL HYPOTHESIS

11.7 OBJ 11-2

DIVERSIVE EXPLORATION

11.8 OBJ 11-2

SPECIFIC EXPLORATION

11.9 OBJ 11-3

EXPECTANCY THEORIES

11.10 OBJ 11-3

THEORY OF
ACHIEVEMENT MOTIVATION

11.11 OBJ 11-3

NEED TO ACHIEVE

11.12 OBJ 11-3

MOTIVATION TO AVOID FAILURE

11.13 OBJ 11-3

RESULTANT MOTIVATION

11.14 OBJ 11-3

THEMATIC APPERCEPTION TEST
(TAT)

11.15 OBJ 11-5

INTRINSIC MOTIVATION

11.16 OBJ 11-5

EXTRINSIC REINFORCERS

11.9 Obj 11-3

explanations of motivation based on what people think will happen if they engage in a particular behavior

11.10 Obj 11-3

McClelland et al.: based on person's assessment of value of a goal; assumes need to achieve source of human motivation

11.11 Obj 11-3

according to Murray, human tendency to try to do something difficult as well and as quickly as possible

11.12 Obj 11-3

basic personality trait in achievement motivation theory; need that causes people to avoid tasks in which they may fail

11.13 Obj 11-3

product of formula that expresses relation of four variables: expectation of success, perceived value of success, and motivation to achieve success and motivation to avoid failure

11.14 Obj 11-3

measures success motivation by examining story a person tells while looking at drawings of ambiguous situations

11.15 Obj 11-5

reinforcement that is an integral part of performing a task

11.16 Obj 11-5

reinforcement that is delivered to a subject after performing a task

11.1 Obj 11-1

effects of reinforcers and punishers or stimuli associated with them that alter the probability of an organism engaging in an activity

11.2 Obj 11-1

state of imbalance, often caused by physiological need, that can energizes behavior; according to Hull, does not provide direction for behavior

11.3 Obj 11-1

notion that the aversive state of imbalance caused by unfulfilled physiological needs motivates behaviors that are reinforcing if imbalance is corrected

11.4 Obj 11-1

according to Hull, a learned behavior that was previously reinforced by drive reduction in the presence of particular stimuli

11.5 Obj 11-1

energizes behavior through an organism's anticipation that performance of a particular behavior will secure the reinforcer

11.6 Obj 11-2

attempt to explain positive and negative reinforcement; organisms seek an ideal (moderate) level of arousal

11.7 Obj 11-2

according to Berlyne, one of two forms of exploration; response to understimulation that increases diversity of stimuli that the organism contacts

11.8 Obj 11-2

according to Berlyne, one of two forms of exploration; response to overstimulation that leads to need fulfillment and decrease of drive level

11.17 OBJ 11-6

LEARNED HELPLESSNESS

11.18 OBJ 11-8

REGULATORY BEHAVIORS

11.19 OBJ 11-8

HOMEOSTASIS

11.20 OBJ 11-8

GLYCOGEN

11.21 OBJ 11-8

GLUCOSTATIC HYPOTHESIS

11.22 OBJ 11-11

ORGANIZATIONAL EFFECTS

11.23 OBJ 11-11

ACTIVATIONAL EFFECTS

11.24 OBJ 11-14

PARAPHILLIA

11.25 OBJ 11-14

TRANSVESTISM

11.26 OBJ 11-14

TRAVESTISM

11.27 OBJ 11-15

INTRASPECIFIC AGGRESSION

11.28 OBJ 11-15

THREAT GESTURES

11.29 OBJ 11-15

APPEASEMENT GESTURES

11.30 OBJ 11-16

PSYCHOSURGERY

11.31 OBJ 11-18

FRUSTRATION

11.32 OBJ 11-19

CATHARSIS

11.25 Obj 11-14

deriving most or all sexual gratification from dressing in the clothes of the opposite sex

11.26 Obj 11-14

strong, abnormal desire to assume the identity of a member of the other sex

11.27 Obj 11-15

attack by an animal upon another member of the same species

11.28 Obj 11-15

action that communicates to another animal an intent to engage in violence before actually doing so

11.29 Obj 11-15

action of an animal threatened by another; signals defeat before an attack begins

11.30 Obj 11-16

removal of brain tissue to alter a person's behavior without direct evidence that the tissue was abnormal or damaged

11.31 Obj 11-18

event that prevents an animal from engaging in a behavior that normally achieves a particular goal; according to Dollard et al., results in aggression

11.32 Obj 11-19

view that if aroused, the aggressive drive must find actual or symbolic outlet; once "released," the aggressive drive will decrease

11.17 Obj 11-6

realization that aversive events cannot be avoided or escaped regardless of what the organism does

11.18 Obj 11-8

a behavior that corrects physiological deficits or imbalances; e.g., drinking, eating, shivering

11.19 Obj 11-8

process of detection and correction of deficits or imbalances;
motivates organism to engage in appropriate regulatory behavior

11.20 Obj 11-8

animal starch—one of two forms of nutrient storage in the body that can later be broken down into glucose

11.21 Obj 11-8

Mayer's theory that hunger occurs with drop in blood level of glucose detected by glucostats that activate neural circuit to makes person hungry and eat

11.22 Obj 11-11

effect of hormones that influences development—for example, of the sex organs and neural circuits in the brain

11.23 Obj 11-11

effect of sex hormones that activate organs or brain circuits that have already developed

11.24 Obj 11-14

"unusual" sexual behavior directed toward an object or body part, such as articles of clothing or hair

CHAPTER 12
Emotion

INTRODUCTION

This chapter considers emotions (Objectives 1-3), their expression and recognition (Objectives 4-12), elicitation (Objectives 13-15), feelings,and cognitive and physiological underpinnings (Objectives 16-21). This chapter is divided into two lessons. Lesson I covers Objectives 1-12, and Lesson II, Objectives 13-21.

CONCEPT CARDS AND EXERCISES

After you have surveyed and read the text, assemble the concept cards located at the end of this chapter. Use them to learn the important terms, then begin reading the text again, one learning objective at a time, and work through the exercises for each lesson. Answers for questions marked with an asterisk are found at the end of the chapter.

SELF TESTS

Each lesson is followed by a multiple-choice self test. After you are proficient with a lesson's concept cards and exercises, take the self test to see whether you have mastered the material. Review those objectives for questions you answered incorrectly.

INTEGRATING QUESTIONS

To challenge yourself further, answer the integrating questions at the end of the chapter. These questions ask you to apply the information you have learned to consider larger theoretical or real-life issues.

LESSON I EMOTIONS: THEIR NATURE, EXPRESSION, AND RECOGNITION

1. Distinguish among emotions, moods and temperament. (pp. 491-492)

1.1 Define emotions, mood, and temperament in your own words.

* 1.2 Distinguish among emotions, mood, and temperament in terms of their duration.

1.3 Give examples of emotions, moods, and temperament.

2. Describe the myth that emotions force people to commit behaviors that they would otherwise not perform. (pp. 492-493)

2.1 Evaluate the validity of the assumptions underlying each of these statements. Explain the reasons for your evaluations.

a) "In the heat of passion I forgot to use birth control and now I'm pregnant."

b) "I'm sorry. I didn't mean what I said. It was just that I was so angry, I had to express it."

c) "I usually can type eighty words per minute. But, I get so anxious when you are watching me that I can only type thirty words per minute."

d) "It's crazy. Whenever I approach one of those high suspension bridges, my heart begins to pound."

* 2.2 Identify four common misconceptions concerning emotions.

3. Describe the problems confronting researchers attempting to study emotions. (pp. 493-494)

3.1 Dr. Feelgood wants to study the emotion of love. Describe some of the difficulties that Dr. Feelgood may encounter.

4. Identify Darwin's contribution to the study of emotions. (pp. 494-495)

4.1 Describe how Darwin viewed the relationship between evolution and emotions.

4.2 Describe the methods Darwin used to study emotions and give reasons why he used these methods.

5. Explain the criticisms raised against Darwin's studies of emotion. (pp. 495-496)

5.1 Describe the criticisms of the methods Darwin used to study emotion.

5.2 Summarize Darwin's conclusions regarding emotions and note two criticisms of his conclusions.

6. Describe illustrators, regulators, and emblems, and explain how they differ from facial

* 6.1 Identify the following as expressions of emotion, illustrators, regulators, or emblems.

a) Maureen was thrilled. She held four aces and knew that she was going to win this poker hand. Nevertheless, her face displayed no emotion.

b) Carrie wrinkled her brow when she did not understand what Ralph was saying.

c) When President Kennedy uttered the words, "Ask not what your country can do for you, but what you can do for your country," he used facial expressions as well as words to convey his message.

Note: Take a moment as Carlson suggests to imagine how you use your facial expressions to regulate conversations.

6.2 Give your own examples of an illustrator, regulator, and emblem.

6.3 Explain how Ekman and Friesen (1971) reconciled Darwin's conclusions regarding emotion with those of his critics.

7. Describe the methods and findings of cross-cultural studies of expression and recognition of emotions. (pp. 496-498)

7.1 Explain why Ekman and Friesen chose to study the South Fore tribe.

* 7.2 Ekman and Friesen studied the ______________ and ______________ of emotion of the South Fore tribe.

7.3 Describe how Ekman and Friesen studied the production and recognition of emotional expression of the South Fore tribe.

7.4 Summarize the results of Ekman and Friesen's studies of the South Fore tribe.

7.5 What are the implications of Ekman and Friesen's studies of the South Fore tribe for Darwin's theory and the criticisms of that theory?

8. Describe the expressions of emotions in blind children and the implications of these observations. (pp. 498-499)

8.1 Do the expressions of blind children support the hypothesis that emotional expressions are innate? Explain the reasons for your answer.

8.2 Describe how the expressions of blind children differ from those of sighted children.

8.3 What role does learning play in these differences?

9. Describe evidence regarding the ways that people control their emotions. (pp. 499-501)

* 9.1 Answer the questions that follow on the basis of this scenario.

Jay was angry with Jennifer, but refused to show it. Jennifer felt nothing towards Jay but pretended to be glad to see him. June was only mildly interested in the conversation but she forced herself to appear very interested. Hank asked Jennifer why she was feigning interest in Jay.

a) Most of these individuals are controlling their emotions through use of

________________ ________________.

b) Identify the controls Jay, Jennifer, and June are using.

c) What does Hank's observation about Jennifer suggest?

9.2 Men and women often differ in their expression of emotion. Review two studies that suggest that these differences may be attributable to conditioning.

9.3 Describe the methods and results of the studies by Ekman et al. of American and Japanese college students.

9.4 What implications do the studies by Ekman et al. have for American executives who conduct business in Japan?

9.5 What implications does the study by Ekman and Friesen (1974) have for determining if someone is lying?

10. Describe the methods, results, and implications of studies of the expression and recognition of emotion in nonhuman primates. (pp. 501-503)

10.1 Explain why we cannot conclude that the recognition of emotions is innate on the basis of cross-cultural studies and observations of blind children.

10.2 Describe the research by Miller and his colleagues. In particular, note

a) the hypothesis.

b) the subjects.

c) the method.

d) results.

e) implications.

10.3 Explain why Miller, Caul, and Mirsky (1967) used isolate monkeys in one of their studies on the communication of emotional states.

10.4 Describe the results that Miller et al. found in the experiments with normal and isolate monkeys.

10.5 What implications do the studies by Miller et al. have in terms of learning and the expression of emotion, the recognition of emotion, and the control of emotion?

10.6 What does the study by Sackett (1970) suggest about learning and the recognition of emotions?

11. Describe two theories of emotion that are based on a functional analysis of emotional behavior. (pp. 503-505)

11.1 List as many emotions as you can. Group the emotions into categories. How do you think these emotions have contributed to the survival of the human species?

* 11.2 _______________ and _______________ each developed theories based on a _______________ analysis of emotional behavior.

* 11.3 How did Tomkins determine that there are nine primary emotions?

* 11.4 List the three positive emotions and the six negative ones identified by Tomkins.

11.5 An acting student is asked to display each of the emotions noted in 11.4. What behaviors should this student display in order to communicate each of these nine emotions?

11.6 Draw and label a diagram of Plutchik's classification scheme of emotions.

11.7 According to Tomkins and Plutchik, how does the expression of emotion contribute to the survival of the human species?

12. Summarize the evidence indicating that emotional expression in humans is a social behavior. (pp. 505-507)

12.1 You observe someone scoring many points playing a videogame. This person does not know you are watching and he does not smile at his success. On the basis of the study by Kraut and Johnson (1979), what can you conclude about this person? Give reasons for your answer.

* 12.2 You feel exhilarated but when you walk into a room in which everyone is somber, you become subdued. Your behavior is a function of _______________.

12.3 What does the study by Field, Woodson, Greenberg, and Cohen (1982) suggest about the question of whether the imitation of emotional expression is learned or innate?

LESSON I SELF TEST

1. Which of the following is arranged from briefest to longest in duration?

   a. affect, emotion, temperament
   b. emotion, mood, temperament
   c. temperament, affect, emotion
   d. mood, emotion, temperament

2. Your textbook author argues that emotions are

   a. unreasonable and irrational.
   b. responses that have gotten out of control.
   c. passive.
   d. often the result of intellectual activity.

3. Identify a problem with theories of emotion that have been based upon experimental data.

   a. They are restricted in scope.
   b. They are based upon faulty premises.
   c. They are based solely upon simulated emotions.
   d. They are limited to nonhuman primates.

4. Who first suggested that human expressions of emotion have evolved from similar expressions in other animals?

   a. William James
   b. Charles Darwin
   c. Stanley Schachter
   d. Paul Ekman

5. How did Darwin study emotions?

   a. He studied the production and recognition of emotion in the South Fore tribe.
   b. He conducted clinical interviews of therapists who treated patients in distress.
   c. He produced fear and other intense responses in subjects through procedures that would be regarded as unethical today.
   d. He asked people living in isolated cultures to perform specific observations of emotional expression.

6. Which of the following had been a criticism of Darwin's study of emotions?

   a. Darwin failed to take into account the universal nature of emotions.
   b. Darwin confused emotional expression with facial movements such as illustrators and emblems.
   c. Darwin failed to recognize that the expression of emotion is not consistent even in Western society.
   d. Darwin overemphasized the role of cognition in emotion.

7. The fierce grimace of the leader of a group of Melanesian tribesmen during a festive ceremony is an example of a(n)

   a. illustrator.
   b. regulator.
   c. emotion.
   d. emblem.

8. Research by Ekman, Friesen and their colleagues distinguishes between

   a. the cognitive and affective components of emotions.
   b. the cultural and universal aspects of emotions.
   c. the superficial and deep meanings of emotions.
   d. the animal and essentially human aspects of emotions.

9. Which of the following is suggested by the research of Ekman and Friesen with the South Fore tribe?

   a. The pattern of facial movements that expresses emotions is wired into the human brain.

b. The pattern of facial movements that expresses emotions is culturally determined.
c. Research with even isolated cultures is biased because of the way investigators phrase their questions to the people.
d. Research with isolated cultures yields inconclusive data because researchers cannot separate illustrators, regulators, and emblems from emotions.

10. What does the research with blind children suggest?

a. The expression of emotion must be learned through the observation of others.
b. Even the feelings associated with emotion must be learned.
c. Social reinforcement is important in maintaining displays of emotion.
d. The data from studies with blind children has yielded inconclusive and contradictory results.

11. Marlene was very interested in the lecture but did not appear to be so because she was afraid her friends would mock her. Marlene's behavior is an example of

a. a regulator.
b. leakage.
c. simulation.
d. masking.

12. What did Miller and his colleagues find in their studies involving cooperative conditioning?

a. Isolate monkeys were not able to express or recognize emotions in other monkeys.
b. Isolate monkeys were as effective as the normal monkeys in avoiding the electrical shock.
c. Isolate monkeys were less able to control their expression of emotion than the normal monkeys.
d. Isolate monkeys were more successful in recognizing emotions in other monkeys than in expressing emotion.

13. The theories of emotion developed by Tomkins and Plutchik look at emotions in terms of their

a. purity.
b. dimensionality.
c. duration.
d. survival value for the species.

14. Kraut and Johnson (1979) observed that people are more likely to express emotion when they

a. are alone and feeling blue.
b. are in the presence of others.
c. feel happy regardless of the situation.
d. have mastered the display rules of the culture.

15. What does the study by Field and colleagues (1982) suggest about the role of imitation in the expression of emotions?

a. The ability to imitate appears to be innate.
b. Infants can express emotions but cannot imitate others' emotion.
c. The recognition as well as the expression of emotions appears to be innate in the human species.
d. Infants who imitate the emotions of adults put a distance between themselves and their own emotions.

Chapter 12

LESSON II: THE ELICITATION AND FEELINGS OF EMOTIONS

13. Describe the nature of stimuli that elicit emotions in humans, and the role of cognition in this process. (pp. 507-509)

* 13.1 Identify three categories of stimuli that elicit emotions in humans.

13.2 How do humans differ from other mammals in the stimuli that elicit emotions and in the feelings and expressions that these stimuli elicit?

13.3 Give an original example of a human emotion that is the product of judgement and one that is primarily an automatic response.

14. Describe Millenson's theory, which classifies emotions according to the nature of the eliciting stimuli. (p. 509)

* 14.1 What are the three dimensions that Millenson suggests are basic to all emotions?

* 14.2 How are these dimensions related?

* 14.3 Compare pure emotions to emotions that are not pure.

14.4 Identify the stimuli that elicit emotions in their pure form.

14.5 Give an example of a pure emotion.

14.6 What changes would be necessary to transform the pure emotion in 14.5 into a less pure emotion?

15. Describe research on the development of expressions of fear of specific predators in vervet monkeys. (pp. 509-510)

15.1 Identify the predators of vervet monkeys.

15.2 How do vervet monkeys respond when they see one of these predators when they are alone? when they are with other monkeys?

15.3 How does the behavior of young vervet monkeys differ from that of the adults?

15.4 What do the observations of Marler et al. suggest about the the roles of nature (heredity) and nurture (learning) in the expression of emotions?

16. Describe the James-Lange theory of emotion and describe and evaluate Cannon's criticisms of this theory. (pp. 511-512)

* 16.1 Arrange the following events into the sequence predicted by the James-Lange theory of emotion.

_____ a) feeling afraid

_____ b) giving a speech

_____ c) voice quavering

16.2 Use the James-Lange theory to explain the cause of the emotion noted in 16.1.

16.3 According to the James-Lange theory of emotion, what could be done to reduce or eliminate the fear noted in 16.1?

* 16.4 The James-Lange theory of emotion is related to a _______________ psychological process known as _______________.

16.5 State in your own words the five objections Cannon offered against the James-Lange theory of emotion.

16.6 Review the evidence that eliminates or minimizes the importance of Cannon's objections to James-Lange theory.

16.7 What does Hohman's research suggest about the relationship between feelings and emotional behavior?

17. Describe the physiological effects of simulated emotion expression and their implications for human communication. (pp. 513-514)

17.1 Make the movements indicated in the textbook's example to simulate fear. What changes, if any, do you observe in yourself?

17.2 Describe the methods and results of the study by Ekman, Levenson, and Friesen (1983).

17.3 Offer two possible reasons as to why particular movements of the facial muscles produce changes in the autonomic nervous system.

18. Describe Schachter's theory of emotion and the studies that tested it. (pp. 514-516)

* 18.1 According to Schachter, _______________ and _______________ of _______________ arousal are necessary for emotion.

18.2 Summarize the three conditions that Schachter believes elicit emotion.

18.3 Draw a chart to illustrate the different conditions subjects were exposed to in Schachter and Singer's (1962) experiment.

18.4 Explain the rationale for the different conditions in the study by Schachter and Singer (1962). In particular, explain why Schachter and Singer

a) administered adrenalin or a placebo to the subjects.

b) informed some subjects to expect side effects and other subjects to expect no or irrelevant side effects.

18.5 Describe the results obtained by Schachter and Singer (1962).

18.6 Summarize the study by Nisbett and Schachter (1966).

18.7 What does the report by Nisbett and Wilson (1977) suggest about people's awareness of their cognitive and psychological processes?

18.8 Explain how the results of the study by Nisbett and Schachter support Schachter's theory of emotion.

18.9 Compare the views of Lazarus, Zajonc, and Schachter regarding emotion.

19. Describe the roles that the hypothalamus, limbic system, and cerebral cortex appear to play in emotions. (pp. 516-518)

* 19.1 According to Cannon, what are the roles of the thalamus and hypothalamus in emotion?

* 19.2 What is the limbic system?

* 19.3 Identify three responses produced by the electrical stimulation of the limbic system.

19.4 What do the studies of people who have brain damage suggest about the role of the cerebral cortex in emotions?

20. Describe the effects of brain damage on emotional expression and recognition. (p. 518)

* 20.1 The _______________ hemisphere plays the more important role in the _______________ and _______________ of emotions than the _______________ hemisphere. The _______________ and _______________ lobes appear to play an important role in the _______________ of emotions and the _______________ lobe plays an important role in the _______________ of emotions.

* 20.2 Identify the reactions of the people below, and explain why reactions have occurred.

__________ a) Ned's left side is paralyzed but he does not seem to care.

__________ b) Tracy suffered brain damage as a result of a car accident. Despite the improvements she has made, she feels terribly depressed.

* 20.3 Damage to the left hemisphere will produce deficits in _______________ recognition and expression, whereas damage to the right hemisphere produces deficits in _______________

recognition and expression.

* 20.4 Identify the area of the brain that probably has been damaged in the following examples.

__________ a) John shows no emotion but is able to tell how others are feeling.

__________ b) Jeremy is able to express anger and pain but he is not able to recognize these emotions in others.

21. Describe studies investigating the hemispheric differences in emotional behavior in normal people. (pp. 518-520)

* 21.1 In the example below, which side of the brain seems to be controlling the speaker? Which side of the brain probably is influencing the person who is being addressed?

"Stop being so emotional. You need to step back and see this situation more objectively."

21.2 Describe the evidence that supports the right and left hemisphere distinctions found in normal people.

LESSON II SELF TEST

1. How do humans differ from other animals in terms of emotions?

   a. in their expression and feeling of emotion
   b. acquisition though conditioning as well as automatic processes
   c. the types of stimuli that evoke emotions
   d. the physiological processes underlying emotion

2. According to Millenson, an emotion is not pure if it is

   a. a combination of two of the following emotions: anger, fear, and pleasure.
   b. produced by a conditioned rather than automatic response.
   c. is not contributing to the survival of the species.
   d. based upon animal instincts.

3. Studying vervet monkeys, Marler et al. found that

   a. the young monkeys must be taught to recognize and respond to predators.
   b. the adult monkeys make the alarm call only when they are alone.
   c. the young monkeys tend to overgeneralize the situations in which they should sound alarm calls
   d. the young monkeys recognize the predators but must be taught how to respond to them.

4. According to the James-Lange theory of emotions

   a. we feel frightened because we tremble.
   b. we tremble because we are frightened.
   c. we feel frightened and tremble simultaneously in response to messages from the brain.
   d. our interpretation of the situation leads to our feelings and expression of fear.

5. Which of the following is a criticism Cannon offered regarding the James-Lange theory of emotion?

a. Emotions produce different visceral states.
b. Cutting the sensory nerves between the internal organs and the central nervous system eliminates emotional behavior.
c. The feedback provided by the viscera is too slow to be the cause of the feeling of emotions.
d. Artificial induction of the visceral changes typical of strong emotions produces such emotions.

6. In the musical, The King and I, Anna whistles a happy tune to help herself overcome her fear. What does the research on simulated emotional expression suggest about this situation?

a. The whistling may distract Anna, but her autonomic nervous system still will register fear.
b. The whistling changes Anna's perception of fear and thus her cognitions but not her physiological arousal.
c. The whistling counterconditions the feeling of fear but not the emotional behavior associated with fear.
d. The whistling changes the activity of Anna's autonomic nervous system.

7. What hypothesis does Carlson, your textbook author, offer as a possible explanation of why a particular pattern of movements of the facial muscles causes changes in the activity of the autonomic nervous system?

a. Feedback from the facial movements is a conditional stimulus that can elicit the autonomic response.
b. Based on evolutionary history, any change in the muscles of the face is indicative of a change of emotion.
c. Cognitive processes as a result of operant conditioning monitor and interpret changes in facial muscles to indicate specific emotions.
d. Changes in facial muscles are caused by unconscious factors that also cause changes in the autonomic nervous system.

8. Schachter's research on the effects of cognition upon emotion suggests that

a. Cannon's criticisms of the James-Lange theory of emotions were correct.
b. emotions are felt only if there is awareness of one's internal bodily states.
c. people know how they feel by identifying the physiological reaction associated with each emotion.
d. people interpret the significance of their physiological reactions, rather than simply experiencing them as emotions.

9. The subjects who tolerated the pain better in the study by Nisbett and Schachter (1966) were those who

a. consciously attributed their increased tolerance of the pain to the effect of the pill.
b. were given a placebo and told that it would increase their heart rate.
c. did not receive the drug and thus could take responsibility for their own reactions to the pain.
d. were told that the drug would enable them to withstand the pain.

10. According to Cannon, the thalamus is to the hypothalamus as

a. emotional feelings are to visceral changes.
b. anger is to joy.
c. conditioning is to judgment.
d. simulation is to stimulation.

11. Stimulation of what part of the human brain is likely to produce feelings of pleasure, anger, fear or rage?

a. hypothalamus
b. limbic system
c. frontal lobe
d. left parietal lobe

12. Case studies of people who have right hemisphere damage suggest that

a. cognition is controlled by the activity of right cerebral cortex.
b. the left hemisphere is capable of taking over control of emotions.
c. the cortex of the right hemisphere specializes in the production or recognition of emotional expressions.
d. emotional behavior is controlled by the right hemisphere and feelings are controlled by the left hemisphere.

13. Which of the following behaviors is likely to be associated with damage to the right posterior frontal cortex?

a. catastrophic reaction
b. inability to recognize other people's emotions
c. inability to understand language
d. inability to use facial gestures to express emotion

14. What does research by Safer and Leventhal (1977) suggest about hemispheric differences in emotional behavior in normal people?

a. that normal people are equally adept at perceiving emotions with the right and left hemispheres of their brain
b. that normal people who are restricted from using both sides of their brains miss salient emotional issues in a situation
c. that the right hemisphere is more accurate in rating the emotional significance of the tone of a voice
d. that the left hemisphere is better at detecting emotional messages through visual channels and the right through auditory channels

15. A friend asserts that he is left brained. What does the research on the hemispheric differences in emotional behavior in normal people suggest if he really is left-brained?

a. He is likely to be far less emotional than he is analytical.
b. He is better at expressing emotions than he is at recognizing emotions in others.
c. He is likely to have far deeper feelings of emotion than are reflected by his emotional behavior.
d. He will be more aware of physiological arousal and thus better able to control it.

INTEGRATING QUESTIONS

1. Identify four myths regarding emotion. Debunk one of these myths by summarizing the psychological theory and research regarding emotions that contradicts that myth.

2. Who do you think made the greatest contribution to the study of emotions—Charles Darwin, William James or Stanley Schachter? Explain the reasons for your answers, making sure that you describe the contributions of each man to the study of emotions.

3. Plutchik theorized that emotions have survival value and suggests that our capacity to express and recognize feelings was shaped by evolution. Examine these hypotheses by considering what would happen to individuals who could not a) express their emotions, b) regulate their emotional expression, and c) recognize emotions in others. (Hint: For ideas on how individuals might behave in these cases, consider the studies of monkeys by

Marler et al. and Miller et al. and the studies of people with various kinds of brain damage.

ANSWERS

1.2 Emotions are shorter lived than moods, which are shorter lived than temperament.
2.2 a) We are not responsible for our emotional behavior. b) Intense emotions disorganize behavior. c) Emotions are unreasonable and irrational. d) Emotions rather than species-typical responses interfere with performance in a technological society.
6.1 a) emblem, b) regulators, c) illustrators
7.2 production, recognition
9.1 a) display rules; b) masking, simulation, modulation; c) Although Jennifer may be controlling her emotions, they show leakage. In other words, her body is sending out cues that allow Hank to infer that her facial and verbal behavior may not reflect her true feelings.
11.2 Tomkins, Plutchik, functional
11.3 through study of types of movements and expressions people exhibit
11.4 interest, enjoyment, and surprise; distress, fear, shame, contempt, disgust, and anger
12.2 imitation
13.1 elicitors that are innate, conditioned or based on cognitions
14.1 fear, anger, pleasure
14.2 related to ability of stimuli to reinforce or punish behavior
14.3 Pure emotion consists of only one dimension; emotions that are not pure consist of two or three dimensions. Both pure and not so pure vary in intensity.
16.1 a) 3, b) 1, c) 2
16.4 social, attribution
18.1 cognition, perception, physiological
19.1 Thalamus produces emotional feelings, and the hypothalamus produces visceral changes associated with emotions.
19.2 section of brain that includes portions of thalamus and hypothalamus
19.3 physiological responses controlled by autonomic nervous system, defensive behaviors, and excited exploratory behaviors
20.1 right, feelings, expression, left, temporal, parietal, perception, frontal, expression
20.2 a) indifference reaction. Damage to right side of brain may interfere with ability to express and feel emotion. b) catastrophic reaction. Right side of brain is not damaged; it allows patient to recognize neurological impairments and experience their emotional significance.
20.3 verbal, emotional
20.4 a) right frontal lobe, b) right temporal and parietal lobes
21.1 speaker—left side, other—right side

Self Test: Lesson I			Self Test: Lesson II		
1.	b	Obj. 12-1	1.	c	Obj. 12-13
2.	d	Obj. 12-2	2.	a	Obj. 12-14
3.	a	Obj. 12-3	3.	c	Obj. 12-15
4.	b	Obj. 12-4	4.	a	Obj. 12-16
5.	d	Obj. 12-4	5.	c	Obj. 12-16
6.	c	Obj. 12-5	6.	d	Obj. 12-17
7.	d	Obj. 12-6	7.	a	Obj. 12-17
8.	b	Obj. 12-7	8.	d	Obj. 12-18
9.	a	Obj. 12-7	9.	b	Obj. 12-18
10.	c	Obj. 12-8	10.	a	Obj. 12-19
11.	d	Obj. 12-9	11.	b	Obj. 12-19
12.	c	Obj. 12-10	12.	c	Obj. 12-20
13.	d	Obj. 12-11	13.	d	Obj. 12-20
14.	b	Obj. 12-12	14.	c	Obj. 12-21
15.	a	Obj. 12-12	15.	a	Obj. 12-21

12.1 OBJ 12-1

EMOTION

12.2 OBJ 12-1

MOOD

12.3 OBJ 12-1

TEMPERAMENT

12.4 OBJ 12-1

AFFECT

12.5 OBJ 12-6

ILLUSTRATOR

12.6 OBJ 12-6

REGULATOR

12.7 OBJ 12-6

EMBLEM

12.8 OBJ 12-9

EXPRESSION OF EMOTION

12.9 OBJ 12-7

RECOGNITION OF EMOTION

12.10 OBJ 12-7

CONTROL OF EMOTION

12.11 OBJ 12-9

DISPLAY RULE

12.12 OBJ 12-9

MASKING

12.13 OBJ 12-9

MODULATION

12.14 OBJ 12-9

SIMULATION

12.15 OBJ 12-9

LEAKAGE

12.16 OBJ 12-10

COOPERATIVE CONDITIONING

12.9 Obj 12-7

identification of how others are feeling by observing their behavior; seems to be primarily a learned ability

12.10 Obj 12-7

modulation of inherited ability to express emotions to fit the culture and the situation

12.11 Obj 12-9

learned patterns that modify expression of emotion

12.12 Obj 12-9

attempt to hide emotion

12.13 Obj 12-9

attempt to exaggerate or minimize expression of emotion

12.14 Obj 12-9

attempt to express an unfelt emotion

12.15 Obj 12-9

expression of true feeling of emotion despite attempt to hide it

12.16 Obj 12-10

experimental conditioning procedure to test expression and recognition of emotion in monkeys

12.1 Obj 12-1

relatively brief subjective feelings associated with persons or situations that are personally significant

12.2 Obj 12-1

subjective feelings that are longer-lived and weaker than emotion

12.3 Obj 12-1

a person's general disposition or typical pattern of affective reaction

12.4 Obj 12-1

feeling that accompanies emotion

12.5 Obj 12-6

facial movements used to emphasize words or phrases; may be mistaken as expression of emotion

12.6 Obj 12-6

facial movements used to control give-and-take in conversations; may be mistaken as expression of emotion

12.7 Obj 12-6

facial expressions that convey a specific meaning within a given culture; may be mistaken by members of other cultures as expression of emotion

12.8 Obj 12-7

how people convey what they are feeling; seems to have been "wired" into the brain

12.17 OBJ 12-16

JAMES-LANGE THEORY

12.18 OBJ 12-19

LIMBIC SYSTEM

12.19 OBJ 12-19

THALAMUS

12.20 OBJ 12-19

HYPOTHALAMUS

12.21 OBJ 12-20

CATASTROPHIC REACTION

12.22 OBJ 12-20

INDIFFERENCE REACTION

12.23 OBJ 12-20

RIGHT HEMISPHERE

12.24 OBJ 12-20

RIGHT POSTERIOR FRONTAL CORTEX

12.25 OBJ 12-20

RIGHT PARIETAL AND TEMPORAL LOBES

12.25 Obj 12-20

portion of brain that appears responsible in part for ability to recognize emotions

12.17 Obj 12-16

theory of emotion; states that emotions are the awareness of bodily sensations elicited by arousing stimuli, e.g., fear because tremble

12.18 Obj 12-19

series of brain structures that include hypothalamus and parts of thalamus; necessary for emotional behavior

12.19 Obj 12-19

according to Cannon, part of brain that receives information from all regions of cerebral cortex and produces emotional feelings

12.20 Obj 12-19

according to Cannon, part of brain that produces visceral changes that accompany emotions

12.21 Obj 12-20

severe anxiety and depression following damage to left hemisphere; presumed to be response to awareness of neurological deficits

12.22 Obj 12-20

nonchalance associated with damage to right hemisphere

12.23 Obj 12-20

half of brain that seems responsible for expression and recognition of emotion

12.24 Obj 12-20

portion of brain that appears responsible for ability to express emotions

CHAPTER 13
Social Psychology

INTRODUCTION

This chapter examines four critical areas of the study of how individuals respond to their social environment. These areas include attribution (Objectives 1-4), attitudes and their formation (Objectives 5-12), social influences (Objectives 13-22), and interpersonal attraction (Objectives 23-24). It is divided into two lessons. Lesson I covers Objectives 1-12 and Lesson II covers Objectives 13-24.

CONCEPT CARDS AND EXERCISES

After you have surveyed and read the text, assemble the concept cards located at the end of this chapter. Use them to learn the important terms, then begin reading the text again, one learning objective at a time, and work through the exercises for each lesson. Answers for questions marked with an asterisk are found at the end of the chapter.

SELF TESTS

Each lesson is followed by a multiple-choice self test. After you are proficient with a lesson's concept cards and exercises, take the self test to see whether you have mastered the material. Review those objectives for questions you answered incorrectly.

INTEGRATING QUESTIONS

To challenge yourself further, answer the integrating questions at the end of the chapter. These questions ask you to apply the information you have learned to consider larger theoretical or real-life issues.

LESSON I: ATTRIBUTION AND ATTITUDES

1. Define attribution and explain its importance to the social psychologist and the implicit psychologist. (p. 528)

1.1 Why do you think a fair number of people would follow a salesperson's advice when he tells them not to buy the more expensive model because it will not last as long as the less expensive one? Explain how attribution, implicit psychology, theories of social behavior and facts enter into people's decision to act upon the salesperson's advice.

1.2 In the following example, identify Dan's expectations and the process by which he formed those expectations. Every person who asked for a raise within the last two weeks was granted the raise. Dan decides that he, too, should ask for a raise.

1.3 Describe the problems with the following application of the covariance method.

a) When Ken met Barbara she did not pay much attention to him. He thought that she was a snob and as a result, has avoided her ever since.

b) During the day the sun turned black. The aboriginal tribe began to dance to their god to restore the sun. The sun soon reappeared.

1.4 Explain how the scientist's use of the covariance method differs from the examples of the covariance method given in question 1.3.

2. Describe the distinction between disposition and situation as explanations for behavior, then describe the sources of explanation people use to make attributions. (pp. 528-530)

* 2.1 Situational factors are _______________ to the person and dispositional factors are _______________ to the person.

* 2.2 On the basis of the examples below what do you conclude about Sarah and Joyce?

a) Two-year-old Sarah did not thank her parents and friends for their birthday presents to her.

b) Twenty-two-year-old Joyce did not thank her parents and friends for their birthday presents to her.

2.3 Looking at your conclusions about Sarah and Joyce in question 2.2,

a) identify the factors you considered in reaching your conclusions.

b) label each of these factors as either situational or dispositional.

c) note the role discounting played in your judgement.

2.4 Identify whether the behaviors below are attributable to internal (dispositional) or external (situational) factors. Then note whether they are examples of consensus, consistency or distinctiveness.

* a) When the minister said rise, everyone in the congregation rose.

* b) Ted did not stand when the national anthem was played at the beginning of the baseball game.

* c) Jack only gets drunk when he goes out with Jason, whom he sees infrequently.

3. Describe the fundamental attributional error, the error of false consensus, and research on these topics. (pp. 530-532)

* 3.1 In the example below, identify a) whether the group attributes your behavior to internal or external factors and b) whether you or the group is likely to make the fundamental attribution error.

You slip while walking down the hall. A group of onlookers sees you slip and they assume you are clumsy.

3.2 Discuss the implications of the study by Ross, Amabile, Steinmetz (1977) for new freshmen's evaluations of college professors?

3.3 What explanations do Jones and Nisbett offer for the fundamental attributional error?

* 3.4 Which of the following is (are) example(s) of false consensus?

a) Joe thinks anyone who eats with chopsticks must be strange.

b) Everyone ate dinner with chopsticks.

c) Everyone except Tim ate dinner with chopsticks.

d) Chu thinks eating with a knife and fork is awkward.

3.5 For the example(s) of false consensus in question 3.4, offer two explanations for the attributional error(s).

3.6 What do the results of the study by Ross, Greene, and House suggest about the way we see the world?

4. Describe the two most important motivational biases in attribution and research on these biases. (pp. 532-534)

* 4.1 How do motivational attributional biases differ from intellectual attributional biases?

4.2 Identify the kind of motivational bias illustrated in each of the following examples and suggest explanations for these biases.

* a) Shortly after eight-year-old Ray told his brother that he wished he were dead, his brother was killed by a bolt of lightning. Ray was not responsible for his brother's death but felt somehow his thoughts caused his brother's death.

* b) Captain Queeg blamed his crew for breaking the tow line. He commended himself when his boat and crew survived the hurricane.

4.3 What implications do the studies by Johnson, Feigenbaum, and Weiby (1964), Beckman (1970), and Ross, Bierbrauer, and Polly (1974) suggest about the perceptions of teachers, parents, and students about the teaching situation?

4.4 Briefly summarize the methods and results of Langer's (1970) study?

5. Describe the nature of the affective and cognitive components of attitudes and how they are formed. (p. 538)

5.1 Define what an attitude is in your own words.

* 5.2 Read this scenario.

Nora took her children to the doctor so they could get the necessary childhood shots. Nora told her children not to be afraid of vaccinations because they were good for them. Nora herself, however, is terrified of shots.

a) What would you expect the attitudes of the children to be regarding vaccinations? In particular, note the affective and the cognitive components of their attitudes.

b) Describe the process by which the affective component of the attitude of Nora's children was formed and maintained.

c) Describe the process by which the cognitive component of the attitude of Nora's children regarding vaccinations was formed and maintained.

6. Identify and describe three factors that can affect the correspondence between a person's attitude and behavior. (pp. 535-536)

* 6.1 List the three factors that affect the correspondence between a person's attitude and behavior.

6.2 Briefly describe the study by Weigel, Vernon, and Tognacci (1974) In particular, note its

a) methods.

b) results.

c) implications.

6.3 Briefly describe the study by Regan and Fazzio (1977). In particular, note its

a) methods.

b) results.

c) implications.

6.4 Speculate why LaPiere (1934) found no correspondence between the attitudes and behaviors of the restaurateurs and innkeepers concerning serving Chinese people.

7. Describe Festinger's theory of cognitive dissonance. (p. 536)

7.1 Briefly summarize Festinger's theory of cognitive dissonance.

* 7.2 In the examples below identify the discrepancies that are likely to produce dissonance.

a) Paul is opposed to capitalism because he believes that it exploits workers. He inherits a family fortune that was built from capitalistic enterprises.

b) Kerstin says she supports environmental issues but she refuses to volunteer in the activities of the Sierra Club, an environmental action group.

* 7.3 Under which circumstances are the characters in 7.2 likely to experience cognitive dissonance?

7.4 According to Festinger's theory, if the characters in 7.2 experience a discrepancy between attitudes and behavior, how are they likely to feel? In general terms, if they felt dissonance, how could they reduce it?

8. Describe the effects of induced compliance and self-esteem on a person's attitudes. (pp. 536-538)

8.1 Define induced compliance in your own words.

* 8.2 In the example below, use cognitive dissonance theory to predict the reactions of the two boys.

Two little boys had a fight. The mother of one of the boys makes him apologize. The other boy's mother asks but does not force her son to apologize. Both boys apologize.

8.3 Describe the research study by Festinger and Carlsmith (1959). In particular,

a) which hypothesis were they testing?

b) what were the research groups?

c) what was found?

d) what are the implications of this study for attitude change?

8.4 Offer reasons derived from the research by Festinger and Carlsmith (1959) to explain why the serving of the Chinese people did not change the attitudes towards Orientals of the innkeepers and restaurateurs studied by LaPiere (1934 and described under Objective 6).

8.5 Summarize the methods, findings, and implications of the study by Steele and Liu (1981).

9. Describe evidence that suggests that induced compliance must produce arousal in order to cause attitude change. (p. 538)

9.1 Describe the study by Croyle and Cooper (1983). Note its

a) method.

b) experimental conditions.

c) results.

d) implications.

9.2 What effect did the sedatives and amphetamines have upon attitude change in the study of induced compliance by Cooper, Zanna, and Taves (1978)?

9.3. What does the investigation by Steele, Southwick, and Critchlow (1981) suggest about the role of alcohol in situations involving cognitive dissonance?

10. Describe the effects of conflict resolution and increased expenditures on attitude change. (pp. 538-540)

10.1 Based on dissonance theory, how will the characters in the following situations react? Explain the reasons for your answers.

* a) Bob has been trying to decide which of two different models of cars to buy. He decides and buys one of these models.

* b) Amy wanted ballet lessons. Although her parents could afford to pay for the lessons, they insisted that Amy use a portion of her allowance to pay for the lessons.

10.2 Describe the study by Aronson and Mills (1959). In particular,

a) note how they created cognitive dissonance in their subjects.

b) describe how subjects who experienced the greatest dissonance seemed to reduce their dissonance.

c) discuss the implications of this study for cognitive dissonance theory.

* 10.3 Conscious deliberation _____ (is/is not) necessary for attitude change to occur through cognitive dissonance.

11. Describe Bem's self-perception theory and compare it to the theory of cognitive dissonance. (pp. 540-542)

* 11.1 In contrast to cognitive dissonance theory, self-perception theory makes _______________ assumptions.

11.2 a) Restate Bem's theory of self-perception in your own words and

* b) note the principles from which it has been derived.

11.3 Review the study by Aronson and Mills (1959) presented in Objective 10. Reinterpret this results of this study in terms of Bem's self-perception theory.

11.4 What implications do the studies on arousal and attitude change (for example, Cooper, Zanna, and Taves (1978) presented under Objective 10) have for the theories of self-perception and cognitive dissonance?

12. Describe the role of impression management in self-reports of attitudes and attitude change. (pp. 542-544)

12.1 Give your own example of impression management.

* 12.2 When a person is persuaded to change his or her opinion, an observer in contrast to the _______________ is likely to rate this person as _______________ attractive and _______________.

12.3 Describe the Braver et al. (1977) study. Note its

a) method.

b) experimental conditions.

c) results.

d) implications.

12.4 Offer reasons as to why subjects behaved differently across the experimental conditions set by Braver et al. (1977).

LESSON I SELF TEST

1. What is the process by which people infer the causes of other people's behavior?

   a. attribution
   b. discounting
   c. derivation
   d. assessment

2. John along with the other members of the press corps stood up when the President entered the room. The attribution we make about John's behavior is based upon __________.

   a. consensus
   b. consistency
   c. distinctiveness
   d. discounting

3. Which of the following is a well-supported rule?

   a. People attribute dispositional factors to themselves and situational factors to other.
   b. To change people's behavior, you first must change their attitudes.
   c. Group decisions tend to be more conservative than individual decisions.
   d. People tend to see their own views as representative of those of the larger group.

4. The referee made identical calls in the two games. In the first game, Jerry's team won and in the second, it lost. Jerry accused the referee of costing his team the second game. Which error best describes Jerry's behavior?

   a. fundamental attributional error

b. illusion of personal causation
c. intellectual bias of false consensus
d. credit for success, blame for failure

5. In contrast to the cognitive components of attitudes, the affective components are

a. less resistant to change.
b. acquired through modeling.
c. acquired through a form of classical conditioning.
d. independent of behavior.

6. Recent research has shown that the relationship between attitudes and behavior is

a. clearer when only the cognitive component of the attitude is measured.
b. fairly strong when specific attitudes and behaviors are measured.
c. strong when attitudes first are inferred from behavior, then measured.
d. when moderately strong attitudes are based on the persuasive arguments of other people.

7. According to Leon Festinger, what motivates people to change their attitudes?

a. discounting
b. consensual validation
c. self-perception
d. cognitive dissonance

8. A high school student argues for the importance of honesty in relationships. Later she tells a guy who she does not want to date that she cannot go out with him because she is washing her hair. She is likely to experience cognitive dissonance if she

a. does not see the relationship between her attitudes regarding relationships and her treatment of this young man.
b. feels guilty that she did not tell this guy the truth.
c. notes that this guy was not worth her time.
d. tells herself that she lied to spare hurting this young man.

9. The psychology department seeks subjects for its research projects. Some students receive course credit for their participation and some do not. Dissonance theory predicts that students

a. who receive course credit will learn more from their participation in the projects.
b. will participate in the experiments if they are asked.
c. who participate in the experiments without course credit will observe themselves and conclude that they are committed to advancing science.
d. who participate for no credit will value even the most boring projects more than students who receive course credit.

10. Which group showed the greatest attitude change in the study by Steele and Liu (1981) of the role of self-esteem in attitude change?

a. those who were paid a large amount for writing an essay against further funding of the handicapped.
b. those who were given the opportunity to aid the handicapped after they had written the anti-handicap essay.
c. those who only wrote the essay against funding programs for the handicapped.
d. those whose self-esteem was high initially.

11. What does the study by Croyle and Cooper (1983) suggest about the relationship between arousal and attitude change?

a. Arousal without the conscious awareness of the subjects will not produce attitude change.
b. Physiological arousal is found in conditions where attitude change has been greatest.
c. Physiological arousal minimizes the effects of induced compliance and thus attitude change.
d. There is no relationship between physiological arousal and attitude change.

12. After much contemplation, Sheila decides to date Ron rather than Roger. Which of the following predictions would cognitive dissonance theory support?

a. Sheila will come to value the attributes Ron has more than the attributes Roger possesses.
b. Sheila will regret the fact that she chose to date Ron rather than Roger.
c. Sheila will continue to date Ron but will fault him for not having Roger's positive attributes.
d. Sheila would like Roger and date him if he would offer her a substantial gift.

13. What can we conclude from the study by Aronson and Mills (1959) regarding initiation rituals?

a. The effect of cognitive dissonance upon attitude change is dependent upon conscious deliberation.
b. There is a boomerang effect such that the more a person does to gain entry into a group, the less that person will participate in the group.
c. People value things at least partly by how much they cost them.
d. The less people have to do to join a group, the more likely they are to join that group.

14. What does self-perception theory hypothesize about attitudes?

a. Attitude change occurs only when there is physiological arousal.
b. People infer their own attitudes from observations of their behavior.
c. Attitudes are formed primarily through classical conditioning.
d. In order for attitudes to change, individuals must experience a motivating aversive drive state.

15. During a job interview you want to show the employer that you belong with this company but also that you have a mind of your own. You acknowledge agreement with about eighty percent of what the recruiter says. You are showing _____ in this interview.

a. induced compliance
b. social facilitation
c. a self-handicapping strategy
d. impression management

LESSON II: SOCIAL INFLUENCE AND INTERPERSONAL ATTRACTION

13. Describe research on the nature of conformity. (pp. 544-546)

13.1 Summarize the classic study by Solomon Asch (1951) by noting its

a) method.

b) results.

c) implications

13.2 Explain how the Asch effect could be conceptualized as a case of impression management.

* 13.3 What do the findings of Scofield (1975) and Fuller and Sheehy-Skeffington (1974) suggest for television advertising and programming?

14. Describe the conditions that facilitate or inhibit bystander intervention. (pp. 546-548)

* 14.1 When a person is in need of assistance, the presence of other people who are not responding with aid _______________ people from giving aid.

14.2 Summarize the bystander intervention study of Darley and Latane (1968) in terms of its

a) methods.

b) results.

c) implications.

* 14.3 What do the bystander intervention studies by Clark and Wood (1972, 1974) suggest?

15. Describe the effects that an audience can have on a person's performance and discuss attempts to explain these effects. (pp. 548-549)

15.1 Define social facilitation in your own words.

* 15.2 Under what conditions will the presence of other people positively influence a person's performance of a task?

* 15.3 Under what conditions will the presence of other people negatively affect a person's performance of a task?

15.4 State Zajonc's explanation of social facilitation, and summarize two experiments that support this explanation.

15.5 Offer a reason as to why the presence of a group increases a person's arousal and cite research evidence to support this reason.

16. Define social loafing, and identify the variables that determine whether social facilitation or social loafing are likely to occur. (pp. 549-551)

16.1 What does the research by Latane, Williams, and Harkins (1979) suggest about the question, "Do people work harder in groups or alone?"

* 16.2 According to Williams, Harkins, and Latane (1981), what affects whether an individual will work as hard in a group as alone?

* 16.3 Offer a behavioral explanation for why identifiability affects a person's performance.

16.4 Describe the methods, findings, and implications of the study by Harkins and Petty (1982).

16.5 What implications can be drawn from the investigation of group effort and persuasive arguments by Petty, Harkins, and Williams (1980)?

17. Describe the research on the principle of reciprocity, including returning favors, atoning for causing harm, and reciprocal concessions. (pp. 551-553)

17.1 Define reciprocity in your own words.

17.2 Identify the conditions, results, and implications of the study on favor giving by Regan (1971).

17.3 Explain the implications of the study by Carlsmith and Gross (1969) regarding atoning for harm.

* 17.4 A college alumni association telephones graduates and first asks them to donate $1000, and then, if refused, asks for a lesser amount.

  a) What strategy is the association using?

  b) On the basis of the study on Cialdini and Ascani (1976) how successful do you predict the association will be?

18. Describe research on the effects of making a commitment. (pp. 553-554)

* 18.1 Identify the techniques used below.

  a) Jill is asked to donate two hours to the a state senator's campaign. She offers the requested assistance. She, then is asked to volunteer four hours a week in the campaign, which she does.

  b) The salesperson offers Jeremy the speakers and the turntable for the same price as the speakers alone. Checking with the manager, the salesperson says he cannot make this offer but can sell the turntable at half price. Jeremy accepts this new offer.

18.2 Summarize the study demonstrating the foot-in-the-door technique by Freedman and Fraser (1966) in terms of its

  a) methods.

  b) results.

  c) implications.

* 18.3 Identify two reasons why commitment increases people's compliance with requests.

18.4 What are the implications of the study by Rittle (1981) for commitment and compliance?

19. Describe research on the difficulty people have refusing the requests of attractive people. (pp. 554-555)

19.1 Why do you think people have difficulty refusing the requests of attractive people? Have you ever had difficulty refusing an offer of an attractive person? Why or why not?

19.2 Give two examples of survey studies that support the hypothesis that individuals have difficulty refusing the requests of attractive people.

19.3 Give an example of a controlled experiment that supports the hypothesis that individuals have difficulty refusing the requests of attractive people.

19.4 Explain the roles classical conditioning and self-esteem play in the difficulty people have refusing the requests of attractive people.

20. Describe research on the effects of authority on compliance. (pp. 555-559)

20.1 Summarize a case study (Cohen and David, 1981) and an experiment (Wilson, 1968) that demonstrate people's tendency to respond to authority.

* 20.2 What did the experimenter in the studies by Milgram (1963, 1964) ask subjects to do and how did the subjects respond?

* 20.3 What effect did the presence of the learner in the same room as the subject have upon subjects' behavior?

20.4 Read the following cases.

Case I: Eichman tried as a Nazi war criminal argued that he was not responsible for the murder of thousands of Jews. He claimed that he was only following orders

Case II: In 1983 a Druse Moslem drove a truck filled with explosives into an American army barracks in Lebanon and killed more than two hundred marines.

a) What do you conclude about these cases?

b) Re-examine your conclusions on the basis of the findings of Milgram's studies.

* c) What role might the fundamental attribution error played in your initial conclusions?

21. Describe research on reactance and its relation to self-esteem. (pp. 559-560)

* 21.1 Explain the reaction of the women of Miami and Tampa towards phosphate detergents in terms of psychological reactance.

* 21.2 In Shakespeare's play, _Romeo and Juliet_, Juliet persists in dating Romeo despite her parents' objections. Explain Juliet's behavior in terms of psychological reactance.

21.3 Donna does not want her three-year-old raiding the cookie jar. What does the study by Brehm and Weintraub (1977) suggest about storing the cookies if Donna's child is male? if she is female?

21.4 What roles do biology and self-esteem play in the phenomenon of psychological reactance? Explain your answer.

22. Describe the conditions under which people's behavior is affected by rational or irrational social influences. (pp. 560-561)

22.1 Refute the arguments that social influence is bad and that all behavior should be under rational, conscious control.

* 22.2 Identify the three variables that Petty, Cacioppo, and Goldman (1981) manipulated in their study of conscious control and persuasion.

22.3 What did Petty, Cacioppo, and Goldman (1981) find in their study of conscious control and persuasion?

* 22.4 Identify three variables that may determine if a person will reflect consciously upon a matter of social influence.

23. Describe research on the effects of positive evaluation, shared opinions, physical appearance, and familiarity on interpersonal attraction. (pp. 562-565)

23.1 Review the investigation by Byrne and Rhamey (1965) on the effects of positive personal evaluations on attraction in terms of its

a) methods.

b) results.

c) implications.

23.2 What implications can be drawn from the study by Geller, Goodstein, Silver, and Sternberg (1974) on the effects of negative evaluation by other people?

* 23.3 Byrne and Nelson (1971) found that similarity in terms of ______________

______________ increased a person's ______________ of a stranger.

23.4 Think about three of your friends and note why you like each of them.

a) Describe how social reinforcement can explain your initial and continued attraction to them.

b) Discuss your attraction to these people in terms of shared opinions, similarity and physical appearance.

23.5 Jerry asserts, "It does not matter what a person looks like. It is what is inside that counts." What does the research on interpersonal attraction suggest about this view?

23.6 Your friend Joe, an average looking guy, wants to become friends with Mary, who is gorgeous. Based on the research on interpersonal attraction, what do you suggest Joe do to befriend Mary? Describe the research studies that support your suggestions.

24. Review research on the role of reinforcement in romantic attraction. (pp. 565-567)

24.1 Do you think liking and loving are fundamentally the same? Offer reasons for your answers.

24.2 Describe the study by Dutton and Aron (1974) that involved males encountering a woman on a bridge. Note their

a) methods.

b) results.

c) interpretation of their results.

24.3 Contrast Dutton and Aron's interpretation of their study with the interpretation based on social reinforcement.

24.4 Describe the evidence that supports the social reinforcement interpretation of Dutton and Aron's bridge study.

24.5 What does the study by Dutton and Aron (1974) involving anticipation of an electric shock suggest about the notions of arousal and negative reinforcement as explanations for attraction?

24.6 Consider the friends you listed in question 23.4. What effect did arousal and negative reinforcement have in shaping these friendships?

LESSON II SELF TEST

1. The Asch effect causes people to

   a. change their perceptions, then their behavior.
   b. behave contrary to their own perceptions.
   c. resist persuasion by a group.
   d. conform if members of the group criticize their behavior.

2. Research has shown that the canned laughter that accompanies comedy shows

   a. causes people to feel psychological reactance and therefore dislike the shows.
   b. is only effective if the show is truly funny.
   c. is effective only if people believe that the laughter is real.
   d. causes people to perceive the material as funnier than it is.

3. How do Latane and Darley explain the phenomenon of bystander intervention?

   a. "man's inhumanity to man"
   b. psychological reactance
   c. social loafing
   d. inhibition by the presence of others

4. According to Zajonc, the presence of an audience increases a person's arousal and thus causes the person to

   a. perform better on complex and challenging tasks.
   b. perform better on well-practiced tasks.
   c. become more self-conscious and prone to errors.
   d. hide and withdraw into the crowd.

5. If it takes one person three days to paint an apartment, it should take three people a third of the time. This equation does not hold; the time savings associated with the additional people is less than expected. This is due to

   a. social loafing.
   b. social facilitation.
   c. induced compliance.
   d. psychological reactance.

6. Fran lost Henry's notes. She helped him look for them, and found someone to lend Henry notes. Fran concluded that she was not such a bad person after all. Fran's conclusion suggests that her compliance was due to a need to

   a. restore reactance.
   b. regain some lost self-esteem.
   c. maintain cognitive dissonance.
   d. provide a refutational defense.

7. Charles asked people to donate $100 to the Red Cross. When they refused, he asked if they would donate $10. Charles is likely to achieve some success in getting people to donate $10 because of

   a. social facilitation.
   b. low-balling.
   c. the foot-in-the-door technique.
   d. reciprocal concessions.

8. Which of the following is a likely explanation of why commitment increases compliance?

   a. It changes a person's self-perception.
   b. It activates social facilitation.
   c. It reduces negative reinforcement.
   d. It minimizes the need for false consensus.

9. Carlson, your textbook author, believes that people comply with the requests of attractive individuals because of

   a. social facilitation.
   b. classical conditioning.
   c. biology.
   d. the fundamental attributional error.

10. The soldiers killed everyone in the village on orders from their sergeant. Milgram's studies would suggest that these soldiers

    a. are cruel, inhumane sadists.
    b. behaved as many ordinary people would by following orders.
    c. confused conformity with obedience.
    d. attributed their behavior to dispositional factors.

11. What does the phenomenon of psychological reactance suggest about how people will respond

to laws requiring the use of seat belts?

a. People will comply eagerly to the request by authority to wear seat belts.
b. People will resent being forced to wear their seat belts.
c. People will use their own judgment to determine the effectiveness of seat belts.
d. People will comply with the law because "everyone else is."

12. Petty, Cacioppo, and Goldman (1981) found that people are influenced by the

a. quality of an argument rather than by the authority of the person presenting the argument.
b. authority of the person presenting an argument rather than the quality of the argument.
c. quality of an argument rather than the authority of the presenter when the issues are important to them.
d. authority of the presenter rather than the quality of the arguments when the issues are important to them.

13. Although they come from widely different backgrounds, Rita and Lisa are friends. The simplest explanation of their friendship is that

a. Rita admires Lisa's grace and Lisa adores this admiration.
b. in college they share the same dorm room.
c. they share many of the same opinions.
d. they serve as sources of reinforcement for each other.

14. Psychological research suggests that when people go on dates arranged through a computer dating service, they are likely to like their date more if the date

a. shares their opinions.
b. is physically attractive.
c. plays hard to get.
d. has a nice personality.

15. Which of the following has been offered as an alternative interpretation of Dutton and Aron's study of the man and woman on a bridge?

a. misattribution of arousal
b. biologically based chemistry
c. psychological reactance
d. negative reinforcement

INTEGRATING QUESTIONS

1. Many common expressions may have a basis in reality. Examine each of the following expressions and review the psychological studies and concepts that support or refute these expressions.

   a. The grass is greener on the other side.

   b. Birds of a feather flock together.

   c. Without a particular spark, love will not occur.

   d. Neither a borrower nor lender be.

   e. Beauty is only skin deep.

2. A friend is running for student body president. Plan a campaign strategy that uses the

information presented in this chapter.

3. People perceive themselves to be rational. Do you think people are rational? Do you perceive yourself to be rational? What does the research and theory on attribution, attitudes, social influences, and attraction suggest about our rationality?

ANSWERS

2.1 external; internal
2.2 a) Sarah is like many other two-year-olds. b) Joyce is rude and inconsiderate.
2.4 a) situational, consensus. b) dispositional, consensus. c) situational, distinctiveness
3.1 a) internal, b) group
3.4 a) false consensus
4.1 Motivational biases are more concerned with processes having personal significance for the individual.
4.2 a) illusion of personal causation, b) credit for success, blame for failure
5.2 a) The children will feel fearful as a result of their mother's fear. Affective—negative (fear); cognitive-positive (shots are beneficial; they prevent disease). b) They will have acquired this fear through vicarious classical conditioning. c) modeling of their mother's words
6.1 specificity of the attitudes, attitudes formed through self-attribution, situation where there are few constraints on behavior
7.2 a) discrepancy between his cognitions and his situation, b) apparent discrepancy between cognition and behavior
7.3 They will experience cognitive dissonance when they are made aware of the discrepancy between their attitudes and behavior.
8.2 Probably the boy who was forced to apologize will hold onto his negative attitude regarding the other boy, whereas this other boy will assume a more favorable attitude towards the first lad and the situation.
10.1 a) Once the decision is made, Bob will assemble facts to support his decision. b) Amy will be more committed to her lessons because she has invested her own resources.
10.3 is not
11.1 fewer
11.2 b) behavioral analysis in terms of reinforcement, punishment and discriminative stimuli that signal the contingencies in the particular situation
12.2 persuader, less, intelligent
13.3 Canned laughter may increase people's liking of the television shows and advertisements.
14.1 inhibits
14.3 In clear emergencies, people are more likely to help.
15.2 perform well-rehearsed tasks
15.3 task is complex and not well learned
16.2 identifiability
16.3 produces contingencies of reinforcement
17.4 a) reciprocal concessions, b) moderately successful
18.1 a) foot-in-the-door, b) low-balling
18.3 changes in self-image and changes in perception of compliance
20.2 The subjects were asked to teach a confederate a word list by shocking him when he made mistakes. Most subjects continued to shock the subject even when he screamed in pain and told them he had a heart condition,
20.3 The learner's presence decreased the likelihood that the subject would administer maximum shock to him, but still over one-third administered shock in this condition.
20.4 We tend to attribute other people's behavior to dispositional causes when their behavior may be more a function of the situation than of their personality.
21.1 Women in Miami felt their freedom to choose was threatened so they became more committed to using phosphate detergents.
21.2 Juliet's freedom to choose was threatened so in response Romeo became even more desirable to her.
22.2 authority, strength of argument, subjects' belief regarding effect upon themselves

Chapter 13

22.4 expert, affect upon their lives, awareness of social influence
23.3 shared opinion, liking

Self Test: Lesson I			Self Test: Lesson II		
1.	a	Obj. 13-1	1.	b	Obj. 13-13
2.	a	Obj. 13-2	2.	d	Obj. 13-13
3.	d	Obj. 13-3	3.	d	Obj. 13-14
4.	d	Obj. 13-4	4.	b	Obj. 13-15
5.	c	Obj. 13-5	5.	a	Obj. 13-16
6.	b	Obj. 13-6	6.	b	Obj. 13-17
7.	d	Obj. 13-7	7.	d	Obj. 13-17
8.	b	Obj. 13-7	8.	a	Obj. 13-18
9.	d	Obj. 13-8	9.	b	Obj. 13-19
10.	b	Obj. 13-8	10.	b	Obj. 13-20
11.	b	Obj. 13-9	11.	b	Obj. 13-21
12.	a	Obj. 13-10	12.	c	Obj. 13-22
13.	c	Obj. 13-10	13.	d	Obj. 13-23
14.	b	Obj. 13-11	14.	b	Obj. 13-23
15.	d	Obj. 13-12	15.	d	Obj. 13-24

13.1 OBJ 13-1

ATTRIBUTION

13.2 OBJ 13-1

IMPLICIT PSYCHOLOGY

13.3 OBJ 13-2

COVARIANCE METHOD

13.4 OBJ 13-2

SITUATIONAL FACTORS

13.5 OBJ 13-2

DISPOSITIONAL FACTORS

13.6 OBJ 13-2

SITUATIONAL DEMANDS

13.7 OBJ 13-2

DISCOUNTING

13.8 OBJ 13-2

CONSENSUS

13.9 OBJ 13-2

CONSISTENCY

13.10 OBJ 13-2

DISTINCTIVENESS

13.11 OBJ 13-3

INTELLECTUAL BIAS

13.12 OBJ 13-3

FUNDAMENTAL ATTRIBUTIONAL ERROR

13.13 OBJ 13-3

FALSE CONSENSUS

13.14 OBJ 13-4

MOTIVATIONAL BIAS

13.15 OBJ 13-4

PERSONAL CAUSATION

13.16 OBJ 13-5

ATTITUDE

13.1 Obj 13-1

inferences individuals develop to explain the causes of people's behavior

13.2 Obj 13-1

private theories of reality that allow people to organize their observations and predict future behavior; usually cannot be expressed in words

13.3 Obj 13-2

procedure for forming hypotheses about cause and effect; when two events vary together or occur together, we suspect cause-effect relation

13.4 Obj 13-2

causes or influences upon behavior external to the individual

13.5 Obj 13-2

features internal to the person such as temperament, mood, personality that are perceived as the causes of that person's behavior

13.6 Obj 13-2

factors in the environment that stimulate (coerce) people to act in a given way

13.7 Obj 13-2

behavior perceived as having been caused by the situation is regarded as revealing little or nothing about the person

13.8 Obj 13-2

behavior shared by many others; assumed caused by situational demands

13.9 Obj 13-2

degree to which person's behavior occurs reliably; consistent behavior attributed to dispositional factors; inconsistent to situational ones

13.10 Obj 13-2

degree to which a situation is presumed to be unusual and responsible for behavior that is unusual for the individual

13.11 Obj 13-3

cognitive biases that lead to inaccurate assessments of people or situations (e.g., fundamental attributional error, false consensus)

13.12 Obj 13-3

attribution of a person's behavior to dispositional causes when the behavior was situationally induced

13.13 Obj 13-3

attributional error; assumption that one's own behavior is representative of a general consensus

13.14 Obj 13-4

biases that have personal significance to individuals and that may lead them to make inaccurate judgments, e.g., illusion of personal causation

13.15 Obj 13-4

belief, whether justified or not, that one's behavior has an effect upon subsequent events

13.16 Obj 13-5

affective belief that may affect behavior; affective component formed by classical conditioning; cognitive, by modeling and other processes

13.17 OBJ 13-5

MODELING

13.25 OBJ 13-15

SOCIAL FACILITATION

13.18 OBJ 13-6

SELF-ATTRIBUTION

13.26 OBJ 13-16

SOCIAL LOAFING

13.19 OBJ 13-7

COGNITIVE DISSONANCE

13.27 OBJ 13-16

IDENTIFIABILITY

13.20 OBJ 13-7

DISSONANCE REDUCTION

13.28 OBJ 13-17

RECIPROCITY

13.21 OBJ 13-11

SELF-PERCEPTION THEORY

13.29 OBJ 13-18

LOW-BALLING

13.22 OBJ 13-12

IMPRESSION MANAGEMENT

13.30 OBJ 13-18

FOOT-IN-THE-DOOR TECHNIQUE

13.23 OBJ 13-13

ASCH EFFECT

13.31 OBJ 13-21

PSYCHOLOGICAL REACTANCE

13.24 OBJ 13-14

BYSTANDER INTERVENTION

13.32 OBJ 13-23

INTERPERSONAL ATTRACTION

13.25 Obj 13-15

positive influence an audience has upon an individual's performance

13.26 Obj 13-16

decrease in individual effort associated with the presence of a group

13.27 Obj 13-16

belief that one's own efforts can be distinguished from those of others, that contingencies of reinforcement exist; if present, social facilitation likely

13.28 Obj 13-17

returning a favor; responding with concession to a concession

13.29 Obj 13-18

sales technique; customer agrees to buy at low price, then is told that price is mistake—higher price is required

13.30 Obj 13-18

sales technique; customer agrees to perform small behavior, then when asked to perform larger behavior, tends to agree since already committed

13.31 Obj 13-21

threat to person's sense of freedom; may cause person to do opposite of what is desired by person perceived as threat

13.32 Obj 13-23

people's tendency to approach other people and evaluate them positively

13.17 Obj 13-5

imitation and adoption of observed behaviors and attitudes

13.18 Obj 13-6

inference about own dispositions as result of observing oneself; attitudes based on this inference provide good predictor of future behavior

13.19 Obj 13-7

Festinger's theory; discrepancy between attitudes, behavior or self-image; leads to discomfort and motivates person to reduce the discrepancy

13.20 Obj 13-7

removal of discomfort that arises from discrepancy between attitudes, behavior, or self-image by eliminating or minimizing the discrepancy

13.21 Obj 13-11

Bem's reaction to cognitive dissonance theory; weak, ambiguous internal cues cause people to examine own behavior to determine their inner states

13.22 Obj 13-12

controlling one's behavior and expressed attitudes to appear in a certain desired way

13.23 Obj 13-13

conformity in response to group solidarity; changes behavior, not attitudes

13.24 Obj 13-14

assistance to a person in need; inhibited by presence of nonresponsive others

CHAPTER 14
Personality

INTRODUCTION

This chapter introduces you to the research on human personality (Objective 1), the trait theories of personality (Objectives 2-3), the assessment and heritability of personality traits (Objectives 4-7), the behavioral/cognitive theories of personality (Objectives 8-11), person perception (Objectives 12-15), and Freud's psychodynamic approach to personality (Objectives 16-21). Lesson I covers Objectives 1-11 and Lesson II, Objectives 12-21.

CONCEPT CARDS AND EXERCISES

After you have surveyed and read the text, assemble the concept cards located at the end of this chapter. Use them to learn the important terms, then begin reading the text again, one learning objective at a time, and work through the exercises for each lesson. Answers for questions marked with an asterisk are found at the end of the chapter.

SELF TESTS

Each lesson is followed by a multiple-choice self test. After you are proficient with a lesson's concept cards and exercises, take the self test to see whether you have mastered the material. Review those objectives for questions you answered incorrectly.

INTEGRATING QUESTIONS

To challenge yourself further, answer the integrating questions at the end of the chapter. These questions ask you to apply the information you have learned to consider larger theoretical or real-life issues.

LESSON I: TRAIT THEORIES, ASSESSMENT OF PERSONALITY TRAITS, BEHAVIORAL/COGNITIVE THEORIES

1. Identify the two kinds of efforts required by research on human personality. (p. 571)

* 1.1 Indicate which of the following illustrates the nominal fallacy.

a) John came to the rescue because he is a good person.

b) When Alison feels pressured by her job, she overeats.

Chapter 14

* 1.2 Consider the example of the nominal fallacy in 1.1. Describe the first step it has met in understanding personality and note the next step it still needs to take.

2. Distinguish between personality types and personality traits by giving examples of each. (p. 571-573)

* 2.1 Use Galen's personality types to identify the personalities in the following examples.

   a) Dan is a slow, steady kind of a guy.

   b) Dean sees a dark lining even in the brightest clouds.

   c) Nan always smiles and has a good word for everyone.

   d) Mark responds poorly to changes. He whines, complains, and lashes out at others.

2.2 Identify the following as examples of personality types or traits. Give reasons for your answers.

   a) He's such a Scorpio.

   b) She's awfully shy.

3. Describe and evaluate the contributions made by Allport, Cattell, and Eysenck to the identification of personality traits. (pp. 573-578)

3.1 Give an original example of a cardinal trait.

3.2 By referring to the cardinal trait you described in 3.1, explain how a central trait differs from a cardinal trait.

* 3.3 Cattell identified sixteen personality traits by using the method of ______________

______________; describe this method.

* 3.4 According to Eysenck's approach, the stereotypical accountant is likely to be a(n)

______________; the stereotypical politician is likely to be a(n)

______________, and the stereotypical hypochondriac is likely to be a(n)

______________.

3.5 Take the four personality types hypothesized by Galen and identify the personality dimensions observed by Eysenck that correspond with these types.

3.6 Cheek and Buss (1981) reported two studies on shyness and sociability. For each study, identity its

   a) hypothesis.

b) methods.

c) results.

d) implications for Eysenck's ideas regarding introversion.

4. Describe the rational and empirical strategies of test construction. (pp. 578-579)

4.1 Suppose you wanted to develop a test to measure the traits of masculinity and femininity. Describe what you would need to do to develop such a test using the

a) rational strategy of measurement.

b) empirical strategy of measurement.

4.2 Describe the factors that would be necessary for the success of your test developed according to the

a) rational strategy of measurement.

b) empirical strategy of measurement.

5. Describe the way the Minnesota Multiphasic Personality Inventory was constructed, its scales, and its applications. (pp. 579-581)

* 5.1 Explain how the Minnesota Multiphasic Personality Inventory (MMPI) is an objective test.

5.2 Describe the a) construction, b) scales, and c) uses of the MMPI.

6. Explain the nature of objective and projective tests, and describe the Rorschach Inkblot Test and the Thematic Apperception Test. (pp. 581-583)

* 6.1 Suppose there were two tests that assessed defensiveness. One was an objective test; the other, projective. How would these test differ?

* 6.2 Explain what makes the Rorschach Inkblot Test and the Thematic Apperception Test (TAT) projective tests.

6.3 Respond to Figure 14.5 as if you were being given the Rorschach and then describe how the following examiners would analyze your response.

a) a psychoanalytically inclined examiner

b) an examiner using empirical methods

6.4 Respond to Figure 14.6 as if you were being given the Thematic Apperception Test.

a) Describe the directions you are following.

b) Describe what features a psychologist would look for in interpreting your responses.

7. Describe the methods, findings, and implications of twin and adoption studies on the heritability of personality traits. (pp. 583-585)

7.1 Describe the study by Loehlin and Nichols (1976). In particular, note the

a) methods.

b) results.

c) implications.

7.2 Summarize the findings of Goldsmith and Gottesman (1981) and Matheny, Wilson, Dolan and Krantz (1981) regarding the stability of personality variables.

7.3 Summarize the results, then identify two implications of the adoption study by Daniels and Plomin (1985).

8. Describe Skinner's radical behaviorism as it relates to personality. (pp. 585-586)

8.1 Define radical behaviorism in your own words.

* 8.2 According to Skinner, behavior is explainable in terms of ______________

________________.

8.3 Joanne is a loving, unselfish child. How would Skinner explain her personality.?

8.4 What are Skinner's positions regarding a) personality structures such as the id and ego and b) the role of heredity in personality?

9. Describe social learning theory and compare it to the radical behavioristic approach to personality. (pp 586-588)

* 9.1 Identify the types of social rewards suggested by the following expressions, and the likely effect of these rewards. Offer reasons for your answers.

a) too much of a good thing

b) It is either right or wrong.

* 9.2 According to Mischel, what are the two most important types of personality characteristics?

* 9.3 Social learning theory emphasizes the effects of ______________ on the ______________ as well as the effects of the ______________ on the person. As a result of these emphases, they make considerable use of the concept of ______________.

9.4 Identify and describe <u>five</u> examples of how social learning theorists use the term <u>self.</u>

9.5 Compare and contrast social learning theory and Skinner's radical behaviorism. Make sure you consider the following issues: observable variables, learning, self, reinforcement, and environment.

9.6 Summarize the classic series of experiments on the roles of observation, learning, and reinforcement as reported by Bandura. Note the experiment's methods, results, and implications.

10. Explain the controversy over the relative importance of traits and situations as predictors of behavior and describe research on this topic. (pp. 588-590)

10.1 Describe Mischel's position regarding the relative merits of traits as predictors of behavior. Offer reasons in support of Mischel's position.

10.2 Review Epstein's response to Mischel's criticism of traits as predictors of behavior.

10.3 Give an example of a powerful situation. Note the likely effect of this situation on the ability of traits to predict behavior.

10.4 Give an example of a powerful trait. Note the effect of this trait on the predictability of behavior.

11. Describe the template method of predicting people's behavior. (pp. 590-591)

* 11.1 Bem and Funder (1978) proposed the ______________ method to ______________ the ______________ of people and ______________.

11.2 Provide and describe a research example of the template method.

11.3 Provide an example of the template method for a person's choice of a date through a computer dating service.

LESSON I SELF TEST

1. The nominal fallacy is an error because it

   a. identifies personality traits without classifying them.
   b. mistakes description for explanation.
   c. explains behavior without analyzing the internal determinants of behavior.
   d. fails to determine the variables that produce and control behavior.

2. What aspect of Galen's theory of personality influences many present theories of personality?

   a. its search for the biological underpinnings of personality
   b. its belief that personality can be measured systematically
   c. its classification of people into different personality types
   d. its avoidance of the nominal fallacy

3. Personality types assume that individual differences

   a. tend to be quantitative.
   b. are best plotted on a curve.
   c. tend to be rational.
   d. tend to be dichotomous.

4. How would a person who is choleric according to Galen's system be classified on Eysenck's dimensions?

   a. stable, introvert
   b. unstable, introvert
   c. stable, extravert
   d. unstable, extravert

5. Cheek and Buss demonstrated that Eysenck's dimension of introversion represents two factors; shyness and sociability. What methods did Cheek and Puss use to arrive at this finding?

   a. factor analysis, empirical strategy
   b. template method, cross-situational reliability
   c. criterion groups, projective tests
   d. rational strategy, objective tests

6. A limitation of the empirical strategy for measuring personality traits is the

   a. validity of the underlying theory.
   b. appropriateness of the criterion group.
   c. correspondence between individuals' responses and their behavior.
   d. the logic of the test items.

7. The Rorschach Inkblot Test controls people's tendency to answer in the socially desirable direction by the ambiguity of its items; the MMPI

   a. avoids social desirability by the specificity of its items.
   b. minimizes social desirability by the range of criterion groups.
   c. minimizes social desirability by the length of the test.
   d. measures social desirability by the inclusion of the validity scales.

8. The Minnesota Multiphasic Personality Inventory is a __________ test whereas the Thematic Apperception Test is a __________ test.

   a. rational; empirical
   b. objective; projective
   c. trait; type
   d. psychoanalytic; factor analytic

9. What does the negligible correlation between biologically unrelated children raised in the same household suggest about the effect of the environment upon a child's personality traits?

   a. The same environment may affect children in different ways.
   b. The environment has no influence.
   c. Environmental factors have less of an influence upon personality traits than do biological

factors.
d. Environmental factors tend to cancel themselves out.

10. Which of the following appear to be most heritable?

a. self-efficacy, self-control
b. egocentrism, introversion
c. neuroticism, sensitivity
d. irritability, activity level

11. Skinner believes that Freudian and other personality theories are wrong because they

a. postulate spirits or moving forces within the person.
b. postulate traits rather than types.
c. underestimate the importance of biological factors.
d. underestimate the importance of dispositional factors.

12. According to Skinner, the way to predict people's behavior is to

a. understand their childhood conflicts.
b. know their reinforcement histories.
c. know their biological heritage.
d. understand their beliefs about themselves.

13. Unlike radical behaviorism, social learning theory postulates that

a. learning can occur in the absence of reinforcement.
b. cognitive concepts are not useful unless they are directly observable.
c. the environment, not the individual, controls the behavior.
d. delay of gratification is determined more by heredity than the environment.

14. Research has found that the relation between personal characteristics and behavior tends to

a. account for only ten percent of the variability of human behavior.
b. be low if the situation is weak.
c. account for thirty percent of the variability of human behavior.
d. be high if the personality trait is stable and heritable.

15. What is the method Bem and Funder proposed for predicting the results of interactions between persons and situations?

a. self-efficacy
b. projective
c. type
d. template

LESSON II: PERSON PERCEPTION AND THE PSYCHODYNAMIC APPROACH TO PERSONALITY

12. Describe how people explain other people's behavior and identify the circumstances under which people are likely to make accurate and inaccurate attributions. (pp. 591-592)

12.1 Define <u>person perception</u> in your own words.

12.2 Identify whether the following describe consensual, consistent, or distinctive behavior patterns.

* a) behavior produced by a powerful trait

* b) behavior produced by a powerful situation

* c) behavior produced by a powerful trait in the face of powerful situations

* 12.3 In laboratory studies people are ______________ at making predictions about other people's traits.

* 12.4 Distinguish between circumscribed and global accuracy.

13. Describe a study that provides an example of behavioral self-confirmation. (pp. 592-593)

* 13.1 When Dana wears jeans, she wears only designer jeans. Her behavior is an example of

_______________ and for her designer jeans are a(n) _______________.

* 13.2 Her new roommate perceives that Dana must be a snob because she wears only jeans that have designer labels. Dana wears these jean because they fit and wear well. On the basis of Broxton's study, speculate on how Dana may respond to her roommate's perceptions and identify the process Dana is likely to follow.

13.3 Summarize the study of behavioral self-confirmation by Swann and Hill (1982) in terms of its methods, results, and implications.

14. Describe the Rotter I-E Scale and the behavior of people who exhibit internal or external locus of control. (pp. 593-595)

14.1 a) Predict how a person who has an external locus of control would plan for retirement.

b) Then predict how a person with an internal locus of control would plan for retirement.

14.2 Describe a circumstance in which having an external locus of control is more desirable than having an internal locus of control.

14.3 Describe the Rotter I-E scale.

* 14.4 Identify two criticisms of the Rotter I-E scale.

14.5 Describe how people who have an internal locus of control and those who have an external locus of control would behave in situations involving manipulation, well-reasoned arguments, attempts at persuasion by authorities, and tasks controlled by luck or skill.

15. Describe how primary control, secondary control, predictive control, and vicarious control affect behavior. (pp. 595-596)

* 15.1 Label the behavior of the following individuals by using the types of control proposed by Rothbaum, Weisz, and Snyder (1982).

    a) Maria was king maker. She acted behind the scenes and helped Kevin win the campaign.

    b) Lisa felt that after their fifth date she would marry Bob, and a year later she did.

    c) Sean abandoned his hopes of becoming a doctor because even though he was a good student, he feared he would not be accepted into medical school.

    d) Michael was a "hanger-on." He did whatever Ed said because he valued his association with him.

15.2 Develop your own examples to the four styles of control described by Rothbaum et al. (1982).

16. Describe Freud's background and the experiences that influenced the development of his psychodynamic theory of personality. (pp. 597-598)

* 16.1 Describe Freud's position with respect to the irrational.

16.2 Provide a brief biographical sketch of Sigmund Freud.

16.3 What conclusions did Freud draw from the case of Anna O? What conclusions have others drawn from this case?

16.4 Describe the methods Freud used to develop and refine his theory of personality.

16.5 Explain how Freud's theory of personality is psychodynamic.

17. Identify and describe the structures of the mind as Freud conceived of them. (p. 598)

* 17.1 Identify the structures of the mind that most control the behaviors in each of the following. Justify your answers.

    a) A child has a temper tantrum because his mother will not buy him a candy bar.

    b) Jen felt guilty when she caught herself wishing her mother dead.

    c) If I finish this homework, then I can watch television.

17.2 Define the terms <u>id</u>, <u>ego</u>, <u>reality principle</u>, <u>superego</u>, <u>ego ideal</u>, and <u>conscience</u> in your own words.

17.3 According to Freud, what produces intrapsychic conflicts?

17.4 Give an original example of a compromise formation.

17.5 The textbook offers one example of a dream as compromise formation. Using the same situation, suggest another dream that has the same latent content but different manifest content.

18. Identify the purpose of a defense mechanism and describe six of the most important ones. (pp. 598-599)

* 18.1 Describe, in general terms, the purpose of the defense mechanisms.

18.2 Although you have limited information, make an educated guess regarding the defenses exhibited in the following situations. Explain the reasons for your answers.

* a) Despite her divorce, Ann is pledged to the family. She campaigns against rights for homosexuals.

* b) Terry could not acknowledge that she no longer wanted to date Ray, who loved her dearly; nevertheless, she lamented to him, "You don't love me anymore."

* c) Bill did not recognize that his work as a war correspondent mirrored his relationship with his parents.

* d) After Joe broke up with Mary, she told herself, "I'm really better off without him."

18.3 Give original examples of the defense mechanisms of repression and conversion.

19. Describe Freud's psychosexual theory of personality development. (pp. 599-601)

19.1 Describe in order of their occurrence the stages of psychosexual development.

* 19.2 Describe in general terms what leads a person to move from one stage of psychosexual development to another.

19.3 According to Freud, how do the psychosexual development of males and females differ?

* 19.4 According to Freud, what happens when a person fails to move fully into the next stage of psychosexual development?

* 19.5 At which stage of psychosexual development is it likely that the following individuals have become fixated?

a) Although Georgia denies it, she is an outrageous flirt.

b) Ed is so stubborn that once he makes his mind, under no circumstances will he reconsider.

c) Morgan always has to have something in her mouth, for example a lock of hair, a cigarette, gum, a cup of coffee.

d) Don't cross Tina because she has a quick and violent temper.

20. Describe the procedure, results, and implications of an experimental test of Freud's concept of repression. (pp. 601-602)

* 20.1 Note at least one negative and one positive assessment of Freud's theory held by most experimental psychologists.

20.2 Summarize the procedures of many experiments that have investigated the existence of repression.

20.3 Describe the study on repression by D'Zurilla (1965) by noting his methods, results and interpretation.

20.4 What other interpretations of D'Zurilla's study are possible, and what do these other interpretations suggest about Freudian theory?

21. Describe modern research on self-deception and the implications of this research for Freud's concept of a defense mechanism. (pp. 602-603)

21.1 Develop your own example of self-deception and describe how this example meets the three conditions necessary for self-deception noted by Gur and Sackheim (1979).

21.2 Summarize the experiment on self-deception by Quattrone and Tversky (1984) in terms of its

a) hypothesis.

b) method.

c) results.

d) implications.

LESSON II SELF TEST

1. What kind of accuracy is most required by person perception?

a. projective
b. consensual
c. global
d. circumscribed

2. Swann and Hill (1982) found that when subjects received feedback that agreed with their own perceptions of themselves, they assumed more of that characteristic. Swann and Hill interpreted their results to be a demonstration of

a. repression.
b. internal locus of control.

c. behavioral self-confirmation.
d. predictive control.

3. If a person answers yes to questions such as "in the case of the well-prepared student there is rarely if ever such a thing as an unfair test," this person most likely has a(n)

a. defensive personality.
b. internal locus of control.
c. tendency towards extraversion.
d. tendency towards secondary control.

4. Which of the following is most characteristic of people who have an external locus of control?

a. They are less willing to change their opinions in the face of well reasoned arguments.
b. They tend to overrate their performance on tasks that are determined by luck.
c. They are influenced more by their peers than by authority.
d. They tend to be less emotionally healthy in environments which they cannot control.

5. When Bob is confronted by tasks of moderate difficulty, he analyzes the task, makes a plan, and works hard to succeed. Which of the following types of control best characterizes Bob's behavior?

a. vicarious secondary control
b. vicarious primary control
c. predictive primary control
d. predictive secondary control

6. Freud's theory of personality is psychodynamic in the sense that

a. motives for people's behavior are usually unconscious.
b. cure requires a re-experiencing of the emotion associated with the cause of the disorder.
c. the nervous system seeks constant stimulation and change.
d. there is an ongoing struggle among various aspects of personality.

7. According to Freud, the guilt an adolescent may feel over masturbation is due to the

a. id.
b. libido.
c. superego.
d. ego.

8. On a conscious level Mark wanted to help people but on an unconscious level he wanted to hurt them. He satisfied both these desires by becoming a surgeon by which he helped people by cutting (hurting) them. Mark's behavior is an example of

a. compromise formation.
b. catharsis.
c. internalized prohibitions.
d. projection.

9. Which of the following is a signal for a defense mechanism?

a. ego-ideal
b. internalized prohibition
c. libido
d. anxiety

10. A mother constantly checks if her healthy infant is breathing. This overprotective behavior may mask the mother's hostility to the child through the defense of

a. repression.
b. reaction formation.
c. projection.
d. sublimation.

11. At what stage is a child likely to say to her mother, "No, I'm Daddy's girl."?

a. anal
b. genital
c. phallic
d. oral

12. According to Freud, a person who received too much or too little gratification during a stage of psychosexual development is likely to become __________ at that stage.

a. cathected
b. introjected
c. fixated
d. comprised

13. D'Zurilla observed that subjects who had been told that their responses indicated latent homosexuality were not able to recall many of the words from this measure of sexuality. How did D'Zurilla interpret his results?

a. as a demonstration of repression
b. interference causing poor recall
c. poor recall due to internalized prohibitions
d. results attributable to decay

14. Identify a serious problem of Freud's theory of personality.

a. Its explanations are simplistic.
b. It is difficult to validate experimentally.
c. It is too complicated for even the educated lay person to understand.
d. It is based on empirical data.

15. Quattrone and Tversky studied how long people could keep their hands immersed in cold water. What did they find?

a. Because people can repress negative information about themselves, they can maintain their level of performance across situations.
b. People who were not fixated at the early stages of psychosexual development were better able to tolerate the cold.
c. People who operated according to the reality principle withstood the cold less well.
d. People's behavior was affected by beliefs that they did not admit to themselves.

INTEGRATING QUESTIONS

1. There have been several attempts to reconcile the psychodynamic and behavioristic approaches to personality. What commonalities, if any, exist between these approaches? What do each of these approaches suggest about such issues as the notion of free will, the role of heredity and environment upon behavior, the problem of committing the nominal fallacy, and the problem of creating adequate tests to assess personality?

2. For each of the following examples, compare and contrast the explanations suggested by Skinner's radical behaviorism, social learning theory, and Freud's psychodynamic theory.

a) Four-year-old Jeremy insists on wearing painter's pants and carrying a lunch bucket, just like his father does.

b) Damian is so concerned that children not be exposed to pornography and other corrupting influences that he had joined the school district's advisory committee. His committee work requires that he examine all sorts of books to determine if they are suitable for children.

c) Cathy took the Rotter I-E and received high scores on the scale measuring internal locus of control.

3. How are person perception, self-deception, and behavioral self-confirmation related?

ANSWERS

1.1 a)
1.2 First, identify trait, then explain it.
2.1 a) phlegmatic, b) melancholic, c) sanguine, d) choleric
3.3 factor analysis
3.4 introvert, extravert, neurotic
5.1 The MMPI has questions that can be answered with either a "Yes" or a "No." There are explicit rules for scoring the test results.
6.1 Objective test—unambiguous questions, usually limited responses, explicit rules for scoring; projective—ambiguous test stimuli onto which subjects "project' their personality
6.2 The test items are ambiguous. Subjects "project" their own ideas and personality onto test items.
8.2 instrumental conditioning
9.1 a) process rewards—too much of this reward is aversive and will reduce person's sociability; b) control reward is bipolar, pleasurable and reinforcing or negative and aversive, likely to affect emotionality, self-esteem, and formality
9.2 those determining how people perceive and categorize situations and how much value they place on social reinforcers and punishers
9.3 person, environment, environment, self
11.1 template, predict, interaction, situation
12.2 a) consistent, b) consensus, c) distinctive
12.3 not good
12.4 global predicts behavior over wide range of situations; circumscribed predicts behavior over limited range
13.1 self-presentation, identity cue
13.2 Dana will do something to indicate that she is not a snob and may explain her reasons for wearing designer jeans. The process she will use is behavioral self-confirmation.
14.4 significance of answers obvious, failure to distinguish between attributions regarding good and bad outcomes
15.1 a) vicarious primary, b) predictive primary, c) predictive secondary, d) vicarious secondary
16.1 Freud claimed much of what we do is irrational.
17.1 a) id, b) superego, c) ego
18.1 to protect the ego from acknowledging unacceptable impulses
18.2 a) reaction formation—warding off own homosexual feelings; b) projection—attributing her own unacceptable negative feelings to Ray; c) sublimation—channeling desires into acceptable avenues; d) rationalization—justify unpleasant situation
19.2 physical development that provided a change in the location of the body most sensitive to "sexual" stimulation
19.4 fixated
19.5 a) phallic, b) anal retentive, c) oral, d) anal expulsive
20.1 positive—stimulated research and clinical practice; negative—difficult to test, concepts not well-defined, not directly observable

Self Test: Lesson I

1. b Obj. 14-1
2. c Obj. 14-2
3. d Obj. 14-2
4. d Obj. 14-3
5. a Obj. 14-3
6. c Obj. 14-4
7. d Obj. 14-5
8. b Obj. 14-6
9. a Obj. 14-7
10. d Obj. 14-7
11. a Obj. 14-8
12. b Obj. 14-8
13. a Obj. 14-9
14. a Obj. 14-10
15. d Obj. 14-11

Self Test: Lesson II

1. d Obj. 14-12
2. c Obj. 14-13
3. b Obj. 14-14
4. b Obj. 14-14
5. c Obj. 14-15
6. d Obj. 14-16
7. c Obj. 14-17
8. a Obj. 14-17
9. d Obj. 14-18
10. b Obj. 14-18
11. c Obj. 14-19
12. c Obj. 14-19
13. a Obj. 14-20
14. b Obj. 14-21
15. d Obj. 14-21

14.1 OBJ 14-1

NOMINAL FALLACY

14.2 OBJ 14-2

PERSONALITY TYPE

14.3 OBJ 14-2

PERSONALITY TRAIT

14.4 OBJ 14-3

INTROVERSION

14.5 OBJ 14-3

EXTRAVERSION

14.6 OBJ 14-3

NEUROTICISM

14.7 OBJ 14-4

RATIONAL STRATEGY

14.8 OBJ 14-4

EMPIRICAL STRATEGY

14.9 OBJ 14-4

CRITERION GROUP

14.10 OBJ 14-5

OBJECTIVE TEST

14.11 OBJ 14-5

MINNESOTA MULTIPHASIC PERSONALITY INVENTORY (MMPI)

14.12 OBJ 14-6

PROJECTIVE TEST

14.13 OBJ 14-6

RORSCHACH INKBLOT TEST

14.14 OBJ 14-6

THEMATIC APPERCEPTION TEST (TAT)

14.15 OBJ 14-8

RADICAL BEHAVIORISM

14.16 OBJ 14-9

PROCESS REWARD

14.9 Obj 14-4

groups that differ on some known dimension; used in empirical strategy of test construction

14.10 Obj 14-5

psychological test that has explicit rules for scoring unambiguous items; usually answer choices restricted

14.11 Obj 14-5

objective test developed by empirical strategy; used in assessment of personality features

14.12 Obj 14-6

psychological test whose items are ambiguous; individuals "project" their personalities onto these items

14.13 Obj 14-6

projective test; say what see in ten inkblots; then identify features in cards that determined what was seen

14.14 Obj 14-6

projective test developed by Henry Murray and C.D. Morgan; tell complete story about each picture card

14.15 Obj 14-8

pure form of behaviorism proposed by B. F. Skinner; behavior explained by operant conditioning

14.16 Obj 14-9

stimuli that involve social stimulation; moderate amount is pleasant, reinforcing; too much or little is aversive

14.1 Obj 14-1

erroneous belief; mistakes description for explanation

14.2 Obj 14-2

divides people according to categories

14.3 Obj 14-2

personality dimension upon which people may vary across the range

14.4 Obj 14-3

according to Eysenck, reserved, inner-directed type

14.5 Obj 14-3

according to Eysenck, outgoing, people-oriented type

14.6 Obj 14-3

according to Eysenck, unstable, quickly aroused, slowly calmed personality type

14.7 Obj 14-4

approach to test construction; begins with theoretical definition of trait

14.8 Obj 14-4

approach to test construction; keeps only those items that discriminate between the criterion groups

14.17 OBJ 14-9

CONTENT REWARD

14.25 OBJ 14-12

CIRCUMSCRIBED ACCURACY

14.18 OBJ 14-9

SELF-CONCEPT

14.26 OBJ 14-12

GLOBAL ACCURACY

14.19 OBJ 14-9

SELF CONTROL

14.27 OBJ 14-13

SELF-PRESENTATION

14.20 OBJ 14-9

DELAY OF GRATIFICATION

14.28 OBJ 14-13

IDENTITY CUE

14.21 OBJ 14-9

SELF-EFFICACY

14.29 OBJ 14-13

BEHAVIORAL SELF-CONFIRMATION

14.22 OBJ 14-10

CROSS-SITUATIONAL RELIABILITY

14.30 OBJ 14-14

LOCUS OF CONTROL

14.23 OBJ 14-11

TEMPLATE

14.31 OBJ 14-14

ROTTER I-E SCALE

14.24 OBJ 14-12

PERSON PERCEPTION

14.32 OBJ 14-15

PRIMARY CONTROL

14.25 Obj 14-12

correct prediction of person's behavior in particular situation

14.17 Obj 14-9

stimuli that involve interpersonal relationships, either reinforcing or aversive

14.26 Obj 14-12

correct prediction of person's behavior across all situations

14.18 Obj 14-9

perception of our own personality and abilities; important concept in social learning theory

14.27 Obj 14-13

person's behavior selected to make particular impression; usually reliable across similar situations

14.19 Obj 14-9

person's ability to withhold normally elicited response; important concept in social learning theory

14.28 Obj 14-13

behavior such as style of dress or musical taste that gives others idea of our personality

14.20 Obj 14-9

self-denial of immediate reward for larger, long-term reward

14.29 Obj 14-13

behavior to correct and confirm our self-concept to others

14.21 Obj 14-9

belief in one's ability to succeed; linked to self-control and self-concept; important concept in Bandura's version of social learning theory

14.30 Obj 14-14

belief as to the causes of one's behavior

14.22 Obj 14-10

measure of consistency of behavior and attitudes across situations

14.31 Obj 14-14

measures belief in internal versus external locus of control

14.23 Obj 14-11

as conceived by Bem and Funder, patterns used to categorize and predict person-by-situation interaction

14.32 Obj 14-15

person's direct control of his or her physical and social environment

14.24 Obj 14-12

process of observations, inferences, and prediction of people's behavior

14.33 OBJ 14-15

SECONDARY CONTROL

14.34 OBJ 14-15

PREDICTIVE CONTROL

14.35 OBJ 14-15

VICARIOUS CONTROL

14.36 OBJ 14-16

PSYCHODYNAMIC

14.37 OBJ 14-16

CATHARSIS

14.38 OBJ 14-17

ID

14.39 OBJ 14-17

LIBIDO

14.40 OBJ 14-17

EGO

14.41 OBJ 14-17

REALITY PRINCIPLE

14.42 OBJ 14-17

SUPEREGO

14.43 OBJ 14-17

CONSCIENCE

14.44 OBJ 14-17

EGO-IDEAL

14.45 OBJ 14-17

SEXUAL INSTINCTIVE DRIVE

14.46 OBJ 14-17

AGGRESSIVE INSTINCTIVE DRIVE

14.47 OBJ 14-17

INTERNALIZED PROHIBITION

14.48 OBJ 14-17

COMPROMISE FORMATION

14.41 Obj 14-17

allows ego to delay gratification of a drive until appropriate goal located

14.42 Obj 14-17

according to Freud, that part of personality that includes ideals andinternalized rules of society; may produce guilt

14.43 Obj 14-17

part of superego; internalized rules and restrictions of society

14.44 Obj 14-17

part of superego; what person would like to be

14.45 Obj 14-17

according to Freud, one of two primary drives; demands outlet in sexual behavior

14.46 Obj 14-17

according to Freud, one of two primary drives; demands outlet in aggressive behavior

14.47 Obj 14-17

impedes expression of instinctual drives and thus prevents self from experiencing guilt

14.48 Obj 14-17

expression of instinctual drives transformed by internalized prohibitions into more acceptable form

14.33 Obj 14-15

control of environment through adaptation to it

14.34 Obj 14-15

tendency to anticipate what will happen in particular situation

14.35 Obj 14-15

tendency to deal with environment by influencing powerful people or by submitting to and identifying with them

14.36 Obj 14-16

struggle between parts of the personality for dominance

14.37 Obj 14-16

according to Freud, relief felt when people emotionally relive situations that produced their symptoms

14.38 Obj 14-17

according to Freud, instinctual, wholly unconscious part of personality; contains libido, provides all psychic energy

14.39 Obj 14-17

primary source of motivation in the id; insistent, nonresponsive to reality demands

14.40 Obj 14-17

according to Freud, part of personality that controls and integrates behavior; voice of reason

14.49 OBJ 14-17

MANIFEST CONTENT

14.50 OBJ 14-17

LATENT CONTENT

14.51 OBJ 14-17

PRECONSCIOUS

14.52 OBJ 14-18

ANXIETY

14.53 OBJ 14-18

DEFENSE MECHANISM

14.54 OBJ 14-18

REPRESSION

14.55 OBJ 14-18

REACTION FORMATION

14.56 OBJ 14-18

PROJECTION

14.57 OBJ 14-18

SUBLIMATION

14.58 OBJ 14-18

RATIONALIZATION

14.59 OBJ 14-18

CONVERSION

14.60 OBJ 14-18

HYSTERIA

14.61 OBJ 14-19

ORAL STAGE

14.62 OBJ 14-19

ANAL STAGE

14.63 OBJ 1-19

EXPRESSIVE PERIOD

14.64 OBJ 14-19

RETENTIVE PERIOD

14.57 Obj 14-18

ego's defense of diverting psychic energy from unacceptable drive to an acceptable one

14.58 Obj 14-18

ego's defense of inventing an acceptable reason for behavior that was performed for less acceptable reasons

14.59 Obj 14-18

ego's defense of transforming intrapsychic conflict into physical symptoms

14.60 Obj 14-18

physical symptom without physical cause; product of conversion

14.61 Obj 14-19

Freud's first stage of psychosexual development; pleasure focused around mouth

14.62 Obj 14-19

Freud's second stage of psychosexual development; pleasure focused around anus and sphincter muscles

14.63 Obj 14-19

early anal stage; pleasure derived from expelling feces

14.64 Obj 14-19

later part of anal stage; pleasure derived from holding in feces

14.49 Obj 14-17

actual story line of dream

14.50 Obj 14-17

meaning of a dream

14.51 Obj 14-17

intermediate system between conscious and unconscious

14.52 Obj 14-18

uncomfortable feeling that is produced by intrapsychic conflict and signals ego to utilize a defense

14.53 Obj 14-18

ego's mechanism to protect self from conflict between parts of personality and the resulting anxiety by distorting reality

14.54 Obj 14-18

ego's defense of motivated forgetting of a discomforting idea, feeling, or memory

14.55 Obj 14-18

ego's defense of replacing threatening idea with its opposite

14.56 Obj 14-18

ego's defense of observing in others one's own unacceptable characteristics that one denies

14.65 OBJ 14-19

PHALLIC STAGE

14.66 OBJ 14-19

OEDIPUS COMPLEX

14.67 OBJ 14-19

IDENTIFICATION

14.68 OBJ 14-19

PENIS ENVY

14.69 OBJ 14-19

LATENCY PERIOD

14.70 OBJ 14-19

GENITAL STAGE

14.71 OBJ 14-19

FIXATION

14.72 OBJ 14-21

SELF-DECEPTION

14.65 Obj 14-19

Freud's third stage of psychosexual development; penis or clitoris focus of sexual energy

14.66 Obj 14-19

boy's attachment to his mother during phallic stage

14.67 Obj 14-19

boy models his behavior on that of father; provides resolution to Oedipus complex

14.68 Obj 14-19

distress girl feels when she discovers she and other females do not have penis; motivates attachment to father in phallic stage

14.69 Obj 14-19

Freud's fourth stage of psychosexual development; sexual feelings submerged

14.70 Obj 14-19

Freud's mature stage of psychosexual development

14.71 Obj 14-19

psychologically stuck at a stage of psychosexual development, due to too much or too little frustration at that stage

14.72 Obj 14-21

unconscious, motivated denial of one of two contradictory beliefs that a person holds

CHAPTER 15
The Nature and Causes of Mental Disorders

INTRODUCTION

This chapter provides an introduction to the nature and causes of mental disorders by considering the classification and diagnosis of these disorders (Objectives 1-3) and by examining some of the so-called neurotic disorders (Objectives 4-9), the antisocial personality disorder (Objective 10), and the psychotic disorders including schizophrenia (Objectives 11-16), and the major affective disorders (Objectives 17-21).

As you study this chapter, it may be easy to recognize yourself in some of these disorders. This phenomenon is known as the medical students' disease because just as medical students are apt to recognize in themselves some of the symptoms of the diseases they study, students of psychology are likely to recognize in themselves behaviors that may appear in more exaggerated, and chronic forms in the disorders they study.

This chapter is divided into two lessons; the first lesson covers Objectives 1-10, and the second lesson covers Objectives 11-21.

CONCEPT CARDS AND EXERCISES

After you have surveyed and read the text, assemble the concept cards located at the end of this chapter. Use them to learn the important terms, then begin reading the text again, one learning objective at a time, and work through the exercises for each lesson. Answers for questions marked with an asterisk are found at the end of the chapter.

SELF TESTS

Each lesson is followed by a multiple-choice self test. After you are proficient with a lesson's concept cards and exercises, take the self test to see whether you have mastered the material. Review those objectives for questions you answered incorrectly.

INTEGRATING QUESTIONS

To challenge yourself further, answer the integrating questions at the end of the chapter. These questions ask you to apply the information you have learned to consider larger theoretical or real-life issues.

LESSON I: CLASSIFICATION AND DIAGNOSIS, NONPSYCHOTIC MENTAL DISORDERS, AND THE ANTISOCIAL PERSONALITY DISORDER

Chapter 15

1. Explain the nature of neuroses and psychoses. (p. 611)

1.1 Explaining the difference between neuroses and psychoses, the instructor said that one involved building sand castles in the sky, the other living in them. On the basis of the textbook description of neuroses and psychoses, identify which is like building sand castles in the sky and which is like living in these sand castles. Explain the reasons for your answers.

2. Describe the merits and disadvantages of classification of mental disorders and summarize research findings on this topic. (pp. 611-613)

* 2.1 Describe how the subjects in Rosenhan's study faked mental illness and how these subjects were viewed by the mental health professionals and by the other patients?

2.2 Describe two ways of interpreting Rosenhan's study, one opposing psychiatric diagnosis and one supporting it.

* 2.3 List three reasons for attempting to classify psychological disorders.

3. Describe DSM-III and discuss its merits and limitations. (pp. 613-616).

* 3.1 What is DSM-III and why was it developed?

3.2 Give examples of the praise and criticism DSM-III has received.

4. Describe the symptoms, incidence, and possible causes of panic disorder. (pp. 616-618)

4.1 The word "neurotic" has been absorbed into everyday language; explain, however, what the word means when it is used by clinical psychologists.

4.2 Identify whether the following are examples of neurotic behavior and explain the reasons for your answers.

a) As she walked down the street on a bright sunny day, she thought people were looking at her and conspiring to get her.

b) Rhonda would not go shopping at the mall because just the thought of going made her break out into a cold sweat.

c) Charles laughingly described himself as a workaholic. When he had nothing he had to do, he felt very uncomfortable.

* 4.3 Two categories of anxiety disorders are 1) ______________, which include

______________, ______________, and ______________, and 2) ______________.

4.4 Describe the types of anxiety experienced by someone suffering from a panic disorder.

4.5 Review the evidence that suggests that panic disorder is caused by a) environmental factors and b) biological factors.

5. Describe the symptoms, incidence, and possible causes of the three subtypes of phobic disorders. (pp. 618-620)

* 5.1 According to DSM-III, there are three subclasses of phobic disorders. They are ______________, ______________, and ______________.

5.2 Give an example of each of the these subclasses of phobic disorders.

5.3 Clara is afraid of shopping in the town's newest and largest mall.

a. When would her fear be considered a phobic disorder?

b. If Clara had a phobic disorder, how might a psychoanalyst explain it?

c. How might a behaviorally oriented therapist explain Clara's phobia?

* d. Offer a hypothesis as to why Clara developed this phobia and others in similar circumstances might not.

6. Describe the symptoms, incidence, and possible causes of obsessive compulsive disorder. (pp. 620-621)

* 6.1 Obsessions involve persistent, unwanted ______________; the two principal kinds of obsessions are ______________ and ______________. Compulsions are repetitive, maladaptive ______________; the most characteristic compulsions involve ______________, ______________, ______________, and ______________.

6.2 Explain how a person who is anxious about an exam uses the thought "Look, I studied and I can't expect any more from myself."

6.3 When would this thought (6.2) become an obsession? What would maintain this obsession?

7. Describe the symptoms, incidence, and sex-linked features of somatization disorder. (pp. 621-623)

* 7.1 Two kinds of somatoform disorders are ______________ and ______________.

7.2 When clinicians diagnose a woman as hysterical what do they mean?

a) Are they being sexist?

b) What symptoms is the woman most likely displaying?

c) If this woman is typical of hysterics, what do you know about her?

7.3 What is the difference between someone who is hysterical and someone who is hypochondriacal?

8. Describe the symptoms, incidence, and possible causes of conversion disorder and distinguish it from related disorders. (pp. 623-635)

* 8.1 In what sense is a conversion disorder a pseudoneurological condition?

8.2 What clues would a clinician use to determine if Kathy had a conversion disorder or was malingering if she developed a muscle spasm whenever her husband made sexual demands upon her?

8.3 In the example above, how would a clinician determine whether Kathy had a conversion disorder, a somatization disorder or a psychosomatic disorder?

8.4 Review the case of the man who became blind when watching his wife nurse their baby. (This case, presented by Hofling, is described in your text in the section on conversion disorders.) Explain the development of the man's blindness in terms of

a) psychoanalytic theory.

b) behavioral theory.

9. Describe the symptoms, incidence, and possible causes of three dissociative disorders. (pp. 625-627)

9.1 Name three kinds of dissociative disorders illustrated in these examples. Offer reasons for your answers.

* a) Found on the beach, Georgia could not remember who she was.

* b) Although the fingerprints were identical, the witness said this meek, mild man did not look, act, or sound like the man who had attacked her.

* c) Finding herself in a new town and not knowing how she got there, Julie began a new life. She was dismayed when someone insisted that he knew her from somewhere else.

* 9.2 What are the possible causes of dissociative disorders?

10. Describe the symptoms and incidence of antisocial personality disorder and describe laboratory research on its causes. (pp. 627-632)

* 10.1 Psychopaths have been called many things. Identify five terms that have been used by diagnosticians to label psychopaths.

10.2 Doing an internship in the county jail, you encounter a charming fellow who you later learn has an antisocial personality disorder.

a) What behaviors is this person likely to display?

b) How might the prison's psychologist explain this person's behavior?

10.3 What does the research suggest about people who have an antisocial personality disorder? In particular, note the studies by Hare (1965 a and b) and Guze and colleagues (1967 and 1973).

LESSON I SELF TEST

1. In contrast to people suffering from neuroses, people who have psychoses

   a. overreact to stress.
   b. have learned disorders.
   c. experience severe disruptions in thought processes.
   d. develop their disorder in order to cope with life's problems.

2. Rosenhan's (1973) study of pseudopatients showed that

   a. distinguishing between real and faked symptoms of mental disorders may be difficult.
   b. the mental health community is unable to distinguish between psychoses and neuroses.
   c. psychiatric diagnoses are worthless.
   d. the psychiatric community invests too much time in diagnosis.

3. Graves' disease is an example of how

   a. recognition of a specific diagnostic category precedes development of a successful treatment.
   b. labeling a person exacerbates the condition and in fact, creates an iatrogenic disorder.
   c. psychiatric diagnoses have proven to be unreliable guides for treatment.
   d. mental health professionals can be tricked by people who are malingering.

4. What is the system most commonly used in North America to classify mental disorders?

   a. Encyclopedia of Behavioral and Psychiatric Diseases
   b. Diagnostic and Statistical Manual III
   c. The Thesaurus of the American Psychiatric Association
   d. There is no system that is used most frequently as psychologists and psychiatrists cannot agree.

5. Washing dishes, Hilda felt adrenalin surge through her body. Her heart was beating so fast, it felt like it was going to burst. Hilda's symptoms may be associated with

   a. a panic disorder.

b. catatonic schizophrenia.
c. a psychosomatic disorder.
d. fugue.

6. Individuals who have the panic disorder are likely to have

a. neurotic mothers who failed to recognize their achievements.
b. a high number of first-degree relatives who are alcoholic.
c. physical symptoms of diseases about which they have heard.
d. adaptive anxiety reactions that were developed through classical conditioning.

7. John panics at the thought of having to take a speech class. It is likely that John suffers from

a. a panic disorder.
b. a simple phobia.
c. a social phobia.
d. agoraphobia.

8. Doreen was afraid that she would pull up her skirt and moon every person she saw. This fear is a(n)

a. compulsion.
b. obsession.
c. phobia.
d. conversion reaction.

9. The obsessive compulsive disorder can best be understood in terms of

a. classical conditioning.
b. defense mechanisms.
c. an unresponsive autonomic nervous system.
d. transformation of unconscious impulses into physical symptoms.

10. The primary symptoms of somatoform disorder are

a. cognitive.
b. physical.
c. affective.
d. psychological.

11. Somatization disorder is also known as

a. a pseudoneurological disorder.
b. hysteria.
c. hypochondriasis.
d. a psychosomatic disorder.

12. After watching any hospital show on television, Janice was convinced that she had the diseases of the patients on these programs. Janice seems to suffer from

a. hypochondriasis.
b. a psychosomatic disorder.
c. a conversion disorder.
d. a dissociative disorder.

13. Individuals who have a multiple personality have a

a. dissociative disorder rather than schizophrenia.

b. personality disorder rather than a mental disorder.
c. psychotic rather than neurotic disorder.
d. pseudoneurological condition rather than a conversion disorder.

14. Psychologists have found that men who are psychopaths are likely to have a higher than average number of female relatives who have a __________ disorder.

a. panic
b. dissociative
c. somatization
d. obsessive compulsive

15. Which of the following is most characteristic of individuals who have an antisocial personality disorder?

a. lack of social graces
b. emotional excitability
c. unresponsiveness of aversive punishment
d. loyalty to the gang

LESSON II: SCHIZOPHRENIA AND THE MAJOR AFFECTIVE DISORDERS

11. Describe the characteristic symptoms of schizophrenia. (pp. 632-634)

11.1 Identify and describe the five behavior patterns illustrated below that are common to the different types of schizophrenia.

* a) My heart is stored in the cedar chest to keep it motherized.

* b) Bo seemed blase when told of his mother's death.

* c) Ray heard voices tell him that he did not deserve to live.

* d) Sue wore out the floor with her pacing.

* e) Henry proclaimed, "I will redeem you. I am the Son of God."

* 11.2 Distinguish between a delusion and an hallucination.

11.3 Distinguish among delusions of grandeur, control, and persecution.

12. Describe the symptoms of the major types of schizophrenic disorders. (pp. 634-636)

* 12.1 The distinguishing feature of catatonic schizophrenia is _______________, and the two extremes of motor disturbance are _______________ and _______________.

12.2 How many of the following statements are needed to determine whether the individual has paranoid schizophrenia or paranoia? Explain the reasons for your answers.

a) Barry thought he was being followed.

b) Barry has worked out a scheme to prevent the people who were following him from kidnapping him.

c) As he was studying his college physics he discovered that lasers mounted on space platforms were disrupting the earth's climate.

d) He had to drop out of college because the lasers started controlling his mind.

12.3 Explain why disorganized schizophrenia is called disorganized.

* 12.4 The former label for disorganized schizophrenia is _______________.

12.5 Compare the schizophreniform disorder and schizophrenia in terms of

a) symptoms.

b) duration.

c) prognosis.

* 12.6 How does undifferentiated schizophrenia differ from catatonic, paranoid, and disorganized schizophrenia?

13. Distinguish between process and reactive schizophrenia and describe research on the childhood behaviors of people who later develop schizophrenia. (pp. 636-637)

13.1 Define <u>process schizophrenia</u> and <u>reactive schizophrenia</u> in your own words.

* 13.2 Consider the case of Roger described in your text in the section on paranoid schizophrenia.

a) Identify those behaviors that predict eventual recovery.

b) Identify those behaviors that suggest a poor recovery.

13.3 Provide the following information about the study by Watt and Lubansky (1976).

a) its purpose

b) the two groups of subjects

c) variables that were examined

e) results

f) implications

14. Summarize the principal findings of the studies on the heritability of schizophrenia. (pp. 637-638)

14.1 Describe the research of Kety, Rosenthal, Wender, and Schulsinger (1968). In particular, note their

a) methods.

b) subjects.

c) results.

* 14.2 What do the studies of adoptive children suggest about the heritability of schizophrenia?

15. Identify the drugs that increase the symptoms of schizophrenia and those that reduce them and describe the biochemical effects of these drugs. (pp. 638-640)

* 15.1 Describe the behavioral effects of excessive use of cocaine and amphetamine on normal people and those who have schizophrenia.

15.2 Relate these behavioral effects to the biochemical effects of these drugs.

* 15.3 What are the behavioral effects of chlorpromazine when administered to individuals who have schizophrenia or amphetamine psychosis?

* 15.4 How does chlorpromazine counter the biochemical effects of cocaine and amphetamine?

16. Describe the negative symptoms of schizophrenia and summarize the evidence that suggests schizophrenia is a neurological disorder. (pp. 640-642)

* 16.1 Contrast the characteristics of schizophrenics who are helped by the antipsychotic drugs with those who are not.

16.2 What do the studies by Stevens (1982 a and b) and Weinberger and Wyatt (1982) suggest regarding the causes of schizophrenia?

16.3 What role does cytomegalovirus appear to play in the development of schizophrenia?

16.4 Identify the similarities between schizophrenia and multiple sclerosis and what they suggest about the causes of schizophrenia.

17. Describe the symptoms and incidence of the major affective disorders. (pp. 642-643)

17.1 Identify and briefly describe four kinds of affective disorders.

18. Describe mania and bipolar disorder and identify the drug used to treat bipolar disorder. (p. 643)

18.1 If you lived with someone who had mania, what would this person be like and how might this person make you feel?

* 18.2 Explain why DSM-III classifies mania as a bipolar disorder.

* 18.3 Identify the drug that has been used effectively in the treatment of bipolar disorder.

19. Describe major depression and distinguish it from dysthymic disorder and grief caused by death of a loved one. (pp. 643-644)

* 19.1 Identify the five cardinal symptoms of depression according to Beck (1967).

19.2 Describe the behaviors that distinguish a person suffering from a major depression from a) normal people, b) those who are bereaved, and c) those who have a dysthymic disorder.

20. Describe the views of psychoanalytic and cognitive theory regarding major depression. (pp. 644-645)

20.1 On one level, a person says to himself, "You fool. You can't do anything right. You couldn't even pay this bill on time."

a) How might psychoanalytic theory explain the behavior of this depressed individual?

b) How might cognitive theory explain this behavior?

* 20.2 Describe three criticisms of the psychoanalytic explanation for depression.

21. Summarize the evidence regarding the relation of heredity, biochemical factors, and sleep cycles to the major affective disorders. (pp. 645-647)

21.1 Louise and David are thinking of adopting Christopher but they are concerned. Christopher's mother suffers from major depression and as a consequence cannot care for him. David and Louise are worried about Christopher's future mental health. Based on the research regarding depression, what can you tell them?

* 21.2 The two forms of biological treatment that have been effective in treatment of major depression are ____________________ and ____________________.

21.3 Describe how tricyclic antidepressant drugs affect the nervous system of laboratory animals.

21.4 A friend has been taking reserpine to control his blood pressure. Since he started the medication he has not seemed as happy and energetic as he used to be. Describe what may be happening with your friend.

21.4 What do the effects of the tricyclic antidepressant drugs and reserpine suggest about possible causes of depression?

21.5 Describe the methods, results, and implications of the studies by Träskman et al. (1981) and Taube et al. (1977).

21.6 What cautions must be taken before we can infer that lowered neurotransmitter levels cause depression? Cite evidence to support your answer.

* 21.7 How do the sleep patterns of people with major depressions compare with a) normal people and b) those who have a dysthymic disorder?

* 21.8 What effect does reducing REM sleep have upon depression?

21.9 What do Goodwin et al. (1982) conclude about the relationship between sleep and depression? On what basis do they draw their conclusions?

LESSON II SELF TEST

1. A person who has schizophrenia

   a. has two or more personalities.
   b. experiences a split between thoughts and feelings.
   c. experiences a breakdown of neurotic defenses.
   d. loses control of perceptual and motor functions.

2. A patient in a mental institution stood for hours with his arms stretched over his head. It is most likely that this person has __________ schizophrenia.

   a. undifferentiated
   b. disorganized
   c. catatonic
   d. paranoid

3. People who have paranoia

   a. are merely suspicious and mistrustful of others.
   b. have delusions of grandeur without feelings of persecution.
   c. are responsive to any attempts to rescue them from their delusions.
   d. have delusions without schizophrenic thought disorders.

4. Which of the following symptoms of schizophrenia is associated with poor prognosis?

   a. hallucinations
   b. changes of personality at onset of schizophrenic episode
   c. thought disturbances
   d. emotional blunting

5. Watt and Lubansky (1966) found that schizophrenic males compared to a control group were evaluated by their high school teachers as

   a. abrasive and antisocial.
   b. more intelligent but less conscientious.
   c. introverted and passive.
   d. impoverished economically and emotionally.

6. The study by Kety et al. of the Danish _folkeregister_ suggests that

a. adopted children become schizophrenic if their adoptive parents have schizophrenia.
b. heredity determines the incidence of acute schizophrenia.
c. process schizophrenia is related to schizophrenia in the biological family.
d. schizophrenia shows no relationship with biological or social factors.

7. Antipsychotic drugs gain their effects by

a. tranquilizing schizophrenics and making them more receptive to therapy.
b. stimulating the attentional system in much the same way cocaine does.
c. blocking dopamine receptors and reducing schizophrenia's positive symptoms.
d. increasing production of norepinephrine to restore brain tissue.

8. Patients with negative symptoms of schizophrenia

a. respond favorably to chlorpromazine.
b. seem to have a loss of brain tissue.
c. have overactive dopamine synapses.
d. tend to be born in the summer months.

9. Schizophrenia is to major depression as

a. obsessions are to delusions.
b. thoughts are to affect.
c. dysthymic disorder is to bipolar disorder.
d. biological is to environmental.

9. Len emerged from his depression with plans to build a better mousetrap. He excitedly described his plans to market this product he had not yet built. Len is probably exhibiting

a. a dysthymic disorder.
b. delusions of control.
c. mania.
d. fugue.

11. The antidepressant drug that is effective in treating bipolar disorder is

a. lithium carbonate.
b. chlorpromazine.
c. serotonin.
d. reserpine.

12. Which of the following is a cardinal symptom of major depression?

a. depression in response to environmental trauma
b. physical complaints
c. negative self-concept
d. delusional thinking

13. According to the cognitive theory of depression, depressed people

a. introject their lost loved ones.
b. magnify and overgeneralize their failures.
c. have experienced symbolic or real losses of loved ones.
d. experience perceptual and attentional deficits.

14. Tricyclic antidepressant drugs reduce depression by

a. prolonging the effects of serotonin and norepinephrine.
b. impairing the activity of norepinephrine synapses.

c. restoring the salt balance in the body.
d. increasing the depth and duration of REM sleep.

15. Research indicates that depression results from underactivity of neurons that secrete serotonin or norepinephrine. This evidence

a. demonstrates that depression is a heritable disorder.
b. rules out environmental effects as causes of depression.
c. suggests that the causes of this underactivity are linked to the causes of depression.
d. supports the contention that depression is the result of introjection.

INTEGRATING QUESTIONS

1. Identify those disorders in which there are differences in the number of males and females affected. Offer possible explanations for these differences.

2. Select a disorder from each of the following categories—anxiety disorders, somatoform disorders, personality disorders, schizophrenia, and major affective disorders and review the evidence regarding the effects of nature (heredity) and nurture (environment) on the development of these disorders.

3. As you studied the various mental disorders, you examined their possible causes. Given these possible causes, what do you think can be done to prevent these disorders?

ANSWERS

2.1 They claimed to have auditory hallucinations. Most were diagnosed as having schizophrenia while in the hospital, and as being in remission when discharged.
2.3 leads to development of effective treatment or cure, suggests different kinds of treatment, develops prognosis for patients and their families
3.1 American Psychiatric Association's Diagnostic and Statistical Manual, third edition; attempt to provide reliable, universal set of diagnostic categories and explicit diagnostic criteria
4.3 anxiety states, panic disorder, generalized anxiety disorder, obsessive compulsive disorder; phobic disorders
5.1 agoraphobia, social phobias, simple phobias
5.3 d) Some people, apparently like Clara, are predisposed by a labile autonomic nervous system to acquire conditioned fears.
6.1 thoughts, obsessive doubt, obsessive fear of doing something that is prohibited; behaviors, counting, checking, cleaning, and avoidance
7.1 conversion disorder, hypochondriasis
8.1 resemble neurological disorders but have no underlying organic pathology
9.1 a) psychogenic amnesia, b) multiple personality, c) fugue
9.2 escape from severe conflicts resulting from intolerable impulses or from guilt from misdeeds
10.1 sociopathic personality, antisocial personality disorder, moral insanity, psychopathic inferiority, and sociopath
11.1 a) neologism, b) emotional withdrawal, c) hallucinations, d) anxiety, e) delusions of grandeur
11.2 Delusion is a belief that is contrary to fact and hallucination is a perception of nonexistent stimuli.
12.1 motor disturbances, catatonic postures, waxy flexibility
12.4 hebephrenia
12.6 symptoms do not fit any one of these categories of schizophrenia
13.2 a) delusions, thought disturbances; b) It appears that his symptoms had existed for a long

time.

14.2 Heredity may create a predisposition to schizophrenia.
15.1 in normal people, may cause temporary psychosis; in psychotics, worsen symptoms
15.3 hallucinations and delusions diminish or cease, thought processes become more coherent
15.4 block dopamine receptors and prevent them from becoming stimulated
16.1 helped: positive—have delusions, hallucinations, thought disorders; not helped: negative—show loss of emotional response, decreased speech, lack of drive, diminished social interaction
18.2 Most people who have mania also have depressive episodes.
18.3 lithium carbonate
19.1 1) sad and apathetic mood, 2) feelings of worthlessness and hopelessness, 3) desire to withdraw from other people, 4) sleeplessness and loss of appetite, 5) change in activity level
20.2 dispute reality of stages and fixation, no explanation why hatred turned inward instead of love, symbolic loss cannot be proven
21.2 electroconvulsive therapy, antidepressant drugs
21.7 In contrast to normals, people with major depression enter REM sleep sooner and have longer periods of REM sleep while dysthymics experience difficulty falling asleep.
21.8 It decreased depression.

Self Test: Lesson I			Self Test: Lesson II		
1.	c	Obj. 15-1	1.	b	Obj. 15-11
2.	a	Obj. 15-2	2.	c	Obj. 15-12
3.	a	Obj. 15-2	3.	d	Obj. 15-12
4.	b	Obj. 15-3	4.	d	Obj. 15-13
5.	a	Obj. 15-4	5.	a	Obj. 15-13
6.	a	Obj. 15-4	6.	c	Obj. 15-14
7.	c	Obj. 15-5	7.	c	Obj. 15-15
8.	b	Obj. 15-6	8.	b	Obj. 15-16
9.	b	Obj. 15-6	9.	b	Obj. 15-17
10.	b	Obj. 15-7	10.	c	Obj. 15-18
11.	b	Obj. 15-7	11.	a	Obj. 15-18
12.	a	Obj. 15-7	12.	c	Obj. 15-19
13.	a	Obj. 15-9	13.	b	Obj. 15-20
14.	c	Obj. 15-10	14.	a	Obj. 15-21
15.	c	Obj. 15-10	15.	c	Obj. 15-21

15.1 OBJ 15-1

NEUROSIS

15.2 OBJ 15-1

PSYCHOSIS

15.3 OBJ 15-2

GRAVES' DISEASE

15.4 OBJ 15-3

DIAGNOSTIC AND STATISTICAL MANUAL III
(DSM-III)

15.5 OBJ 15-4

ANXIETY DISORDERS

15.6 OBJ 15-4

PANIC DISORDER

15.7 OBJ 15-4

ANTICIPATORY ANXIETY

15.8 OBJ 15-4

FIRST DEGREE RELATIVE

15.9 OBJ 15-5

PHOBIC DISORDERS

15.10 OBJ 15-5

AGORAPHOBIA

15.11 OBJ 15-5

SOCIAL PHOBIA

15.12 OBJ 15-5

SIMPLE PHOBIA

15.13 OBJ 15-6

OBSESSIVE-COMPULSIVE DISORDER

15.14 OBJ 15-6

OBSESSION

15.15 OBJ 15-6

COMPULSION

15.16 OBJ 15-7

SOMATOFORM DISORDERS

15.9 Obj 15-5

category of anxiety disorders characterized by excessive fear of specific objects or situations

15.10 Obj 15-5

phobic disorder; fear of being alone or in open or public places

15.11 Obj 15-5

phobic disorder; fear situation in which open to public scrutiny

15.12 Obj 15-5

general phobic disorder involving irrational fear of particular objects or situations

15.13 Obj 15-6

anxiety disorder characterized by repetitive thoughts and behaviors that guard against anxiety

15.14 Obj 15-6

persistent thoughts involving doubt or uncertainty or fear of doing a prohibited act

15.15 Obj 15-6

behavior, often unwanted, that is performed repetitively, presumably to ward off anxiety

15.16 Obj 15-7

mental disorder; physical symptoms or complaints that have no organic basis

15.1 Obj 15-1

mental disorder in which behavior is inappropriate and maladaptive; exaggeration of reaction of "normal" people

15.2 Obj 15-1

mental disorder marked by severe disruptions in thought processes

15.3 Obj 15-2

mental disorder caused by oversecretion of thyroxin; characterized by irritability, restlessness, confused, rapid thought processes

15.4 Obj 15-3

American Psychiatric Association's manual of mental disorders, third edition

15.5 Obj 15-4

psychological disorder characterized by tension, overactivity of autonomic nervous system, fear of impending disaster and danger

15.6 Obj 15-4

psychological disorder characterized by anxiety attacks and physical symptoms associated with anxiety

15.7 Obj 15-4

worry experienced by persons who have panic disorder that they will experience a panic attack

15.8 Obj 15-4

a person's parents, children, and siblings; studied to determine heritability of mental disorders

15.17 OBJ 15-7

SOMATIZATION DISORDER

15.18 OBJ 15-7

HYSTERIA

15.19 OBJ 15-7

HYPOCHONDRIASIS

15.20 OBJ 15-7

SYMPTOM

15.21 OBJ 15-7

SIGN

15.22 OBJ 15-8

CONVERSION DISORDER

15.23 OBJ 15-8

PSEUDONEUROLOGICAL DISORDER

15.24 OBJ 15-8

MALINGERING

15.25 OBJ 15-8

PSYCHOSOMATIC DISORDER

15.26 OBJ 15-9

DISSOCIATIVE DISORDER

15.27 OBJ 15-9

PSYCHOGENIC AMNESIA

15.28 OBJ 15-9

FUGUE

15.29 OBJ 15-9

MULTIPLE PERSONALITY

15.30 OBJ 15-10

ANTISOCIAL PERSONALITY DISORDER

15.31 OBJ 15-10

PSYCHOPATHY

15.32 OBJ 15-11

SCHIZOPHRENIA

15.25 Obj 15-8

real, organic illnesses, caused or made worse by psychological factors

15.26 Obj 15-9

one or more parts of awareness separate from other parts; regarded as reaction to severe conflict

15.27 Obj 15-9

serial dissociative reaction; unable to recall former events and conflicts

15.28 Obj 15-9

form of amnesia in which person flees from old life and begins new life somewhere else

15.29 Obj 15-9

dissociative disorder; individual has two or more different personalities at least one of which is unaware of the other personalities

15.30 Obj 15-10

personality disorder in which individual displays no or little regard for laws and social mores and experiences no guilt

15.31 Obj 15-10

condition of individual who has an antisocial personality disorder

15.32 Obj 15-11

psychosis characterized by disordered thoughts, delusions, hallucinations, and often bizarre behaviors

15.17 Obj 15-7

a somatoform disorder characterized by vague physical symptoms in absence of physical disease

15.18 Obj 15-7

older term for somatization disorder

15.19 Obj 15-7

preoccupation with one's body, and imagined development of various physical disorders

15.20 Obj 15-7

reports of feelings or perceptions people make to their physicians

15.21 Obj 15-7

objective evidence such as observations of physical malfunctions

15.22 Obj 15-8

a somatoform disorder; involves physical complaints without organic basis

15.23 Obj 15-8

condition characterized by physical complaints resembling neurological disorders but with no physical basis

15.24 Obj 15-8

faking an illness to gain an advantage; e.g., escape military service

15.33 OBJ 15-11

NEOLOGISM

15.34 OBJ 15-11

DELUSION

15.35 OBJ 15-11

HALLUCINATION

15.36 OBJ 15-12

UNDIFFERENTIATED SCHIZOPHRENIA

15.37 OBJ 15-12

CATATONIC SCHIZOPHRENIA

15.38 OBJ 15-12

WAXY FLEXIBILITY

15.39 OBJ 15-12

PARANOID SCHIZOPHRENIA

15.40 OBJ 15-12

PARANOIA

15.41 OBJ 15-12

DISORGANIZED SCHIZOPHRENIA

15.42 OBJ 15-12

WORD SALAD

15.43 OBJ 15-12

SCHIZOPHRENIFORM DISORDER

15.44 OBJ 15-12

ACUTE SCHIZOPHRENIC EPISODE

15.45 OBJ 15-13

PROCESS SCHIZOPHRENIA

15.46 OBJ 15-13

REACTIVE SCHIZOPHRENIA

15.47 OBJ 15-15

CHLORPROMAZINE

15.48 OBJ 15-15

DOPAMINE HYPOTHESIS

15.41 Obj 15-12

psychosis characterized by silly, inappropriate behavior; usually progressive and irreversible

15.42 Obj 15-12

scrambled, disorganized communication characteristic of disorganized schizophrenia

15.43 Obj 15-12

display of schizophrenic behaviors for a short period of time

15.44 Obj 15-12

former label of schizophreniform disorder

15.45 Obj 15-13

Bleuler's term for chronic schizophrenia with no easily identifiable precipitating factor

15.46 Obj 15-13

Bleuler's term for schizophrenia that developed in response to environmental crisis; quick onset and recovery

15.47 Obj 15-14

antipsychotic drug that blocks dopamine receptors and alleviates schizophrenic symptoms (delusions, hallucinations, etc); trade name, thorazine

15.48 Obj 15-15

argues that schizophrenia caused by excess activity of the neurotransmitter dopamine in the brain

15.33 Obj 15-11

new and meaningless words; frequently coined by schizophrenics

15.34 Obj 15-11

irrational belief characteristic of schizophrenia; feel others persecuting or attempting to control or feel oneself an important person

15.35 Obj 15-11

perception of stimuli that are not present; characteristic of schizophrenia

15.36 Obj 15-12

psychotic disorder in which delusions, hallucinations, and disorganized behavior are present; symptoms do not meet criteria for other schizophrenias

15.37 Obj 15-12

schizophrenia characterized by motor disturbances—either immobility or wild activity

15.38 Obj 15-12

ability of catatonic schizophrenics to be molded into and hold bizarre positions

15.39 Obj 15-12

psychosis characterized by delusions and thought disorders

15.40 Obj 15-12

psychosis characterized by delusions without the thought disturbances of schizophrenia

15.49 OBJ 15-16

POSITIVE SYMPTOMS

15.50 OBJ 15-16

NEGATIVE SYMPTOMS

15.51 OBJ 15-16

CYTOMEGALOVIRUS (CMV)

15.52 OBJ 15-17

MAJOR AFFECTIVE DISORDERS

15.53 OBJ 15-17

BIPOLAR DISORDER

15.54 OBJ 15-17

MAJOR DEPRESSION

15.55 OBJ 15-17

DYSTHYMIC DISORDER

15.56 OBJ 15-17

CYCLOTHYMIC DISORDER

15.57 OBJ 15-18

MANIA

15.58 OBJ 15-18

LITHIUM CARBONATE

15.59 OBJ 15-20

INTROJECT

15.60 OBJ 15-21

ELECTROCONVULSIVE THERAPY (ECT)

15.61 OBJ 15-21

TRICYCLIC ANTIDEPRESSANT DRUGS

15.62 OBJ 15-21

RESERPINE

15.63 OBJ 15-21

5-HIAA

15.64 OBJ 15-21

MHPG

15.57 Obj 15-18

wild, exuberant, unrealistic behavior characteristic of a phase of bipolar disorder

15.58 Obj 15-18

drug of choice in treatment of bipolar depression

15.59 Obj 15-20

product of psychological incorporation of another person into one's personality

15.60 Obj 15-21

electroshock treatment of depression; causes seizures

15.61 Obj 15-21

alleviates symptoms of depression; probably by facilitating activity of norepinephrine and serotonin synapses

15.62 Obj 15-21

drug that impairs activity of norepinephrine and serotonin synapses; can cause depression

15.63 Obj 15-21

produced when serotonin is broken down; lower levels in brains of suicide attempters

15.64 Obj 15-21

produced when norepinephrine is broken down; low levels in urine of patients with affective disorders

15.49 Obj 15-16

hallucinations, delusions, and thought disorders of schizophrenia; good prognosis if present in schizophrenic

15.50 Obj 15-16

schizophrenic symptoms such loss of emotional response, decreased speech, lack of drive, diminished social interaction; poor prognosis

15.51 Obj 15-16

herpes-like virus; evidence of presence found in brains of some schizophrenics

15.52 Obj 15-17

severe disturbances of emotions

15.53 Obj 15-17

affective disorder; alternates between mania and depression

15.54 Obj 15-17

affective disorder marked by profound and prolonged sadness, hopelessness

15.55 Obj 15-17

depression that is deeper or longer than normal; unlike major depression, no delusions and not as severe

15.56 Obj 15-17

affective disorder resembling bipolar disorder without the severity, delusions, and hallucinations

CHAPTER 16
The Treatment of Mental Disorders

INTRODUCTION

This chapter examines historical and contemporary treatment of mental illness. Among the contemporary therapies examined there are the insight therapies (Objectives 2-3), behavior therapy (Objectives 4-10), the cognitive behavior therapies (Objectives 11-12), group psychotherapy (Objective 13), the biological treatments (Objectives 14-17), and eclectic therapy (Objective 18). Also covered is an evaluation of therapies and therapists (Objective 19). The chapter is divided into two lessons. Lesson I covers Objectives 1-10, and Lesson II, Objectives 11-19.

CONCEPT CARDS AND EXERCISES

After you have surveyed and read the text, assemble the concept cards located at the end of this chapter. Use them to learn the important terms, then begin reading the text again, one learning objective at a time, and work through the exercises for each lesson. Answers for questions marked with an asterisk are found at the end of the chapter.

SELF TESTS

Each lesson is followed by a multiple-choice self test. After you are proficient with a lesson's concept cards and exercises, take the self test to see whether you have mastered the material. Review those objectives for questions you answered incorrectly.

INTEGRATING QUESTIONS

To challenge yourself further, answer the integrating questions at the end of the chapter. These questions ask you to apply the information you have learned to consider larger theoretical or real-life issues.

LESSON I: HISTORICAL BACKGROUND AND INSIGHT AND BEHAVIOR THERAPIES

1. Describe the history of attempts to treat mental disorders, including the development of psychotherapy. (pp. 653-657)

1.1 Describe trephining and exorcism in terms of their

a) methods.

b) effects.

c) underlying assumptions.

* 1.2 Compare the ideas of Johann Wier and Saint Vincent de Paul with the beliefs about mental disorders held by most Europeans prior to the eighteenth century.

* 1.3 Describe how viewing mental disorders as illnesses affected treatment of the mentally ill.

* 1.4 Which of the following is an example of the effects of Pinel's reforms?

a) Without punishment from others, patients developed self-inflicted punishments to drive out their demons.

b) With the removal of the chains and other restrictions, there was bedlam—a rise of noise and fighting among patients.

c) An atmosphere of peace and quiet allowed some psychotic patients to get better on their own.

1.5 Identify the following men—Mesmer, Charcot, and Freud in terms of their use of hypnosis as a therapeutic tool.

2. Describe psychoanalysis and explain the problems of evaluating it scientifically. (pp. 657-660)

2.1 Define insight therapy in your own words, then explain how psychoanalysis is an insight psychotherapy.

2.2 Identify the aspects of psychoanalysis displayed in these responses by clients (C) or therapists (T), then explain the reasons for your answers.

* a) C: "Well, let's see I lost my train of thought. It doesn't matter. What I was going to say was not important."

* b) C: "You sit there so smug and indifferent. You do not know how much it hurts to spill your guts out and get no response."

* c) C: "That's funny talking about that makes me think of how my father used to give me my Saturday night bath and tell me how fat and ugly I was."

* d) T: "In contrast to your previous dreams, this, your first dream of being inside your own home suggests you are achieving self-acceptance.

* e) T says to himself: "This patient's whining reminds me of my baby sister's demands for attention," then feels anger towards the patient.

2.3 Which of the following people would be likely to complete psychoanalysis successfully and offer reasons for your answers?

a) Alan, a thirty-year-old physician who is willing to invest in himself for hopes of future happiness.

b) Barbara, a bright, articulate woman who has slipped in and out of psychosis.

c) Carl, who is mildly retarded and whose treatment is being funded by a rehabilitation program.

d) Diane, a movie star who has tried a number of therapies in the past.

2.4 At the end of therapy the psychoanalyst concluded that the client no longer needed to deny her feelings of inferiority. Discuss whether this conclusion indicates success from the perspective, of (1) the therapist and (2) a critic of psychoanalysis.

2.5 Summarize, in your own words, the limitations of psychoanalysis, making sure to consider the criticisms noted by Luborsky and Spence (1978) and Wachtel (1977) and those regarding the escape clause that is used when psychoanalysis does not work.

3. Describe client-centered therapy and attempts to evaluate its usefulness. (pp. 660-663)

* 3.1 What effect would the following events have on self-actualization? Explain the reasons for your answer.

a) A young boy who has been told repeatedly when he has been upset or hurt that "boys don't cry."

b) An adolescent whose mother says to her, "I am worried about you. You don't seem to be having much fun these days."

3.2 Describe the goals of client-centered therapy and the methods it uses to achieve those goals.

* 3.3 Explain why client centered therapy is <u>not</u> really non-directive by referring to Truax's analysis of client-centered therapy sessions.

3.4 Identify and describe two limitations of client-centered therapy.

4. Describe behavior therapy and compare its approach with that of insight therapies. (pp. 663-664)

4.1 Identify whether the therapists below are likely to be insight-oriented therapists or behaviorists. Give reasons for your answers.

* a) "What do you think that means?"

* b) "Let's look at the specific events that preceded your feelings of pain and anxiety."

* c) "If we treat the behavior, the underlying problem remains and will be expressed by a new symptom."

* d) "What happened in childhood is important only in so far as it has shaped a person's reinforcement history."

4.2 Argue against the following statement. Give examples to support your argument.

Because behavior therapy is concerned with observable or quantifiable behavior and psychoanalysis is concerned with the more inaccessible unconscious, it is reasonable to conclude behavior therapists do not need as much skill, sensitivity, and training as psychoanalysts do.

5. Describe systematic desensitization and aversive classical conditioning. (pp. 664-666)

5.1 Give an original example of a problem that could be treated effectively by systematic desensitization.

5.2 Describe the steps that would be followed in applying systematic desensitization in the example you offered in question 5.1.

* 5.3 Identify the necessary component(s) for effective systematic desensitization.

5.4 Describe the procedures and probable effect if in vivo desensitization were used in the example in questions 5.1 and 5.2 instead of vicarious desensitization.

5.5 Describe aversive classical conditioning and situations in which it is likely to be used.

6. Describe the use of reinforcement and punishment in instrumental therapy procedures and identify the drawbacks and ethical problems with the use of aversive procedures. (p. 666)

6.1 In high school John never studied. In college he will need to study about two hours daily in order to do well enough to remain in school. Describe how shaping could be used to help John increase his study time.

6.2 Jan persists in putting herself down. She tells herself that she is dumb and ugly. How could punishment be used to eliminate these self-deprecating thoughts?

* 6.3 In which of the following situations would punishment be an appropriate behavior change technique. Explain the reasons for your answer.

a) Lynne does not want her toddler near the stove because she fears the baby might get hurt. When the baby goes near the stove Lynne says, "No," and gives the baby a light swat.

b) John continues to disrupt the class with shouts and fights. The teacher punishes him by giving him more homework.

7. Describe the use of covert reinforcement and punishment procedures. (pp. 666-668)

7.1 Describe how covert reinforcement and punishment could be used in the case of a diabetic who voraciously consumes chocolates but must eliminate them from his diet.

8. Explain how modeling may be used in behavior therapy. (pp. 668-669)

8.1 "I'm tired of being stepped on by everyone else. I've got to stand up for my rights." Describe how modeling could be used to help this client become more assertive.

* 8.2 Describe two different kinds of situations in which modeling may be used successfully.

* 8.3 Offer at least two reasons for why modeling is effective.

9. Describe the nature of token economies and the difficulties encountered in implementing them. (pp. 669-670)

* 9.1 The token that can be exchanged for goods and services becomes a(n) ______________ ______________.

9.2 Describe the likelihood of success in the token economy described below. Explain the reasons for your answers.

When patients came to breakfast dressed, washed, and shaved, they were given tokens to be exchanged later for privileges. An aide gave three tokens to one resident, one to another, and none to a third.

9.3 Summarize the study by Paul and Lentz (1977) in terms of its

a) experimental and control groups.

b) results.

c) implications.

10. Describe the evaluation of behavior therapy. (pp. 670-672)

* 10.1 Sally told her friend that she is undergoing systematic desensitization to eliminate her fear of bridges. Her friend, a strong proponent of psychoanalysis, warned her that if she did not uncover the underlying cause of her fear, she would experience other symptoms when she got rid of her bridge phobia. How would behavior therapists respond to her friend's concern?

10.2 Speculate upon the high recidivism of residential treatment programs for juvenile offenders.

10.3 Describe a way to maintain the behavior change of the juveniles referred to in question 10.2.

10.4 In addition to knowing behavioral techniques, behavior therapists must know ethics. Describe two general situations in which ethical considerations suggest that behavior therapy is not appropriate.

LESSON I SELF TEST

1. One benefit of Pinel's reforms was that

   a. many patients recovered with little, if any, treatment.
   b. fewer patients died from infections due to trephining.
   c. the tranquilizing chair speeded the recovery of depressed patients.
   d. patients' psychoses were reduced through mesmerism.

2. Insight therapy assumes

   a. there is widespread abnormality among people.
   b. insight is necessary but not sufficient for a cure.
   c. people learn maladaptive thought patterns and behaviors.
   d. most forms of mental illness have a biological basis.

3. Psychoanalysts regard transference neurosis as

   a. an indication that the client is resisting therapy.
   b. an aid to understanding conflicts rooted in childhood.
   c. the result of the therapist's lack of empathy.
   d. the patient's failure to transfer intellectual understanding into emotional insight.

4. The client-centered therapist attempts to

   a. create a discrepancy between the client's real and ideal selves to motivate client change.
   b. offer the client conditional positive regard.
   c. help the client pay attention to his or her own feelings.
   d. show the client new, adaptive behaviors.

5. What did Truax observe when he studied tapes of Carl Rogers' therapy sessions?

   a. Rogers appropriately reinforced clients' statements of progress.
   b. Once people began to heed their own feelings, as Rogers had hypothesized, maladaptive behaviors automatically ceased.
   c. Rogers provided clients with non-directive support and unconditional positive regard.
   d. Client-centered therapy is better suited that psychoanalysis to the treatment of psychotic individuals.

6. In contrast to psychoanalysis, behavior therapy

   a. requires less skill and training on the part of the therapist.
   b. places greater emphasis on the biological underpinnings of behavior.
   c. has been supported in the research lab but not in clinical settings.
   d. argues that insight is not a necessary or sufficient precondition for change to occur.

7. Your friend describes her therapy, "We paired relaxation with increasingly more anxiety producing events." Your friend probably is describing

   a. psychodrama.
   b. transactional analysis.
   c. systematic desensitization.
   d. a token economy.

8. Applied to the treatment of a person with a shoe fetish, aversive classical conditioning

a. attempts to establish an unpleasant response to shoes.
b. punishes the person every time he looks at shoes and feels sexually stimulated.
c. rewards the person for thinking about shoes in a nonsexual way.
d. restricts the kind of shoes that the person finds stimulating.

9. Punishment is the preferred treatment when

a. the client demonstrates negative attitudes toward the therapist.
b. it is difficult to figure out how to reinforce behaviors that can replace the undesired behavior.
c. the client does not respond to positive reinforcement.
d. the undesirable response is injurious to the client.

10. The therapist asked Judy, who was having difficulty sticking to her diet to imagine that as she reached for certain fattening, non-nutritious foods she could feel the vomit beginning to form in her mouth. What technique is the therapist using?

a. in vivo desensitization
b. covert punishment
c. symptom substitution
d. behavior rehearsal

11. By their example, sponsors in Alcoholics Anonymous show other alcoholics how to maintain their sobriety. This feature of Alcoholics Anonymous is an example of

a. reinforcement.
b. aversive classical conditioning.
c. modeling.
d. shaping.

12. What did Paul and Lentz (1977) observe in their study of a token economy used with hospitalized patients who had severe, chronic schizophrenia?

a. Once transferred to community-based facilities, the patients could not function without the token reward system.
b. The token economy may work in principle but it was too difficult to put into practice.
c. More patients in the experimental group in contrast to the control group were discharged from the hospital.
d. Surprisingly, the token economy was able to effect cures in 20 percent of the cases.

13. Which of the following is an example of symptom substitution?

a. Marilyn chewed gum to prevent herself from biting her fingernails.
b. Chuck imitated the way Richard stammered and added a few facial tics of his own.
c. When criticized for coming late to the meeting, Cindi stopped coming to the meeting.
d. Linda stopped starving herself, but she became visibly more anxious and nervous around people.

14. Behavior changes produced by behavior therapy may be short-lived in that

a. soon after one symptom is eliminated, another emerges.
b. clients are unable to reinforce themselves and maintain the behavior change.
c. behaviors learned in the therapy situation may not generalize to everyday life.
d. clients unconsciously resist changing their behavior.

15. Which of the following is an inappropriate use of behavior therapy?

a. To reduce the patient's uncontrollable violent outbursts, part of his limbic system was removed.

b. The client's alcoholism was treated before his problems with domestic violence were treated.
c. The client was asked to imagine herself covered with vomit whenever she reached for a cigarette.
d. Required by the court to seek therapy, the Peeping Tom was presented with pictures of windows and women and then given electric shocks.

LESSON II: BEHAVIORAL THERAPIES AND BIOLOGICAL TREATMENT

11. Describe and evaluate rational-emotive therapy. (pp. 672-675)

* 11.1 Read the following scenario and use the A-B-C's of rational-emotive therapy to label each statement.

1. The promotion Fran had wanted was given to someone else.

2. Fran was hurt, angry, and felt miserable about this promotion.

3. Fran felt that if she did not get this promotion she would never get anywhere with this corporation.

11.2 How would rational-emotive therapists explain Fran's negative feelings and how might they work with Fran?

11.3 Compare rational-emotive therapy and client-centered therapy in terms of directiveness, empathy, and unconditional positive regard.

11.4 Compare rational-emotive therapy and psychoanalysis in terms of the focus of therapy, the root of the client's problems, and the relationship between therapist and client.

* 11.5 For what kinds of people is rational-emotive therapy recommended?

12. Describe and evaluate cognitive behavior therapies using a combined approach. (pp. 675-677)

12.1 Identify how most cognitive behavior therapies using the combined approach differ from

a) rational-emotive therapy.

b) behavior therapy.

* 12.2 Darlene worked with a cognitive behavior therapist to overcome her fear of public speaking. As a by-product of the therapy, she found that she felt less shy and more assertive. How would Bandura explain this effect?

12.3 How could self-talk be used to help someone who felt anxious without cause during an exam?

12.4 Does behavior change because cognitions change or do cognitions change because behavior changes? Discuss these questions in terms of cognitive behavior therapy, then behavior therapy.

12.5 How do the cognitive behavior therapies differ from the insight therapies?

13. Describe and evaluate group psychotherapies. (pp. 677-681)

* 13.1 Offer at least four advantages of group therapy.

13.2 Describe the drama in psychodrama.

* 13.3 Which of the following is an example of mirroring?

a) John slowed down his pace, lowered his volume to match Melinda's and repeated her words.

b) Lee said to Randy, "Your fist is clenched; your upper lip is quivering, and you mean to tell me that you are not angry?"

13.4 Describe the assumptions underlying family therapy.

13.5 Give examples of strategies structural family therapists use to achieve their therapeutic goals.

13.6 Describe and evaluate one type of group behavior therapy.

14. Describe the effects of antipsychotic drugs, their usefulness in treating schizophrenia, and their possible side effects. (p. 681)

* 14.1 Describe the symptoms antipsychotic drugs alleviate.

14.2 Offer an explanation why the antipsychotic drugs are effective.

* 14.3 Antipsychotic drugs fail to ______________ between the dopamine-secreting neurons associated with ______________ and, presumably, ______________ and the dopamine-secreting neurons controlling ______________.

14.4 Describe the effects of this failure of the antipsychotic drugs to discriminate between the two types of receptors noted in question 14.3.

15. Identify the drugs used to treat depression and anxiety and discuss their effects and usefulness. (pp. 681-682)

* 15.1 Identify two types of drugs used to treat affective disorders.

15.2 Note the uses and the dangers of the two antidepressant drugs identified in question 15.1.

* 15.3 _______________ and _______________ are two kinds of tranquilizers or _______________ _______________.

15.4 Identify three positive uses of the antianxiety drugs.

15.5 When does use of the antianxiety drugs become abusive?

16. Describe electroconvulsive therapy, its benefits, and its drawbacks. (pp. 682-684)

16.1 Describe how electroconvulsive therapy is administered.

* 16.2 For which mental disorder does ECT seem effective?

* 16.3 Which aspect of electroconvulsive therapy appears necessary for therapeutic results?

16.4 Under which circumstances does use of ECT seem justified?

17. Describe psychosurgery procedures, the disorders they have been employed to treat, and their benefits and drawbacks. (pp. 684-686)

* 17.1 How does psychosurgery differ from other forms of brain surgery?

17.2 Describe the conclusions of the U.S. National Commission for the Protection of Human Subjects of Biomedical and Behavioral Research regarding the effectiveness of psychosurgery in treating thought disorders and affective disturbances.

17.3 Describe the therapeutic goal and uses of the prefrontal lobotomy.

17.4 How does a cingulotomy differ from a prefrontal lobotomy?

17.5 When is a cingulotomy likely to be used? For which patients is it likely to be effective?

18. Describe the eclectic approach to psychotherapy. (p. 687)

18.1 Define the word <u>eclectic</u> in your own words.

18.2 Describe what makes a therapist eclectic.

19. Describe the four major difficulties encountered in evaluating psychotherapies, the results of such studies, and the conclusions that may be drawn with respect to the factors that lead to successful outcomes. (pp. 687-690)

19.1 Identify and describe four problems psychologists confront when they attempt to evaluate psychotherapy scientifically.

19.2 Summarize the results of Eysenck's research on the effectiveness of psychotherapy.

* 19.3 Smith and her colleagues (1980) used _______________ to evaluate the effectiveness of psychotherapy as reported in many research studies.

19.4 Smith et al. (1980) concluded that psychotherapy offers positive benefits. Describe what benefits psychotherapy offers and identify the therapies that offer these benefits.

* 19.4 In a study on the factors that influence the outcome of psychotherapy, Luborsky, Chandler et al. (1971) investigated three general factors. These are _______________ variables, _______________ variables, and _______________ variables.

19.5 Identify the seven patient variables associated with positive therapy outcomes and discuss why these variables may lead to therapeutic success.

* 19.6 Identify the treatment variable associated with therapeutic success.

19.7 Offer an alternate explanation why the number of therapy sessions is associated with treatment efficacy.

19.8 Identify the three therapist variables associated with therapeutic success.

19.9 Explain how empathy works according to researchers such as Fix and Haffke (1976) and Strupp and Hadley (1979).

LESSON II SELF TEST

1. Which of the following conceptualizations correctly reflects the analysis of emotions provided by rational-emotive therapy?

   a. When Karen did not return his call, John felt awful.
   b. Because John thought his life would be incomplete without Karen, he felt miserable.
   c. John felt that Karen was a rotten person because she did not return his call.
   d. When the relationship ended, John felt he might never find anyone as good as Karen.

2. Marcia survived a messy divorce with the aid of therapy. After which she felt confident that she could handle anything life would give her. How would Bandura regard Marcia's increased confidence?

   a. self-efficacy
   b. ego involvement
   c. unconditional positive regard
   d. conditioned reinforcement

3. According to Minuchin, a couple with children in order to be healthy must regard themselves first as

   a. parents to their children.
   b. children to their parents.
   c. allies of their children.
   d. spouses to each other.

4. Like group therapy, family therapy

   a. overcomes the problems associated with insight therapy.
   b. has been proven to be effective.
   c. observes the interaction of group members.
   d. is based on the premise that the only way to produce change in an individual is to change his or her environment.

5. Given to schizophrenics, the antipsychotic drugs

   a. cure hallucinations and delusions.
   b. apparently block the dopamine receptors in the brain.
   c. stimulate the synapses that control attentional processes.
   d. reactivate the cingulum bundle in the brain.

6. A negative side effect of tricyclic antidepressant drugs is

   a. tardive dyskinesia.
   b. confusion and memory loss.
   c. blood toxicity.
   d. elevated blood pressure.

7. DiMascio and colleagues studied the effects of psychotherapy and tricyclic antidepressant drugs in the treatment of acute depression. They found that

   a. drug treatment was more effective than psychotherapy.
   b. the antidepressant drugs improved the patients' moods and therapy reduced their anxiety.
   c. psychotherapy reduced suicidal thoughts and the drugs reduced the sleep and appetite disturbances.
   d. together or alone, psychotherapy and drug treatment were equally effective.

8. The therapeutic effect of electroconvulsive therapy is due to the

   a. placebo effect.
   b. seizures.
   c. convulsions.
   d. induction of REM sleep.

9. Electroconvulsive therapy has been shown effective in the treatment of

   a. insomnia.
   b. anxiety disorders.
   c. major depression.
   d. schizophrenia.

10. In the novel <u>One Flew Over the Cuckoo's Nest</u>, McMurphy, a patient who stirred up other patients, has psychosurgery. After surgery he shows apathy, and severe blunting of emotions. It is likely that he had

    a. a cingulotomy.
    b. electroshock therapy.
    c. tardive dyskinesia.
    d. a prefrontal lobotomy.

11. Describing her approach to therapy, the psychologist emphasized a need to form a positive relationship with the client, to look at how clients perceive their world, and to help them change their behavior. The form of therapy this psychologist practices is likely to be

    a. psychoanalytic.

b. client-centered.
c. rational-emotive.
d. eclectic.

12. A significant difficulty in evaluating the efficacy of therapy is

a. developing appropriate control groups.
b. recording therapy sessions.
c. finding clients willing to participate in research projects.
d. classifying the techniques used by different therapists.

13. Like Pinel in the eighteenth century, Eysenck in the 1950's found that

a. psychotherapy cannot be evaluated scientifically.
b. most forms of treatment of mental illness do more harm than good.
c. drug therapy is more effective than the talk therapies.
d. many patients improve without treatment.

14. Which of the following statements indicates the kind of person who would benefit most from psychotherapy?

a. The fewer the sessions, the better the cure.
b. The brighter the therapist, the quicker the cure.
c. The best get better.
d. Anxiety drives a person away from therapy.

15. Which of the following is the best description of effective empathy?

a. demonstrating warmth and understanding by tuning into the client
b. feelings of concern and care that good therapists seem to have been born with
c. mirroring the client's words to let the client know that you are listening and care
d. communicating positive regard and liking for the client

INTEGRATING QUESTIONS

1. Compare and contrast psychoanalysis, client-centered therapy, and cognitive behavior that uses a combined approach in terms of their therapeutic goals, methods, and probable outcomes.

2. Develop a list of questions individuals should ask themselves and then therapists as they look for a psychotherapist.

3. If you were to seek psychotherapy, what kind of therapist would you prefer? Consider both the personal aspects and theoretical orientation of the therapist.

ANSWERS

1.2 Wier and de Paul disputed the commonly held belief that mentally ill people were either witches or were possessed by the devil.
1.3 Initially patients were treated not much better than before the belief about mental illness had changed.
1.4 c)
2.2 a) resistance b) transference neurosis c) free association d) dream interpretation e) countertransference
3.1 a) cause child to develop discrepancy between his real and ideal selves b) mother's

acceptance will stimulate adolescent to examine her behavior and feelings with the effect of stimulating self-actualization.

3.3 Rogers selectively responded to clients' statements by reinforcing those indicating progress; therefore, client-centered therapy is not entirely non-directive.
4.1 a) insight b) behaviorist c) insight d) behaviorist
5.3 pairing of anxiety-producing stimuli with relaxation
6.3 a) appropriate. Punishment protects child from more serious injury, burns. b) inappropriate because not likely to be effective and may cause John to dislike teacher and respond poorly to teaching.
8.2 to establish new behaviors such as exercise routines and to eliminate fears
8.3 one, watch behavior, imitate it and be reinforced and two, experience vicarious extinction of own emotional responses
9.1 conditioned reinforcer
10.1 Research indicates that symptom substitution does not occur.
11.1 1. A, significant activating event; 2. C, emotional consequence; 3. B, belief system
11.5 people who are self-demanding and feel guilty; alcoholics
12.2 self-efficacy
13.1 more economical; therapist can observe rather than merely infer clients' interpersonal behavior; social pressure of group; modeling and insight from hearing others
13.3 b)
14.1 delusions, hallucinations
14.3 discriminate, attention, schizophrenia, movement
15.1 tricyclic antidepressants, lithium carbonate
15.3 Librium, Valium, antianxiety drugs
16.2 depression
16.3 seizure
17.1 performed in absence of obvious organic damage
19.3 meta-analysis
19.4 patient, therapist, treatment
19.6 number of treatment sessions

Self Test: Lesson I

1.	a	Obj. 16-1
2.	c	Obj. 16-2
3.	b	Obj. 16-2
4.	c	Obj. 16-3
5.	a	Obj. 16-3
6.	d	Obj. 16-4
7.	c	Obj. 16-5
8.	b	Obj. 16-5
9.	d	Obj. 16-6
10.	b	Obj. 16-7
11.	c	Obj. 16-8
12.	c	Obj. 16-9
13.	d	Obj. 16-10
14.	c	Obj. 16-10
15.	d	Obj. 16-10

Self Test: Lesson II

1.	b	Obj. 16-11
2.	a	Obj. 16-12
3.	d	Obj. 16-13
4.	c	Obj. 16-13
5.	b	Obj. 16-14
6.	d	Obj. 16-15
7.	c	Obj. 16-15
8.	b	Obj. 16-16
9.	c	Obj. 16-16
10.	d	Obj. 16-17
11.	d	Obj. 16-18
12.	a	Obj. 16-19
13.	d	Obj. 16-19
14.	c	Obj. 16-19
15.	a	Obj. 16-19

16.1 OBJ 16-1

TREPHINING

16.2 OBJ 16-1

MESMERISM

16.3 OBJ 16-2

INSIGHT THERAPY

16.4 OBJ 16-2

PSYCHOANALYSIS

16.5 OBJ 16-2

FREE ASSOCIATION

16.6 OBJ 16-2

RESISTANCE

16.7 OBJ 16-2

TRANSFERENCE NEUROSIS

16.8 OBJ 16-2

COUNTERTRANSFERENCE

16.9 OBJ 16-2

TRAINING ANALYSIS

16.10 OBJ 16-3

CLIENT-CENTERED THERAPY

16.11 OBJ 16-3

IDEAL SELF

16.12 OBJ 16-3

REAL SELF

16.13 OBJ 16-3

UNCONDITIONAL POSITIVE REGARD

16.14 OBJ 16-3

NON-DIRECTIVE

16.15 OBJ 16-5

SYSTEMATIC DESENSITIZATION

16.16 OBJ 16-5

IN VIVO

16.1 Obj 16-1

early therapy technique designed to permit evil spirits to leave the victim's head through holes drilled in the person's head

16.2 Obj 16-1

type of hypnotism based on Anton Mesmer's theory of animal magnetism

16.3 Obj 16-2

approach to therapy that assumes understanding of the causes of one's problems will lead to a cure

16.4 Obj 16-2

form of insight therapy developed by Sigmund Freud; attempts to uncover unconscious conflicts stemming from childhood

16.5 Obj 16-2

psychoanalytic technique; client says what comes to mind, regardless of how ridiculous or irrelevant; suppresses defense mechanisms, reveals unconscious

16.6 Obj 16-2

in psychoanalysis, client's failure to free associate indicates areas significant to client's problem

16.7 Obj 16-2

in psychoanalysis, client acts toward therapist in ways similar to relations with dominant childhood figures, evidence for causes of conflicts

16.8 Obj 16-2

therapist feelings towards patient; may interfere with the analysis and therefore must be guarded against.

16.9 Obj 16-2

psychoanalysis undertaken by future analyst to work out conflicts to prevent countertransference when analysts treating patients.

16.10 Obj 16-3

developed by carl Rogers to help clients attend to their own feelings so that their innate tendencies toward goodness can emerge

16.11 Obj 16-3

the way a person would like to be; if based on others' evaluations, person may ignore own instincts for goodness

16.12 Obj 16-3

way the person actually is; if discrepant from ideal self, person will be unhappy and dissatisfied

16.13 Obj 16-3

expression of acceptance, care, and support of the person that provides environment for individuals to self-actualize

16.14 Obj 16-3

former label of client-centered therapy; actually, client-centered therapist selectively reinforces client's healthy statements

16.15 Obj 16-5

developed by Wolpe, pairs relaxation with visualization of a hierarchy of fears, successful in eliminating neurotic fears and phobias

16.16 Obj 16-5

performing desensitization or other behavioral technique using real rather than imagery exposure

16.17 OBJ 16-5

AVERSIVE CLASSICAL CONDITIONING

16.18 OBJ 16-7

COVERT REINFORCEMENT

16.19 OBJ 16-8

MODELING

16.2Ø OBJ 16-8

BEHAVIORAL REHEARSAL

16.21 OBJ 16-9

TOKEN ECONOMY

16.22 OBJ 16-1Ø

SYMPTOM SUBSTITUTION

16.23 OBJ 16-1Ø

SELF-CONTROL

16.24 OBJ 16-11

COGNITIVE BEHAVIOR THERAPY

16.25 OBJ 16-11

RATIONAL-EMTOIVE THERAPY

16.26 OBJ 16-11

SIGNIFICANT ACTIVATING EVENT
(A)

16.27 OBJ 16-11

EMOTIONAL CONSEQUENCE
(B)

16.28 OBJ 16-11

BELIEF SYSTEM
(C)

16.29 OBJ 16-11

FULL ACCEPTANCE

16.3Ø OBJ 16-12

SELF-EFFICACY

16.31 OBJ 16-12

SELF-TALK

16.32 OBJ 16-13

PSYCHODRAMA

16.25 Obj 16-11

developed by Albert Ellis; teaches clients to abandon irrational thinking for rational thinking

16.26 Obj 16-11

according to Ellis, an event that people interpret erroneously as the cause of emotions

16.27 Obj 16-11

according to rational-emotive therapy, feelings that result from people's interpretations of an event

16.28 Obj 16-11

according to Ellis the collection of ideas that a person uses to interpret the meaning of an event

16.29 Obj 16-11

feeling based on the rational belief one is worth something and should not be measured against impossible standards; goal of rational-emotive therapy

16.30 Obj 16-12

cognitive concept that one is capable of achieving one's goals; may generalize from successful therapy

16.31 Obj 16-12

private behavior often targeted for change in cognitive behavior therapy

16.32 Obj 16-13

form of structured group therapy developed by Moreno; clients pretend to be members of play cast and act out problems under direction of therapist

16.17 Obj 16-5

technique to eliminate undesired behavior by pairing unpleasant stimulus with stimulus that produces or is associated with undesired behavior

16.18 Obj 16-7

imaginary pairing of reinforcement with a desired response to increase probability of that response

16.19 Obj 16-8

observing and imitating the behavior of another which in therapy is followed by reinforcement

16.20 Obj 16-8

client practices behavior demonstrated by therapist to handle particular interactions with other people

16.21 Obj 16-9

system of awarding tokens for performance of certain tasks; tokens can be exchanged for desired items or privileges

16.22 Obj 16-10

psychoanalytic belief: elimination of symptom without addressing underlying causes will lead to another symptom; disputed by behavior therapists

16.23 Obj 16-10

use of reinforcement and punishment by individuals to manage their own behaviors

16.24 Obj 16-11

therapy that believes change in behavior is produced by change in beliefs and perceptions

16.33 OBJ 16-13

MIRRORING

16.34 OBJ 16-13

STRUCTURAL FAMILY THERAPY

16.35 OBJ 16-13

MARITAL SUBSYSTEM

16.36 OBJ 16-14

ANTIPSYCHOTIC DRUGS

16.37 OBJ 16-14

TARDIVE DYSKINESIA

16.38 OBJ 16-15

ANTIDEPRESSANT DRUGS

16.39 OBJ 16-15

ANTIANXIETY DRUGS

16.40 OBJ 16-16

ELECTROCONVULSIVE THERAPY (ECT)

16.41 OBJ 16-17

PSYCHOSURGERY

16.42 OBJ 16-17

PREFRONTAL LOBOTOMY

16.43 OBJ 16-17

CINGULECTOMY

16.44 OBJ 16-17

CINGULUM BUNDLE

16.45 OBJ 16-18

ECLECTIC PSYCHOTHERAPY

16.46 OBJ 16-19

META-ANALYSIS

16.41 Obj 16-17

treatment of mental disorder in the absence of obvious organic damage by means of brain surgery

16.42 Obj 16-17

psychosurgical procedure that disconnects the frontmost portion of brain

16.43 Obj 16-17

psychosurgical procedures designed to disconnect thoughts and emotions by cutting the cingulum bundle

16.44 Obj 16-17

band of nerve fibers connecting prefrontal cortex with limbic system

16.45 Obj 16-18

selecting those techniques and theories that seem most effective in describing and treating a given client

16.46 Obj 16-19

statistical procedure for estimating magnitude of experimental effects reported by published studies; used in Smith et al. report on effectiveness

16.33 Obj 16-13

psychodrama technique in which a group member acts out a particular maladaptive pattern of behavior that is displayed by another member

16.34 Obj 16-13

developed by Salvador Minuchin, focuses on the organization of relationship within the family

16.35 Obj 16-13

in structural family therapy, the husband and wife; healthier if spouse relationship rather than parental role primary

16.36 Obj 16-14

control delusions and hallucinations of schizophrenics by blockingdopamine receptors in brain

16.37 Obj 16-14

movement disturbance involving facial muscles; caused by prolonged use of antipsychotic drugs

16.38 Obj 16-15

several kinds; tricylics used for major depressions, also helpful for agoraphobia and panic disorders; lithium carbonate used in bipolar disorders (manic phase)

16.39 Obj 16-15

tranquilizers used to reduce anxiety; examples: Valium and Librium

16.40 Obj 16-16

a treatment for major depression in which electric current is passed through the body and produces a seizure